CAMBRIDGE

Brighter Thinking

GCSE for OCR

COMPUTER SCIENCE
Student Book

David Waller
Course consultant: Ann Weidmann

CAMBRIDGE
UNIVERSITY PRESS

University Printing House, Cambridge CB2 8BS, United Kingdom

Cambridge University Press is part of the University of Cambridge.

It furthers the University's mission by disseminating knowledge in the pursuit of education, learning and research at the highest international levels of excellence.

www.cambridge.org
Information on this title:
www.cambridge.org/9781316504031 (Paperback)
www.cambridge.org/9781316504055 (2 Year Online Subscription)
www.cambridge.org/9781316609965 (Site Licence Online Subscription)
www.cambridge.org/9781316503997 (Paperback + 2 Year Online Subscription)

© Cambridge University Press 2016

First published 2016

Printed in the United Kingdom by Latimer Trend

A catalogue record for this publication is available from the British Library

ISBN 978-1-316-50403-1 Paperback
ISBN 978-1-316-50405-5 2 Year Online Subscription
ISBN 978-1-316-60996-5 Site Licence Online Subscription
ISBN 978-1-316-50399-7 Paperback + 2 Year Online Subscription

Additional resources for this publication at www.cambridge.org/education

Contents

Introduction

Computers and our lives

There isn't any area of our lives that isn't dependent on computers. There was probably a computer involved when you were born and most likely there will be when you die. And in between, computers will have an impact on every single aspect of your life. It's easy to think computers are in control of so much of our lives. But of course they aren't. It's the people who control the computers who are in charge. Controlling the computers is what this GCSE is all about.

Why learn Computer Science?

Learning about computers and how to use them is important. But that is not a good enough reason for you to study computer science. You could just as well say that you need to learn how cars are made before you drive one, or learn how to build a house before you live in one. Obviously learning how to use and do things is important but education is about much more than that.

Computational thinking

You should study computer science because it affects your brain and the way you think. Computer science is all about formulating, tackling and solving problems in a particular and unique way. A computer scientist coined the term 'computational thinking' for the way in which problems are analysed and solutions are created and tested. And the solutions must be explained clearly and unambiguously because they are going to be carried out by a computer – a mindless machine. If it can't understand an instruction it doesn't pause and try to work it out. It just stops and refuses to budge!

So studying computer science will develop your **problem-solving abilities** – which will be useful in whatever you choose to do after your GCSEs. It will help your **clarity of communication**. And it will also develop your **creativity** – anyone can paint any old picture, but creating a masterpiece takes skill, creativity and work. In the same way, producing a creative solution to a problem in an elegant, efficient way needs these same skills.

How to use the book

The book is divided into 15 chapters which cover all of the content listed in the specification.

At the start of each chapter are the expected **learning outcomes** – what you should understand and be able to do by the time you reach the end of the chapter.

Throughout the text there are **activities** for you to complete. These will help you to see if you understand the ideas covered in the text and are able to apply the concepts to solve problems.

Each chapter contains a **challenge**. This is where you can use computational thinking, creativity and your coding skills to produce solutions for larger, real-life problems.

There are **real-life examples** at the start of each chapter and throughout, to help you understand how computer science is important to everyday life.

There are features throughout the book to help you build knowledge and improve your skills:

Tip

Tip boxes provide helpful hints.

Maths skills

Maths skills boxes highlight the key mathematical skills that you'll need for computer science.

Key term

Important computer science terms are written in **orange**. You can find what they mean in the **Key term** boxes and also in the **Glossary** at the back of the book.

Remember

These appear near the end of each section to help your understanding. Look back at these useful summaries to **remember** for your revision and before completing the final challenge in each chapter.

Watch out

Watch out boxes help you to avoid making common mistakes.

WORKED EXAMPLE

Worked examples guide you through model answers to help you understand methods of answering questions.

Practice questions

Practice questions give you a taste of how your knowledge and skills will be assessed.

Working on Cambridge Elevate

Cambridge Elevate is the platform which hosts a digital version of this student book. If you have access to this digital version you can annotate different parts of the book, send and receive messages to and from your teacher and insert weblinks, among other things.

As you work through the student book, you will find links to Cambridge Elevate. You can use these to watch animations explaining concepts from the book, complete interactive activities and download worksheets to help you reinforce your learning.

Watch the bubble sort algorithm animation on Cambridge Elevate

Download Worksheet 1.1 from Cambridge Elevate

Complete Interactive Activity 1a on Cambridge Elevate

There are also links to additional activities on Cambridge Computing Online to help expand your learning.

Complete the Cambridge Computing Online activity

Why algorithms?

Algorithms run our world! In every area algorithms are used to decide what action should be taken in a particular circumstance and as computers can consider all the possibilities far more quickly than a human brain, they are becoming more important to the running of the world. Here are just a few examples.

- In a game of chess, when each player has made 3 moves, there are over 9 million possible moves available; after 4 moves there are over 288 billion possible moves. Computers have the ability to consider all these possible moves far more quickly than humans. That is why no chess grandmaster has beaten a top computer chess algorithm since 2005.

- Algorithms are used by financial organisations to trade shares on the stock market. A computer following an algorithm can decide which deal to make far more quickly than a human and a split second difference can be worth millions of pounds.

- Closely guarded algorithms are used for Internet searches to make them quicker and the results more relevant to the user. They will even auto-complete the search terms based on previous searches.

Algorithms are used to control automatic-pilot systems in airplanes. You have probably been piloted by an algorithm!

What is an algorithm?

An algorithm is a step-by-step procedure for solving problems. It is something that can be followed by humans and computers.

We use algorithms to carry out everyday tasks, often without thinking about them. For example, an algorithm to solve the problem of getting ready for school might be:

Watch out

In an algorithm, the order in which the tasks are carried out is very important to its success or failure. For example, this algorithm would not be very successful if 'shower' was placed after 'get dressed'. The sequence is very important.

Get out of bed.
Shower.
Get dressed.
Turn on kettle.
Put bread in toaster and turn on.
Wait for kettle to boil and make tea.
Wait for bread to toast, butter it and add marmalade.
Drink tea and eat toast.
Gather school books and put in bag.
Put on shoes and coat.
Leave the house.

Key terms

sequence: the order in which tasks are to be carried out

sub-tasks: small steps making up a larger task

The algorithm shows the sequence of tasks. Different people will design different algorithms, as they will do things in a different order, meaning there can be many solutions to the same problem. Some of these tasks could also be further divided into sub-tasks as they may be made up of smaller steps.

For example, 'showering' could involve many different steps: turning on the shower, setting the correct temperature etc. If all the possible sub-tasks were included, the complete algorithm would get very large and complicated.

ACTIVITY 1.1

Create an algorithm for someone who has never made a cup of tea before to follow in order to make one successfully. Compare it with other members of your group and note any differences in sequence and sub-tasks.

Complete the Cambridge Computing Online activity
www.cambridge.org/links/kose4001

Download Worksheet 1.1 from Cambridge Elevate

The getting to school example might seem pretty easy. Like a typical algorithm, it is just a list of steps. However, here is part of another algorithm, which is part of a recipe to make a perfect meringue.

1. Tip 4 large egg whites into a large clean mixing bowl (not plastic).
2. Beat them on medium speed with an electric hand whisk.
3. Keep beating until the mixture resembles a fluffy cloud and stands up in stiff peaks when the blades are lifted.
4. Now turn the speed up and start to add 115g caster sugar, a dessert spoonful at a time, until there is none left.
5. Continue beating for 3–4 seconds between each addition.

SEQUENCE

SEQUENCE

ITERATION

SELECTION

ITERATION

SELECTION

SEQUENCE

In addition to *sequence*, this algorithm has two new elements: iteration and selection.

Iteration means doing things over and over again. The cook has to beat the mixture and then stop and ask themselves if it resembles a fluffy cloud. If it doesn't they have to beat again, check again, beat again, check again etc. until they are convinced they have made a fluffy cloud. There is also repetition when adding the sugar. It has to be added a spoonful at a time until there is none left.

Selection means making decisions. In other words, as well as doing things over and over again, they have to make a decision. Does it resemble a fluffy cloud?

 Key terms

iteration: when a task is repeated until there is a required outcome

selection: a question is asked, and depending on the answer, the program takes one of two courses of action

 Complete Interactive Activity 1a on Cambridge Elevate

ACTIVITY 1.2

Using *sequence*, *selection* and *iteration*, write an algorithm that a person (who has never done this before) could follow in order to successfully prepare a bath with the water at the correct temperature. Annotate the algorithm to indicate sequence, iteration and selection.

You could set it out as shown, where the first four tasks have been done for you.

`Put plug in the bath.`	Sequence
`Turn on hot tap.`	Sequence
`Is the water at the correct temperature?`	Selection
`Turn cold tap until water is at the correct temperature.`	Iteration

What makes a successful algorithm?

The two most important criteria are:

- *Correctness*: it successfully solves the problem.

- *Efficiency*: it solves the problem in the least possible time.

List A is the 'getting up' algorithm we looked at earlier. **List B** is similar but with the sequence slightly altered.

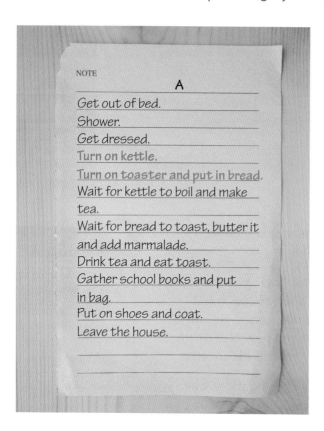

List B is more efficient as it could be implemented in less time. The kettle and the toaster are turned on before taking a shower and so the water will boil while the person is showering. There will be no waiting time.

An algorithm for a computer

Now let's look at a simple algorithm that we could create for a computer to follow, instead of a human. Computers are ideal for obeying orders and carrying out actions over and over again; in fact, that is their main function.

It is important for the temperature in a shopping mall to be kept at a set value. It will keep the shoppers comfortable and it will help to prevent condensation on glass shop windows and slippery floor surfaces. Here is an algorithm intended to be used to control the temperature in a shopping mall and maintain a temperature of 20 °C.

1. Check the temperature.

2. If the temperature is greater than 20 °C then turn off heaters and open the ventilators.

3. If the temperature is less than 20 °C then turn on heaters and close the ventilators.

4. Go back to instruction 1.

This is a simple algorithm but it includes the basic building blocks:

- *Sequence*: there is a list of instructions in the correct order.

- *Selection*: the 'if' statements in instructions 2 and 3 allow a decision to be made and action taken.

- *Iteration*: instruction 4 instructs the computer to go back to instruction 1 and so the sequence will run over and over again indefinitely.

 Remember

1. An algorithm is a step-by-step procedure for solving a problem in a finite number of steps.
2. The basic building blocks of algorithms are sequence, selection and iteration.
3. The criteria for a successful algorithm are correctness and efficiency.
4. An algorithm must be translated into a programming language before it can be executed by a computer.

Flow diagrams

Flow diagrams can be used to represent algorithms visually.

They use symbols connected by arrows to show the flow of the algorithm.

The symbols used are:

This represents the start or end point of the flow diagram. You always start your flow diagram with this symbol and use it to finish the flow diagram.	
You use this to represent data input or data output. For example it could be a number or name entered by a user.	
You use this where a decision has to be made. It is also called selection. It will contain a question, for example 'Is the temperature greater than 20 °C?' If it is then an arrow will point to a task to be carried out and if it isn't then an arrow will point to a different action.	
You use this to represent a process that must be carried out by the algorithm. In this example it is used as a result of one of the questions which has been asked, e.g. 'Turn on the heaters' or 'Turn off the heaters'.	

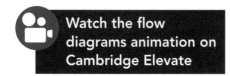

Watch the flow diagrams animation on Cambridge Elevate

WORKED EXAMPLE

Here is the flow diagram of an algorithm to calculate the area of a rectangle:

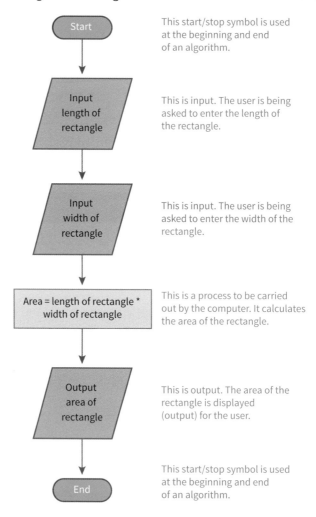

There are two inputs of the dimensions of the rectangle, a process to calculate the area and an output of the area.

In this example there is just *sequence*: a list of tasks to be performed.

Complete Interactive Activity 1b on Cambridge Elevate

ACTIVITY 1.3

At the end of each day an ice cream seller calculates how much money he has collected. Assuming that the ice creams all cost the same amount, draw a flow diagram of an algorithm that would output the total amount collected during the day.

WORKED EXAMPLE

Here is a flow diagram of an algorithm to identify a vertebrate animal. It includes *sequence* and *selection*.

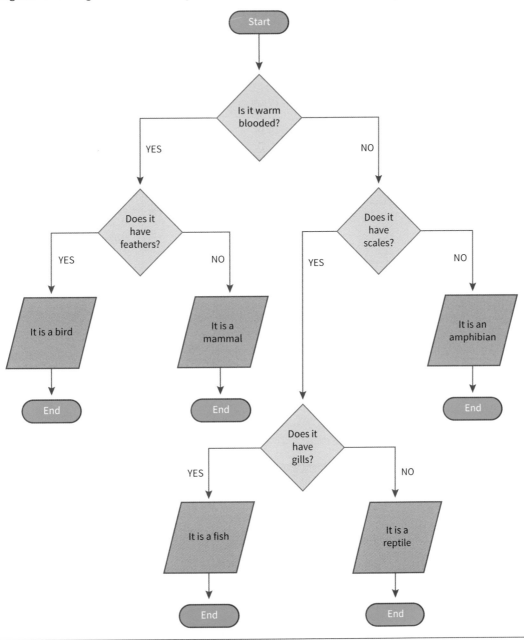

 Complete Interactive Activity 1c on Cambridge Elevate

ACTIVITY 1.4

A teacher is marking his students' test papers on a computer. If they achieve over 50% he would like the message 'Very well done' displayed. If they achieve over 90%, they should also receive a second message stating 'This is an excellent result'. If they score 50% or lower, the message will be 'You must try harder next time'.

Draw a flow diagram of an algorithm that would output these messages.

WORKED EXAMPLE

A flow diagram to represent the algorithm to control the temperature of the shopping mall that we mentioned earlier would look like this. It contains *sequence*, *selection* and *iteration*.

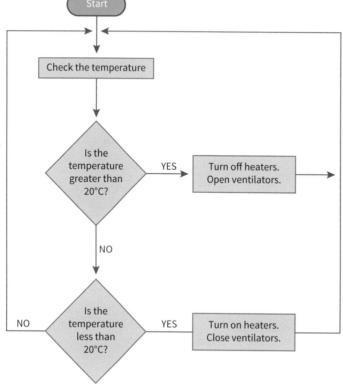

There are three **processes**: one to check the temperature in the mall and two to either turn off the heaters and open the ventilators, or turn them on and close the ventilators.

There are two **decisions**: is the temperature greater or is it less than 20 °C? Both are needed as the temperature could in fact be equal to 20 °C.

There are only two possible answers for each decision question: *yes* or *no*, and the arrows show the relevant action to be taken depending on the answer.

Iteration is shown in the flow diagram as the arrows always lead the flow back to the first process. So the algorithm will repeat over and over again indefinitely.

As the algorithm repeats forever, no end symbol is required.

 Key terms

decision: when a question is asked (as in *selection*) the answer will lead to one or more different alternative actions

process: action that is taken, sometimes as a result of a decision, in order to achieve a desired outcome

ACTIVITY 1.5

Draw a flow diagram to illustrate an algorithm for making a cup of tea.

It should include sequence, selection and iteration.

(**Hint**: Look back at your answers for Activity 1.1.)

Input and output

In some of the previous examples, user input was required and information was output to the user.

A common request for user input is to enter a password.

WORKED EXAMPLE

Here is a flow diagram of an algorithm to authenticate a user's password.

When a user enters a password it has to be confirmed that it is the same as the one stored; it has to be authenticated.

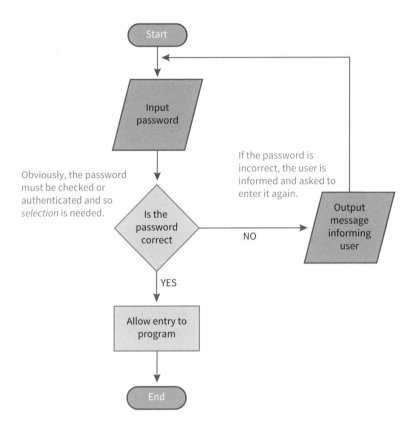

Obviously, the password must be checked or authenticated and so *selection* is needed.

If the password is incorrect, the user is informed and asked to enter it again.

In this flow diagram there is *iteration*. If the password is incorrect then, in this particular algorithm the user is asked to enter it again, and again, and again, forever or until it is correct.

 Download Worksheet 1.2 from Cambridge Elevate

Now assume that the user is given three attempts and then the account is locked.

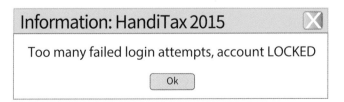

WORKED EXAMPLE

Here is a flow diagram to authenticate a password and lock the account after three incorrect attempts.

The algorithm will have to keep a count of the number of attempts that have been made.

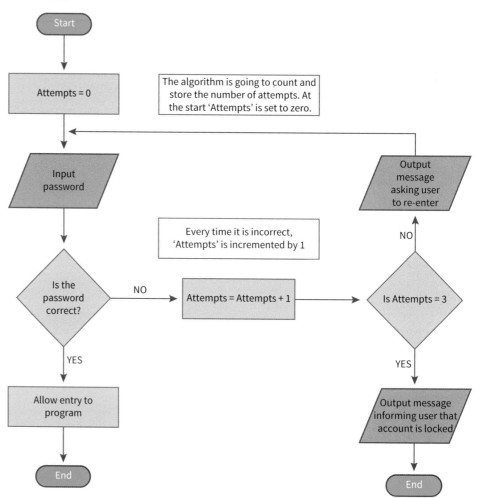

In this algorithm we have used a container called 'Attempts' to keep a count of the number of attempts that have been made.

When incorrect attempts are made, the value of 'Attempts' changes. It doesn't keep the same value throughout the algorithm; it can change because it is a variable.

At the first attempt it is changed to 1, on the second attempt to 2 and to 3 on the third attempt.

If three attempts are made then the container 'Attempts' equals 3 and if there is still no correct password then the account is locked.

Containers like 'Attempts' are used in algorithms to store values that can change as the algorithm is running. As the values they contain can change, they are called variables.

Key term

variable: a container which is used to store values such as the number of attempts

Download Worksheet 1.3 from Cambridge Elevate

ACTIVITY 1.6

The following flow diagram shows the algorithm used to create usernames for a school network.

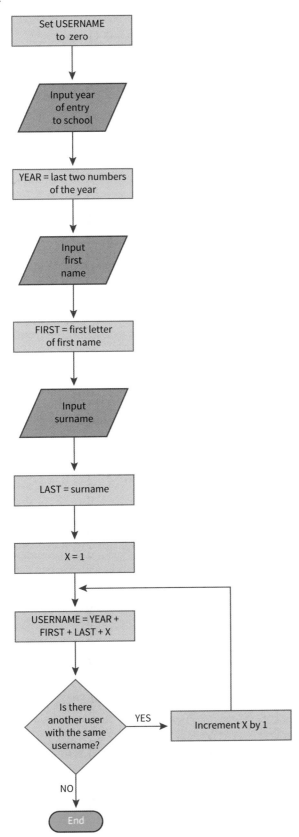

11

Follow the algorithm shown in the flow diagram and then answer the following questions.

a. Identify and list the variables that have been used in this algorithm.

b. State the usernames that the flow diagram will give to the following pupils (assume that there are no other pupils with the same username):

   i. Catherine Jones who joined the school in 2005.

   ii. Fred Green who joined the school in 2006.

c. A pupil has been given the username of 03SSmith13.

   State four facts that you can work out from this username.

Pseudocode

As we have seen, flow diagrams make algorithms easy for people to understand. However, computers can't understand flow diagrams they can only understand programming languages.

In addition to flow diagrams algorithms can also be expressed using pseudocode.

Pseudocode is a kind of structured English for describing algorithms. It is a generic, code-like language that can be easily translated into any programming language.

Writing in pseudocode helps you to concentrate on the *logic* (the process) and *efficiency* of your algorithm before you have to start thinking about the code that you will be using. It is important to check that you have included all the stages in your process as it is easier to spot anything missing at this stage than when you have carefully translated it into code!

There are many different varieties of pseudocode; some programming teams or organisations have their own versions of pseudocode. However, all pseudocode must be able to express the basic programming constructs that we will be looking at.

Variables

Before we look at examples of algorithms expressed in pseudocode, we should look at variables in more detail.

As we mentioned above, a variable can be changed and manipulated as an algorithm is running.

So that programmers can keep track of variables, they are given names or identifiers.

An algorithm might contain many variables and so it is important to give them meaningful identifiers.

If you were creating an algorithm that stores people's ages it would be sensible to name or identify that variable as 'Age' and not something like 'X' or 'Y'.

Key term

pseudocode: a language that is similar to a real programming language, but is easier for humans to understand although it doesn't actually run on a computer. It can easily be converted to a regular programming language

Tip

Have a look through the OCR Pseudocode Guide to familiarise yourself with the commands and keywords that are needed.

Key term

identifier: the 'name' given to a variable

Choosing variable identifiers

Variable identifiers should be as descriptive as possible so that anyone reading the code will be able to see what they represent. For example, look at these identifiers:

X = 10

and

distanceToSchool = 10

Anyone reading the code would know immediately what the value '10' represented in the second example.

Here are some golden rules for choosing variable identifiers.

1. Shorter identifiers are easier to type and spell. A longer identifier could easily be misspelt.

2. Longer identifiers may be used if they are more descriptive of the data they represent.

3. Some identifiers may be reserved words used by the programming language and cannot be used e.g. 'print'.

4. In many programming languages identifiers cannot begin with a number.

Naming conventions

Again, it is important for all variables to be written in a similar way throughout an algorithm. This makes the program consistent and easy to understand. This is even more important when a team of programmers is working on the same project.

- A commonly used convention is to use *camel case* (also known as CamelCase or camelCase) for compound words.

  e.g.

  FirstName, LastName.

  Often the first word is given a lower case initial, e.g.

  firstName, lastName.

- An alternative is to use an underscore. This method is often called *snake case*.

  e.g. first_name, last_name.

Assigning values to variables

All variables have to be given or assigned a value. This is done in *assignment statements*. It is done differently in different varieties of pseudocode.

Tip

People have variables! We all have a variable that is given the identifier 'Age' and stores the length of time we have been alive. It changes every second but is celebrated when it changes at the end of a year. So you could say 'Happy variable change!'

Our pulse rate, blood pressure and temperature are also our variables.

The school stores variable data about you in variables identified as 'Year' and 'Tutor Group'. Their values change each school year.

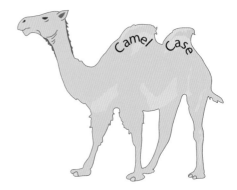

Tip

Study the OCR Pseudocode Guide to see how assignment is made in the variety of pseudocode that you will be using.

Key term

assigning: giving a variable a value

Here are two examples, one that assigns a number, and the other that assigns text.

Code

```
myAge = 21

myName = "David"
```

Several variables can be assigned in the same statement:

Code

```
myAge = 21, myName = "David"
```

Watch out

Unfortunately the = operator is used to assign variables and this can cause confusion. In this case it does not mean 'equal to'. It means 'assign the variable this value'. It can be assigned other values as the program is running.

Constants

Key term

constant: a value that does not change while the program is running

A constant is a value that cannot be altered by the program during normal execution: the value stays the same.

Tip

Constants are also given identifiers.

For example a constant identified as 'conversionFactor' could be assigned the value of 0.39. It could then be used to convert a distance in centimetres into inches:

Code

```
lengthInInches = lengthInCm * conversionFactor.
```

Remember

1. A variable is a value that can change while a program is running.
2. Variables are given names, called identifiers.
3. Variable identifiers should be descriptive of the data they are storing e.g. age or firstName and not identifiers such as X or Y.
4. Variables should be written in a consistent way, e.g. they should all be camel case or all snake case and not a mixture of the two.
5. Variables are assigned a value using the = symbol.
6. Constants are values that cannot be altered as a program is running.

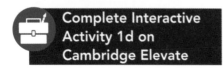

Complete Interactive Activity 1d on Cambridge Elevate

OK. Now back to using pseudocode.

WORKED EXAMPLE

The first flow diagram we looked at illustrated an algorithm to find the area of a rectangle. Here it is expressed in pseudocode. It asks a user for the width and the length of a rectangle. It then calculates the area and prints it to screen.

Where variables are first assigned a value, they are shown in red.

`length = input ("Please enter the length")`	This is how the pseudocode allows users to input data. Note how the prompt text is enclosed in speech marks. The variable 'length' will be assigned the value entered by the user.
`width = input ("Please enter the width")`	The variable 'width' will be assigned the value entered by the user.
`area = length * width`	The variable 'area' will be assigned the value of the variable 'length' multiplied by the variable 'width'.
`print area`	The value stored by the variable 'area' is printed on the screen.

Adding comments

When writing pseudocode it is a good idea to add comments to explain to others, and often to remind yourself, what the code is intended to do.

To separate these comments from the actual code, two forward slashes **//** are used.

The pseudocode example used above could have been commented in the following way:

Code ———

```
length = input("Please enter the length") // Ask the user
for the length of the rectangle

width = input("Please enter the width") // Ask the user for
the width of the rectangle

area = length * width // Find the area by multiplying the
length by the width

print (area)  // output the area
```

Tip

Check the commands and keywords used in the OCR Pseudocode Guide.

Tip

The printed message could have been made more user-friendly by including some text rather than just the area value.

To do this the text would have to have been included in speech marks to show that it is literal text and not a variable name. It would then have to have been joined to the variable 'area'.

```
print("The area is "
+ area)
```

The computer will print the literal text "The area is " and then the value for the variable 'area' as they have been joined together (concatenated) using the '+' symbol.

Key term

comment: a piece of information for the programmer. It doesn't form part of the program and is not executed by the computer. It is for information only

ACTIVITY 1.7

Write the pseudocode to ask a user to enter their name and their age. It should then print the following message:

```
Hello (name entered). You
are (age entered) years
of age.
```

You should add comments to your code.

Keywords

If you look through the Pseudocode Guide you will see words like 'print', 'for', 'next', 'if' and 'endif', which are used in commands. They are *reserved words* or *keywords* as they have specific meanings for the language and therefore cannot be used as variable identifiers.

Operators

The algorithm you wrote in Activity 1.7 just printed out the data a user had input. Often you want the computer to do something with that data, usually a calculation.

In the worked example the values of two variables were multiplied together to find the area:

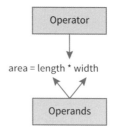

An operator is a symbol that tells the computer to perform a specific action on the data and manipulate it in a particular way. The data on which it performs the action is called an operand.

Key terms

operator: the symbol that tells the computer what to do

operand: the data the operator is working on

 Watch the arithmetic, relational and Boolean operators animation on Cambridge Elevate.

Arithmetic operators

These are operators we have been using all our mathematical lives. The following list shows the most common arithmetic operators:

Operator	Function	Example
+	**Addition:** add the values together.	3 + 6 = 9 firstResult + secondResult
-	**Subtraction:** subtract the second value from the first.	6 - 3 = 3 dailyProfit - dailyCosts
*	**Multiplication:** multiply the values together.	3 * 6 = 18 length * width
/	**Real division:** divide the first value by the second number and return the result including decimal places.	13/3 = 4.333 totalSweets/totalChildren
DIV	**Quotient:** like division, but it only returns the whole number or *integer*.	13 DIV 3 = 4 totalSweets\totalChildren
MOD	**Modulus:** this will return the remainder of a division.	13/3 = 4 remainder 1. Therefore: 13 MOD 3 = 1
^	**Exponentiation:** this is for 'powers of'.	3^3 = 27. It is the same as writing 3^3.

Order of operations

In computer programming the order of precedence (the order in which you do each calculation) is the same as in mathematics and science.

To change the order of operations, parentheses are used.

 Key term

parentheses: brackets

Therefore:

$$13 \times (3 + 6) = 13 \times 9 = 117$$

Multiplication and division are carried out before addition and subtraction. Brackets are calculated before multiplication and division.

ACTIVITY 1.8

Using pseudocode, create an algorithm that will ask a user to input the diameter of a wheel.

It should then calculate the area (assume pi is 3.142) and output the result.

 Complete Interactive Activity 1e on Cambridge Elevate

Relational operators

Let's look again at the temperature control in the shopping mall.

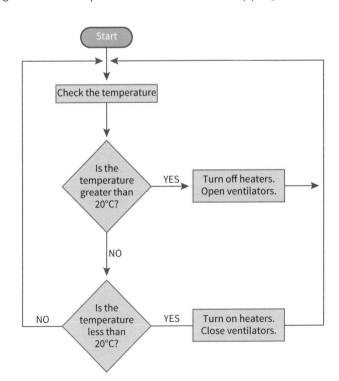

 Tip

- In a division such as 13/3 the '13' is called the *dividend* and the '3' is called the *divisor*.

- The *quotient* is the number of times the divisor divides into the dividend; in this case 4 times.

- The DIV operator returns just the quotient and so in some pseudocode dialects it is called *integer division* and the symbol used is a backslash: \.

 Maths skills

Remember BIDMAS!

This is how the following would be evaluated:

$$3^3 \times 6 + (16 - 7)$$

Brackets $\quad 3^3 \times 6 + (9)$

Indices $\quad 9 \times 6 + (9)$

Division

Multiplication $\quad 54 + (9)$

Addition $\quad 63$

Subtraction

$$13 \times 3 + 6 = 45 \text{ and not } 117$$

 Maths skills

The area of a circle can be found by the formula pi × r^2 where **r** equals the radius.

In this flow diagrams two questions are being asked:

'Is the temperature greater than 20°C?'

and

'Is the temperature less than 20°C?'

Key term

relational operator: an operator that compares two items of data, e.g. <, >, =

We used two different relational operators: greater than and less than. Relational operators test the relationship between two values. As they compare the values they are sometimes called *comparison operators*.

Operator	Function	Example
==	**Equal to**: checks if two values are equal. Note that the double equals sign are used (==) to differentiate it from assigning a value to a variable when one equal sign is used.	length == width
!=	**Not equal to**: checks to see if two values are not equal.	temperature != 20
<	**Less than**: checks to see if one value is less than another.	temperature < 20
>	**Greater than**: checks to see if one value is greater than another.	temperature > 20
<=	**Less than or equal to**: checks to see if one value is less than or equal to another.	temperature <= 20
>=	**Greater than or equal to**: checks to see if one value is greater than or equal to another.	temperature >= 20

Complete Interactive Activity 1f on Cambridge Elevate

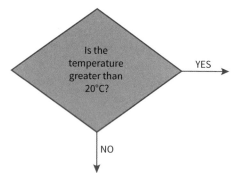

As mentioned above we used two of these operators in the flow diagram for the algorithm to control the temperature of a shopping mall.

If the temperature is greater than 20°C then one course of action is carried out and if it isn't then something else is done.

We can rewrite this using the 'if', 'then' and 'else' statement in the pseudocode.

Code ────────────────────────

```
if the temperature is greater than 20°C then turn off
the heater and open the ventilators.

else do something else.
```

If we put both of the selections together we could write:

Code ────────────────────────

```
if the temperature is greater than 20°C then turn off
the heater and open the ventilators.

if the temperature is less than 20°C then turn on the
heater and close the ventilators.

else go back and check the temperature.
```

When the computer is running a program coded from these 'if' statements, it will run both of them. But if the first one is true, it doesn't need to run the second one as the temperature can't be greater than and less than 20 °C at the same time!

The computer will be wasting time. The algorithm is inefficient!

Therefore another term, 'elseif', is used.

In this example, **x** is actually equal to 2.

Inefficient algorithm	Efficient algorithm
if x = 1 do this	if x = 1 do this
if x = 2 do this	elseif x = 2 do this
if x = 3 do this	elseif x = 3 do this
if x = 4 do this	elseif x = 4 do this
if x = 5 do this	elseif x = 5 do this
if x = 6 do this	elseif x = 6 do this
else do this	else do this
endif	endif

In this example it won't make much difference as there were only six 'if' statements but in large programs there might be hundreds or thousands of 'if' statements and going through them all would waste a significant amount of time.

Tip

When 'if' statements are used, each one will be checked even when the correct condition has been found.

However, 'elseif' statements will not be checked after the correct condition has been found.

Tip

If you study the Pseudocode Guide you will see that 'if', 'then', 'elseif' and 'else' are written in lower case.

You should also notice that after the statements are used, the checking is stopped using the 'endif' statement.

WORKED EXAMPLE

A teacher would like a program that allows her to enter three test results and calculate the average.

If the average is 50 or above it should output the message 'Pass' and if it is below 50 the message 'Fail'.

```
test1= input("Please enter first test result.")

test2= input("Please enter second test result.")

test3= input("Please enter third test result.")
```

The user is asked to input the three test results which are stored in the variables test1, test2 and test3.

```
average = (test1 + test2 + test3)/3
```

The average is calculated and stored in the variable 'average'. Notice how the additions are in brackets to ensure that they are done first.

```
if average >= 50 then

        print ("Pass")
```

This 'if' statement checks to see if the average is equal to or greater than 50. If it is the message "Pass" is output.

```
else

        print ("Fail")
```

There is no need for another 'if' statement as if the average is not 50 or above it must be less than 50. Therefore an 'else' statement is used.

```
endif
```

In the pseudocode dialect that we are using, an 'endif' statement must be placed at the end of the selection block of code.

Indentation

It is considered good practice to indent statements that occur within an 'if' statement.

Some programming languages demand it but most will accept it if you don't. Indentation helps to show the logic in your algorithm.

The statements above should be set out in the following way:

Code ————————————————————————

```
if average >= 50 then
        print("Pass")        This is indented as it is dependent
                             on the 'if' statement.
else
        print("Fail")        This is indented as it is dependent
                             on the 'else' statement.
endif
```

ACTIVITY 1.9

Create an algorithm, expressed as pseudocode, that asks a user to enter a number between 1 and 10.

Complete Interactive Activity 1g on Cambridge Elevate

If the number is 5 or less the message: (the number input) " is a low number." is output to the screen and if it is over 5 the message: (the number input) " is a high number." is output.

ACTIVITY 1.10

A teacher created an algorithm to automatically generate one comment for a student's test result based on the score out of 10.

```
score = input("Please enter the test result.")

if score < 5 then

     print("You must try harder next time.")

elseif score > 5 then

     print("You have gained half marks.")

elseif score > 7

     print("This is a good result.")

elseif score > 8

     print("This is an excellent result.")

endif
```

The teacher input a score of 9 and expected the message 'This is an excellent result.' to be printed. However, the comment produced was not as he expected. What would have been generated? Explain why this was the case.

Boolean operators

These operators are named after George Boole, a 19th century English mathematician who formulated an algebraic system of logic.

They are sometimes referred to as logical operators.

Look at this Venn diagram, which shows the number of rainy and sunny days in a fortnight.

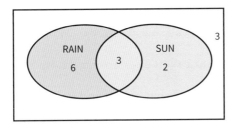

There were 3 days where there was RAIN **AND** SUN.

There were 6 days where there was RAIN **AND NOT** SUN.

There were 2 days where there was SUN **AND NOT** RAIN.

There were 11 days where there was SUN **OR** RAIN (6 with rain only, 2 with sun only and 3 where there were both.).

The words underlined in bold are all Boolean operators.

Key term

logical operator: operator such as AND, OR, NOT, which performs a Boolean operation on some inputs

Tip

The instructions that follow 'if' statements and are executed as a result of the 'if' statements should be indented. Look at the examples to see how this is done.

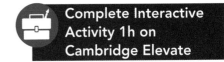

Complete Interactive Activity 1h on Cambridge Elevate

Operator	Function	Example

AND	**Logical AND operator** If all of the operands are true then the condition becomes true.	```if length > 6 AND width > 3 then```
		
		``` area = length * width```
		
		```else```
		
		``` print("Rectangle is not large enough.")```
		
		```endif```
		
		Note: In this example the length must be greater than 6 AND the width must be greater than 3 to work out the area.

OR	**Logical OR operator** If any of the operands are true then the condition becomes true.	```if score < 0 OR score >100 then```
		
		``` print("The score is invalid.")```
		
		```endif```
		
		Note: In this example if the score entered is less than 0 OR if it is greater than 100 it will not be accepted.

NOT	**Logical NOT operator** Used to reverse the logical state of the operand.	```if NOT (length >= 6 AND width >= 3) then```
		
		``` print("Rectangle is not large enough.")```
		
		```endif```
		
		Note: This produces the same result as the first example.

Tip

Study the OCR Pseudocode Guide as you read through the following algorithm so that you understand the command words and how they have to be used.

WORKED EXAMPLE

A student would like to select a suitable T-shirt from local shops. The colour could be red, blue or white, the size should be medium and the shop must be no more than 10 miles away.

Create an algorithm to help the student find suitable T-shirts.

```
colour = input("Enter colour of T-shirt.")

size = input("Enter size as S, M or L.")

distance = input("Enter distance to shop in miles.")
```

The user is asked to input the T-shirt colour and size and the distance to the shop. The values entered are stored in variables.

```
if(colour == "red" OR colour == "blue" OR colour == "white")
AND size == "M" AND distance <= 10 then
```

The 'if' statement is used to select the desirable characteristics.

The items for colour selection are enclosed in brackets so that they are evaluated together.

```
print("This T shirt is suitable.")
```

If all of the variables meet the criteria, then this message is printed

```
else
```

```
print("No. This T shirt is not suitable.")
```

If all the variables do not meet the criteria, then this message is printed.

```
endif
```

The 'endif' statement must be placed after the 'if', 'else' code.

 Download Worksheet 1.4 from Cambridge Elevate

 Complete Interactive Activity 1i on Cambridge Elevate

ACTIVITY 1.11

An 11 to 18 school would like you to design software to help with student administration. The software should allow the user to input the first name and the surname of each student and then their year and tutor group.

In each year there are four tutor groups: red, green, blue and yellow so that, for example, a tutor group is designated as 7 red or 9 blue.

Create an algorithm that would allow a user to enter these details and check that the data entered is acceptable, i.e. check that the year group or tutor group entered actually exists.

'Nested if' statements

The 'if … elseif … else' statements are sometimes referred to as *nested if statements* as the 'elseif' and 'else' statements run inside the overall 'if' statement.

But strictly speaking, 'nested if' should refer to two complete 'if' statements, one running inside the other.

WORKED EXAMPLE

A shop gives a discount of 5% on purchases over £100 up to a maximum of £50. If the discount would be greater than this it has to be reduced back to £50.

```
purchase = input("Please enter the money spent in £.")
```

The user is asked to enter the purchase price.

```
if purchase > 100 then
```

If the purchase price is greater than £100 the discount is calculated.

```
        discount = purchase / 100 * 5

        if discount > 50 then
```

The 'nested if' is then used to check if the discount is more than 50.

Notice how the second 'if' statement is indented.

```
                discount = 50
```

If the discount is more than £50 it is reduced back to £50.

```
        endif
```

endif for the inner 'if'.

```
endif
```

endif for the outer 'if'.

Complete the Cambridge Computing Online activity
www.cambridge.org/links/kose4002

Download Worksheet 1.5 from Cambridge Elevate

Switch/case

As well as the 'if … elseif … else' statements, switch/case is another method that can be used for selection. It is very useful where users have to select an item from a list.

WORKED EXAMPLE

In a multiple choice question there are four possible answers, labelled **A**, **B**, **C** and **D**. To select their answer the users have to enter one of those letters. They will then be informed if they are correct or incorrect. There should also be a method to inform them if they enter a letter other than the four allowed. (In this example the correct answer is option **C**.)

Using 'if … elseif … else' statements, this could be coded as:

```
answer = input("Please select an option.")

    if answer == "A" then

        print("Sorry. That is incorrect.")

    elseif answer == "B" then

        print("Sorry. That is incorrect.")

    elseif answer == "C" then

        print("Well done. That is the correct answer.")

    elseif answer == "D" then

        print("Sorry. That is incorrect.")

    else

        print("That option is not recognised.")

    endif
```

Using switch/case it would be coded as:

```
answer = input("Please select an option.")

switch answer:

    case "A":

        print("Sorry. That is incorrect.")

    case "B":

        print("Sorry. That is incorrect.")

    case "C":

        print("Well done. That is the correct answer.")
```

```
    case "D":

        print("Sorry. That is incorrect.")

    default:

        print("That option is not recognised.")

endswitch
```

ACTIVITY 1.12

A student is writing code to ask a user to enter the month number, e.g. 1 = January and 12 = December. The user should then receive a message giving the name of the month.

Write an algorithm in pseudocode, using switch/case statements, to solve this problem.

Practice questions

1. Using pseudocode examples, explain the following terms:

    a. variables
    b. relational operators
    c. Boolean operators
    d. 'nested if' statements

Complete Interactive Activity 1j on Cambridge Elevate

Your final challenge

*   'We drive anywhere' is a taxi firm who have the following criteria when working out the customer charge.

Between 8am and 8pm the following rules apply:

1. £3 for the first mile and £2 for every additional mile.

2. If there are more than 4 passengers there is a charge of £2 for each extra passenger.

Between 8pm and 8am, the overall charge is doubled.

a. Design an algorithm that will allow the taxi drivers to input the required information and will then output the total charge.

b. Display your algorithm as a flow diagram and as pseudocode.

Download Self-assessment 1 worksheet from Cambridge Elevate

2 Iteration

Learning outcomes

By the end of this chapter you should be able to:

- explain what is meant by iteration
- explain the difference between definite and indefinite iteration
- use for loops
- use while loops
- use do … until loops
- use nested loops
- analyse algorithms using trace tables
- use iteration when designing algorithms.

Challenge: write an algorithm for a computer game

- The computer games industry is huge, with over 50% of the British and United States population regularly playing.
- Top selling games earn more than Hollywood blockbusters and have 'red carpet' premieres.
- Your challenge is to write an algorithm for a new computer game!

Why iteration?

Iteration is the act of repeating a process until there is a desired result.

- Iteration is used in education. We repeat activities and assessments, to master a new topic. That is the desired result.
- We learn poetry or the script of a play by repeating the lines over and over again until we can quote them without making any mistakes. That is the desired result.
- When we practise sports skills we are using iteration. We execute actions over and over again until we can perform them perfectly every time, like always scoring from the penalty spot! That is the desired result.

What is iteration used for?

We mentioned iteration when we looked at simple algorithms using flow diagrams. We use iteration in our daily lives for actions such as learning to do something: it is called practice!

Everything we learn, from walking, to sport, to driving a car, requires iteration until we have mastered the skills.

Key term

iteration: a procedure or a set of statements or commands is repeated either for a set number of times or until there is a desired outcome

We do the action over and over again until we can do it properly or better than we did before. In a computer program, iteration is used so that a section of code is repeated to check on a condition, e.g. the temperature, until it reaches one that the programmer has selected, e.g. temperature equals 20 °C.

Program constructs that cause iteration are called loops and there are several different types of loop. Loops are explained in detail in the following sections.

 Complete the Cambridge Computing Online activity www.cambridge.org/links/kose4003

There was even a popular film made about iteration.

The film *Groundhog Day* is about a person caught in a loop (Visit the IMDb website to watch a trailer of the film).

For a range of time he has to live the same day over and over again.

He has to live the same day over and over again *until* there is a desired outcome.

While he does the unwanted action he has to go back and start all over again.

All of the words in red used to describe the film are also used in algorithms, pseudocode and actual programming languages.

 Key term

loop: part of a program where the same activity is specified once and then repeated for a fixed number of times or until a condition is met. Usually the condition is stated within the loop itself

Definite iteration
In these types of loops, the number of iterations is known before the execution of the loop is started, e.g. it may be set to three or five times and it will execute that number of times, whatever the conditions, unless there is a command to break out of the loop.

Definite iteration can be run with a 'for' loop and also with a 'while' loop.

 Key term

execution: when a program or part of a program is run by the computer

For loop
Basically this states 'For a set number of times, do something'.

An example written in pseudocode:

Code

```
for index = 0 to 10
```
There is a for statement with a variable (in this case with the identifier 'index') and the range of values it must count through.

```
    print(index)
```
The action that should be done at each iteration.

```
next index
```
An end statement to trigger the next turn of the loop.

In this case the printed output would be:

0   1   2   3   4   5   6   7   8   9   10

Complete the Cambridge Computing Online activity
www.cambridge.org/links/kose4004

While loop

Definite iteration can also be accomplished using a while loop set for a predetermined number of turns.

An example in pseudocode:

Code

`index = 0`	The variable index is initialised as 0.
`while index < = 10`	While 'index' is less than or equal to 10, it will be printed.
`  print("The number is "` `+ index)`	
`index = index + 1`	At each turn of the loop, index is incremented by 1.
`endwhile`	The 'endwhile' statement is placed at the end of the loop and will transfer the processing back to the top of the loop. The loop will run while the condition (<=10) is still true.

The 'while' and 'for' loops can both be used for definite iteration and produce the same result.

It is just personal preference as to which one a programmer will use.

Tip

The print statement could just have been index but text has been added to make it more user friendly. Notice how the added text is in speech marks and the statements are joined by '+' symbols.

WORKED EXAMPLE

Write an algorithm in pseudocode to ask a user to input a number. The algorithm should then print out the times table for that number.

`number = input("Please enter a number:")`	The user is asked to enter a number for the times table. It is stored in a variable called 'number'.
`for index  = 1 to 12`	The 'for' loop is started.
`    print(index + " x " + number + " = " +` `    number*index)`	This is printed while the loop is running.
`next index`	The end of the loop.

The text to be printed looks quite complicated but we have met all of the constructs before. Let's go through them. We will assume that the user entered the number 9 and index has reached a value of 6.

```
print(index + " x " + number + " = " + number*index)
```

What will be printed	Explanation
6	Index is now equal to 6
6 x	As we have already seen, a '+' in a print statement will join two items together. In this case it will add the letter 'x' to stand as a multiplication sign.
6 x 9	Now 'number' is added. That is the number 9.
6 x 9 =	Now the equals symbol is added.
6 x 9 = 54	Now 54 is added as that is equal to number*index or 9*6.

 Download Worksheet 2.1 from Cambridge Elevate

 Complete Interactive Activity 2a on Cambridge Elevate

Indefinite iteration

In indefinite iteration (also known as conditional iteration), the number of iterations is not known before the loop is started. The iterations stop when a certain condition becomes true or false. There are two main variants of this type of loop, depending on where in the block of code the comparison is made.

While loop

The loop continues *while* a certain condition remains true.

The condition is checked *before* the code is executed.

It is written as:

Code ———————————————————————

```
while a condition is true

    …

    Block of code to be executed

    …

endwhile
```

ACTIVITY 2.1

Write the above algorithm using a while loop.

WORKED EXAMPLE

A while loop can be used to check if a password is correct by comparing it with one that is stored.

`storedPassword = password stored in the system`	The password stored in the system is assigned to the variable 'storedPassword'.
`password = ""`	The variable 'password' is going to be used in the while loop and it must be declared before the loop is set up. It is given the value of an empty text string by using the speech marks with nothing between them as the while loop is going to run while the string is empty.

`while password == ""`	The while loop is started and will run while the variable 'password' has the value of an empty string.
`password = input("Please enter a password.")`	The user is asked to enter the password.
`if password != storedPassword then`	This checks the password variable against the stored password. It is checking to see if it is **not** equal to it (!=).
	This selection ('if' statement) is nested within the while statement.
	We could also have written this as:
	`If NOT(password == storedPassword)`
`password = ""`	If the passwords do not match then the password variable is changed to empty text so that the loop will run again.
`endif`	This ends the if block.
`endwhile`	This ends the while loop and directs processing back to the while statement.
	This loop will run forever until the correct password is entered and the loop will be exited.

In Chapter 1 there is a flow diagram illustrating an algorithm that allows a user only three failed attempts before stopping the program. The pseudocode above could be modified to allow this.

Code

`storedPassword = password stored in the system`	The password stored in the system is assigned to the variable 'storedPassword'.
`attempts = 0`	The variable 'attempts' is assigned the value of 0.
`password = ""`	
`while password = "" AND attempts <3`	This time there are two conditions for the loop to run. The variable 'attempts' has to have a value of less than 3 i.e. 0, 1 or 2.
`password = input("Please enter a password.")`	
`if password != storedPassword then`	
`password = ""`	
`attempts = attempts +1`	As they are not the same, the variable 'attempts' is increased by 1.
`endif`	
`endwhile`	

ACTIVITY 2.2

A student wants to find the sum of a series of numbers. Write an algorithm that would allow them to enter the numbers needed and would then print out their sum. (Hint: how could the algorithm be informed that all of the numbers had been input?)

 Complete Interactive Activity 2b on Cambridge Elevate

Do … until loops

The do … until loop is similar to the while loop but the comparison is not done until the end of the code block.

It is written as:

Code

```
do (or repeat)
      execute this code
until this condition is met
```

Because the condition is checked at the end of the code block, it is always run at least once.

The loop will run while the condition remains unmet.

WORKED EXAMPLE

The password entry example could be written using a do … until loop.

Code	Explanation
`storedPassword = password stored in the system`	The password stored in the system is assigned to the variable 'storedPassword'.
`attempts = 0`	
`do`	
`    password = input("Please enter a password")`	
`        attempts = attempts + 1`	The variable 'attempts' is incremented by 1. So it will equal 0, then 1 and finally 2.
`until password == storedPassword OR attempts = 2`	The loop will run until the password is correct, or 'attempts' is equal to 2, as when attempts = 2 the user will have had 3 attempts.

 Tip

The do … until loop is more efficient than the while loop. For both, the variable 'password' has to be introduced before the comparison is made. In the while loop it has to be introduced before the loop code block because the comparison is made at the start, but for the do … until, where the comparison is not made until the end, it can be introduced by the 'input' statement in the code block. Therefore fewer lines of code are needed!

Download Worksheet 2.2 from Cambridge Elevate

WORKED EXAMPLE

A client would like an algorithm for a computer game with the following specification:

- The computer generates a random number between 1 and 100.

- The user is asked to enter a number.

- If the guess is too high, then they are told 'Your guess is too high.'

- If the guess is too low, then they are told 'Your guess is too low.'

- If the guess is correct, then they are told that they are right.

`mysteryNumber = a random number between 1 and 100`	There isn't a 'random number' method in the OCR pseudocode and so we will just use this statement.
`guess = 0`	The variable 'guess' is assigned the value of 0.
`while guess == 0`	A while loop is set to run while 'guess' is equal to 0.
`guess = input("Please enter a number between 1 and 100.")`	The user is asked to input a number that is assigned to the 'guess' variable. Therefore 'guess' is no longer equal to 0.
`if guess > mysteryNumber then`	If the guess is greater than the random number …
`guess = 0`	… 'guess' is changed back to 0 so that the loop will run again and …
`print("Your guess is too high.")`	… the user is informed.
`elseif  guess < mysteryNumber`	If the guess is less than the random number …
`guess = 0`	… 'guess' is changed back to 0 so that the loop will run again and …
`print("Your guess is too low.")`	… the user is informed.
`endif`	This ends the if block.
`endwhile`	This ends the while loop and processing is sent back to the start if 'guess' has been changed back to 0.
`print("Well done. You guessed correctly!")`	If the guess is equal to the random number then the variable 'guess' will not be equal to 0 and so the loop will be exited and this print statement will be executed.

ACTIVITY 2.3

The client would now like an improvement to the game. They would like the user to be given an option to play the game again: 'press the Y' key to play the game again and any other key to exit.

Adapt the code above to incorporate this and, as an added extra, print a message for the user when they finally quit the game. Add comments to explain how your algorithm works.

Nested loops

One loop can be run inside another loop. This is referred to as 'nesting', so they are called 'nested loops'. You can also have nested 'if' statements.

WORKED EXAMPLE

The following algorithm will print out all of the times tables from 2 to 12.

`for index = 2 to 12`	The first 'for' loop is set up to run from 2 to 12.
`  print("This is the " + index " times table")`	This prints a message telling the user which times table is being printed.
`    for times = 2 to 12`	The second, inner loop is set up, also to run from 2 to 12.
`print(times  + " x " + index + " = " + index*times)`	The second loop will run from 2 to 12 and each time will multiply the value for 'index' by the value for 'times'.
`    next times`	This ends the inner loop.
`next index`	This ends the outer loop.

Therefore:

- The first loop runs and index = 2.

- A message is printed saying that this is the index times table.

- The second loop starts with times = 2 and index is multiplied by times (2 x 2).

- The second loop now runs to completion, i.e. times = 3, then times = 4, etc.

- When the second loop has finished, control is given back to the first loop, which runs for a second time with index = 3.

- This continues until index = 12.

So the second loop has to work much harder. For every single turn of the first loop it has to do 11!

It does 122 to the first loop's 11.

```
This is the 2 times table
2 × 2 = 4
3 × 2 = 6
4 × 2 = 8
5 × 2 = 10
6 × 2 = 12
7 × 2 = 14
8 × 2 = 16
9 × 2 = 18
10 × 2 = 20
11 × 2 = 22
12 × 2 = 24
This is the 3 times table
2 × 3 = 6
3 × 3 = 9
4 × 3 = 12
5 × 3 = 15
6 × 3 = 18
7 × 3 = 21
8 × 3 = 24
9 × 3 = 27
10 × 3 = 30
11 × 3 = 33
12 × 3 = 36
```

 Download Worksheet 2.3 from Cambridge Elevate

ACTIVITY 2.4

Write an algorithm like the one shown above but allow the user to input the range of tables they want, e.g. from 5 to 9. Explain how your algorithm works.

Infinite loops

These are also called 'endless loops' because they go on repeating and never stop. Sometimes they are intentional, for example if you want the algorithm to check the temperature over and over again, forever (or until there is an override to exit the loop). But infinite loops are often unintentional mistakes. A common cause is to place a condition in a while loop that will always be true.

Code

```
index = 1
while index <10
  print(index)
endwhile
```

In this example, the programmer has forgotten to increment the variable index before the end of the loop. It will always remain with the value of 1, therefore it will always be less than 10.

Code

```
index = 1
while index <10
  print (index)
  index = index -1
endwhile
```

In this example, the programmer has incremented the variable index before the end of the loop but has written –1 instead of +1 so it will always be less than 10.

Remember

1. Iteration means that a procedure or a set of statements or commands is repeated a set number of times or until there is a desired outcome.
2. In definite iteration, the number of iterations is known before the execution of the loop is started, and can be run with for loops and while loops.
3. In indefinite iteration (conditional iteration), the number of iterations is not known before the loop is started. The number of iterations depends on a condition becoming true or false.
4. Conditional while loops run until a condition becomes false.
5. Do … until loops run until a condition becomes true.
6. While loops are tested at the start of a loop.
7. Do … until loops are tested at end of a loop.
8. Nested loops runs completely inside another loop.
9. Infinite loops run forever. They might be deliberate or accidental.

Complete Interactive Activity 2c on Cambridge Elevate

Trace tables

When programs are being coded, errors often occur. Some of these may be syntax errors (mistakes with the way that the code is written). Each programming language must be written in a particular way and use certain keywords.

Programming languages have rules of grammar, just like any other language.

Algorithms do not suffer these errors. They are written in pseudocode, for human use, and are not meant to be understood by a computer. Therefore, pseudocode is far more forgiving. You could have incorrect capital letters, missing punctuation marks and missing indents and it would still be understandable because it will be followed by a human, instead of a computer.

Algorithms and their expression in pseudocode are intended to allow a programmer to create a logical solution to a problem that can then be translated into any actual programming language that a computer can understand.

Algorithms can suffer from the second type of error: logical error. There might be a blip in the programmer's thinking and the algorithm doesn't produce the output or solution expected. For example, a while loop might have been set up incorrectly, or an if block doesn't select what it was expected to select.

One way to trap these errors is to do a dry run of the algorithm using sample data that can be tracked through the algorithm using a trace table.

Analysing the algorithm with a trace table will show whether it achieves what it was intended to, i.e. whether it is fit for purpose.

A trace table has columns for each of the variables and rows for each of the steps in the algorithm.

Key term

syntax error: a grammatical mistake in the code, which could be caused by a misspelling, e.g. 'prnit' instead of 'print' or by missing colons, semi-colons or brackets

Watch out

When you write computer code, you must make sure that you use exactly the right keywords. Otherwise your program might not run correctly.

Key terms

dry run: the program is run on paper and each stage is carefully analysed to see what values the various variables, inputs and outputs have. At this stage, a computer is not being used

trace table: while the dry run is being worked through, a table is drawn up showing the values of each variable, input and output and how they change as the program is running. A trace table has columns for each of the variables and rows for each of the steps in the algorithm

Tip

When you are writing pseudocode, always try to use the correct punctuation. That will help you later when you are writing the computer code in a particular language.

WORKED EXAMPLE

Here is a trace table for the nested loop algorithm above (but so that it isn't too large it will just cover the times tables for 2).

```
for index = 2 to 2

  print("This is the " + index "times table.")

  for times = 2 to 12

      print(times + " x " + index + " = " + index * times)

  next times

next index
```

index	Output	times	Output
2	2		
2		2	4
2		3	6
2		4	8
2		5	10
2		6	12
2		7	14
2		8	16
2		9	18
2		10	20
2		11	22
2		12	24

There are two loops; one for 'index' and an inner loop for 'times'.

When the outer loop starts, index is equal to 2.

The next command is to output the value of index.

Then times runs in a loop from 2 to 12.

On each turn of this loop, the value of index*times has to be output. While the inner loop is running, the value of index remains at 2.

WORKED EXAMPLE

This algorithm should allow the user to input numbers over and over again and the sum of the numbers is found. The loop will stop when the user enters a zero as the loop runs while number is greater than 0. (It would also stop if the user entered a negative number.)

```
total = 0

input number

while number > 0

    total = total + number

    input number

endwhile

print(total)
```

This algorithm could be tested with sample data such as 3, 13, 21, 28, 0.

The trace table would be:

total	number	Output
0	3	
3	13	
16	21	
37	28	
65	0	65

At the start, total = 0 and the first test number, 3, is entered.

Therefore total = 3 when the second number, 13, is added.

The loop should stop when the user enters 0. At that time the total should be 65 and that will be the output.

WORKED EXAMPLE

Here is another algorithm.

```
Y = 2

for X = 1 to 6

    Y = Y + X

next X

print(Y)
```

X	Y	Output	Explanation
1	2		When the loop starts, X becomes 1 and Y already is equal to 2.
2	3		When X is incremented to 2, Y is equal to 3 (2+1) from the previous loop.
3	5		When X is incremented to 3, Y= 3 + 2 from the previous loop.
4	8		
5	12		Explanations as above.
6	17		
6	23	23	The final value of Y is output.

 Download Worksheet 2.4 from Cambridge Elevate

ACTIVITY 2.5

Use a trace table to track the variables and the output from the following algorithm.

```
turns = 0

X = 3

while turns < 22

  X = X * 3

  turns = turns + 3

endwhile

print(X)

print(turns)
```

Here is the start of the trace table.

turns	X	Output
0	3	
0	9	
3	9	

 Tip

At the start, turns = 0 and X = 3.

On each turn of the loop X is changed to X * 3 and turns is changed to turns + 3.

The loop will run while turns < 22.

Complete Interactive Activity 2d on Cambridge Elevate

Remember

1. Trace tables use sample data to track the values of variables through an algorithm.
2. Trace tables have columns for variables and outputs and rows for steps in the algorithm.

Efficiency of algorithms

Different programmers will create different algorithms to solve the same problem: for every problem there can be many solutions.

Although they might successfully solve the problem, some algorithms might be more efficient than others: they might have fewer lines of code and produce the solution in less time. In Chapter 5 we will be looking at algorithms for sorting and searching data and seeing that some can do it far more quickly than others.

Software development

Creating an algorithm is only one stage in developing software to meet the needs of a particular situation. In Chapter 5 we will be looking in detail at all of the stages that need to be carried out in order to achieve a successful outcome. Briefly, they are:

- identification and analysis of the problem
- design
- implementation
- testing
- documentation
- evaluation
- maintenance.

In this chapter we have only looked at stages within the design phase. It is crucial to get the design of the solution right before proceeding to coding, which is done during the implementation stage.

Implementation

This is the stage where the algorithm, either in a flow diagram or pseudocode, is translated into an actual programming language. Pseudocode allows the programmer to concentrate on the logic of the solution without having to think about the way the actual programming language has to be written with its rules and syntax.

It's a bit like making notes of your ideas and then writing them out in 'proper' English with all the correct spellings, punctuation marks and rules of grammar.

Key term

efficiency: efficiency can be assessed by:

- how long it takes a program to generate a result
- how much code has been written to generate the result
- how much processor time and memory it uses

WORKED EXAMPLE

Here is the algorithm of the guessing game that we looked at earlier.

`mysteryNumber = a random number between 1 and 100.`	There isn't a 'random number' method in the OCR pseudocode and so we will just use this statement.
`guess = 0`	The variable 'guess' is assigned the value of 0.
`while guess == 0`	A while loop is set to run while 'guess' is equal to 0.
`  guess = input("Please enter a number between 1 and 100.")`	The user is asked to input a number, which is assigned to the 'guess' variable. Therefore 'guess' is no longer equal to 0.
`  if guess > mysteryNumber then`	If the guess is greater than the random number …
`    guess = 0`	… guess is changed back to 0 so that the loop will run again and …
`    print("Your guess is too high.")`	… the user is informed.
`  elseif  guess < mysteryNumber`	If the guess is less than the random number …
`    guess = 0`	… guess is changed back to 0 so that the loop will run again and …
`    print("Your guess is too low.")`	… the user is informed.
`  endif`	This ends the if block.
`endwhile`	This ends the while loop and processing is sent back to the start if guess has been changed back to 0.
`print("Well done. You guessed correctly!")`	If the guess is actually equal to the random number then the variable 'guess' will not be equal to 0 and so the loop will be exited and this print statement will be executed.

Now we will look at how the guessing game algorithm could be implemented in two different programming languages.

Python

Python is a programming language that was first released in 1991 and has become the most widely used language for teaching computer science in schools and universities. Python users have developed modules and libraries of functions so that it can be used for web and Internet development, database access and networking.

WORKED EXAMPLE

Pseudocode	Python code

```
Pseudocode

mysteryNumber = a random number between
1 and 100.

guess = 0

while guess == 0

   guess = input("Please enter a number

   between 1 and 100.")

   if guess > mysteryNumber then

     guess = 0

     print("Your guess is too high.")

   elseif  guess < mysteryNumber

     guess = 0

     print("Your guess is too low.")

   endif

endwhile

print("Well done. You guessed correctly!")
```

```
Python code

import random

mysteryNumber = random.randint(1, 100)

guess = 0

while (guess == 0):

   guess = int(input("Please enter a number

   between 1 and 100: "))

   if guess > mysteryNumber:

     guess = 0

     print("Your guess is too high.")

   elif guess < mysteryNumber:

     guess = 0

     print("Your guess is too low.")



print("Well done. You guessed correctly!")
```

Notice the following differences:

1. This language has its own terminology for generating a random number.

2. For the while loop there is no endwhile. Python uses indentation to show when a block starts and ends.

3. Python also uses indentation for if blocks.

4. Also notice how these commands:

   ```
   while(guess==0):

   if guess > mysteryNumber:
   ```

   require a colon after their statements. This is an example of the language's syntax.

5. Also notice how the program has to be told that the value that is input is in fact an integer number:

   ```
   guess = int(input("Please enter a number between
   1 and 100: "))
   ```

   More syntax!

Key term

syntax: the rules of spelling, punctuation and grammar of a language so that the meaning of what is being communicated is clear (humans can make allowances if the rules are broken, but computers can't!)

JavaScript

JavaScript is a computer programming language commonly used to create interactive effects in web browsers. It is used with HTML to produce interactive web pages. HTML provides the user interface and JavaScript provides the brains.

When the correct number is entered.

An actual loop does not have to be programmed because the user is doing it manually. All that is needed is code attached to the action buttons.

Code

```
mysteryNumber = Math.floor((Math.random() * 100) + 1);
```

WORKED EXAMPLE

This code is executed when the 'Try it' button is pressed.

JavaScript code	Explanation
`var m = document.getElementById('message');`	This line creates a variable for the text box on the page where the messages will be displayed. Notice how a variable needs the 'var' keyword. This isn't needed in Python.
`var guess = document.getElementById('myguess').value;`	This stores the number (value) that the user has just entered in an entry box named 'myguess'.
`if(guess > mysteryNumber) {`	An if statement. Notice how the block of the if statement is enclosed in braces (curly brackets).
`m.innerHTML = ('Your guess is too high. Try again.');`	This is the message displayed if the guess is too high.
`document.getElementById('myguess').value = '';`	This blanks the entry box ready for the next entry.

```
}
```
Brace at end of if block.

```
else if (guess < mysteryNumber) {

m.innerHTML = ('Your guess is too low. Try again.');

document.getElementById('myguess').value = '';

}
```
This block checks if the number entered is too small.

```
else {

m.innerHTML = ('Well done. You guessed correctly!

Would you like another go?');

}
```
If the number is not too large or not too small, it must be just right!
The user is told and asked if they want to try again.

Remember

1. There can be many different algorithms to solve a particular problem.
2. Some algorithms are more efficient than others in terms of execution speed, amount of code and how much computer memory is needed.
3. Algorithms displayed as flow diagrams or pseudocode have to be coded into programming languages.

The algorithm in the worked examples is interpreted differently for these two programming languages, which produce different visual displays, but the basic logic is the same. And that basic logic was developed by the algorithm.

Complete Interactive Activity 2e on Cambridge Elevate

Practice question

1. Complete the trace table for the following algorithm.

```
number_1 = 3

number_2 = 2

total = 0

for X = 1 to 5

        number_1 = number_1 * X

        number_2 = number_2 *( X + 1)

        total = number_1 + number_2

next X

print(total)
```

number_1	number_2	total	Output
3	2	0	
3	4	7	

Tip

As there is no command in the OCR pseudocode for generating a random number, you can use the same method that we used earlier.

Your final challenge

You have been asked to create an algorithm for a game with the following specification:

- The player starts the game with £5.
- Each round of the game costs 20p. If the player has not got 20p then they are informed and have to quit the game.
- For each game, the player has to roll three dice with six faces with numbers 1 to 6.
- If two dice have the same number then the player wins £1.
- If all three dice have the same number then the player wins £2.
- The player is informed if they have won any money and how much.
- They are also told how much money in total they have.
- The player is asked after each game whether they want to play again or quit.
- If they quit they are told how much money they have.

Your task is to create an algorithm for this game, and you can illustrate it using either a flow diagram or pseudocode.

Even if you are going to present your solution in pseudocode, a flow diagram might be useful for determining the information flow. The start of a possible flow diagram is provided.

- Read through the specification until you understand exactly what you have to do.
- Make notes about the key points.

Here are some initial ideas:

- £5.00 to start the game.
- Ask if they want to play.
- Check if they have at least 20p.
- Deduct 0.20 if they play.
- Roll three dice.
- Check numbers on dice.
- Check if they have won any money.

Remember to:

- List the variables that you will use.
- List the inputs and outputs that will be required.
- Where will selection and iteration be required?

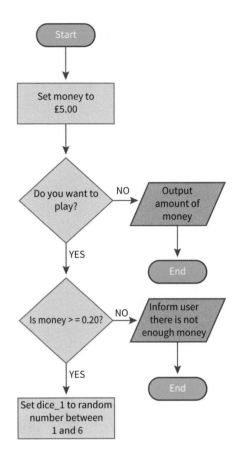

 Download Self-assessment 2 worksheet from Cambridge Elevate

3 Boolean logic

Learning outcomes

By the end of this chapter you should be able to:

- create truth tables for Boolean operators
- draw AND, OR and NOT logic gates
- combine logic gates into logic circuits
- create truth tables for logic circuits.

Challenge: design logic circuits to solve a control problem

- In Chapter 1, we looked at Boolean operators using the keywords AND, OR and NOT. We saw how these could be combined to create logic in an algorithm and returned one of two values: true or false.
- Your challenge is to design logic circuits to solve a control problem in a healthy drinks factory.

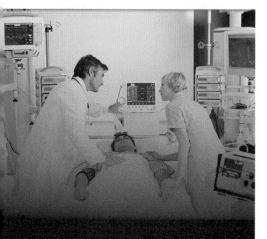

Logic gates can make a difference between life and death as they can monitor patients and trigger YES/NO alarms if there is a problem.

Why Boolean logic?

- Automatic security lights rely on logic gates to know when to switch on and off.

- Sensors used with logic gates can trigger actions, e.g. windows shut automatically when it rains.

- Boolean logic is used to evaluate whether a condition is true or false.

Boolean logic

Boolean logic is very important to computer science because of the way in which computers work.

Computers operate as digital devices using transistors, which are either on or off. The transistors either transmit an electric current (on) or they do not (off). These two states of on or off can be used to represent the two conditions of true (on) or false (off). The two states are also represented by the digits 1 and 0.

Compound statements

Transistors can be combined into logic circuits in order to solve problems using Boolean logic.

When multiple Boolean operators are used in a statement (a compound statement), it can be tricky to work out if the condition for the statement as a whole is true or false.

For example, if we wanted to select red or blue, medium-sized T-shirts from a shop no more than 10 miles away and we could write it as:

Code

```
if(colour = "red" OR colour = "blue") AND size = "M" and
distance <= 10 then …
```

This is a compound statement. In this instance, if all of the above specifications are met then the condition is true and if they are not then the condition is false. But if we wanted any colour except pink, the statement would read:

Code

```
if(NOT colour = "pink") AND size = "M" and distance <= 10
then …
```

This makes it more difficult to work out at a glance whether the statement is true or false.

Truth tables can help as they show all the possible results of each sub-statement (true or false), and then the combined results for the whole statement.

Truth tables

The way in which Boolean operators reach their decision about whether statements are true or false can be shown using truth tables.

WORKED EXAMPLE

Look at the following 'if' statement:

```
if X == 3 AND Y == 6 then
        print("They are correct.")
endif
```

In order for the message to be printed X **must** equal 3 and Y **must** equal 6.

For the compound statement to be true **both** sub-statements **must** be true.

This can be shown in a truth table.

X	Y	X AND Y
T	T	T
F	T	F
T	F	F
F	F	F

Now let's use a truth table for a real-life example.

Boolean logic is used in burglar alarm systems.

Key terms

compound statement: a statement where Boolean operators are combined and work together to examine if several conditions are true or false

true or false: indicate whether a logical statement is correct or incorrect; this could be represented in a computer as 1s (true statements) and 0s (false statements) respectively

truth table: a table that shows all the possible combinations of outputs which can occur with all of the different possible inputs; usually used with logic problems

Tip

There are four possible combinations for the two values. Using the AND operator, both must be true for the compound statement to be true.

We only want the alarm to sound if:

We have turned it on **AND** the door is open.

The truth table will look like this:

Turned on	Door open	Alarm sounds
T	T	T
F	T	F
T	F	F
F	F	F

So 'alarm sounds' is true only if both of the other statements are true.

WORKED EXAMPLE

Now look at the following 'if' statement where they are joined by the OR operator.

```
if X == 3 OR Y == 6 then

        print("That is OK.")

endif
```

In this case if only one of them is true, the statement will be true and the message will be printed.

The truth table will look like this:

X	Y	X OR Y
T	T	T
F	T	T
T	F	T
F	F	F

WORKED EXAMPLE

In the following 'if' statement the NOT operator has been used.

```
if NOT (X == 3 AND Y == 6) then

        print("Conditions are met.")

endif
```

The NOT negates or reverses the statement in brackets. So the statement will be printed whenever X does not equal 3 AND Y does not equal 6, i.e. whenever they are not both true at the same time.

It reverses the results of the AND truth table.

Tip

Remember from Chapter 1 that == means 'equals to'.

Tip

There are four possible combinations for the two values. Using the OR operator, only one must be true for the compound statement to be true.

Tip

Using the NOT with the AND operator reverses the logic of the AND statement.

If the AND statement is false then the NOT AND statement will be true and vice versa.

The truth table will look like this:

X	Y	NOT (X AND Y)
T	T	F
F	T	T
T	F	T
F	F	T

 Complete the Cambridge Computing Online activity
www.cambridge.org/links/kose4005

ACTIVITY 3.1

Create the truth table for the following 'if' statement.

```
if NOT (X == 3 OR Y == 6) then

    print("Conditions are met.")

endif
```

 Complete Interactive Activity 3a on Cambridge Elevate

Logic gates

We can use our brains to work out the results of logical operations and use truth tables for assistance. The microprocessors in computers, however, are physical, digital devices without brains and they use transistors operating as electrical switches to calculate whether complex conditions are true or false.

These transistors can be wired together to form logic gates.

Each logic gate has one or more *inputs* and an *output*. An electric current that is output represents the binary digit 1 (or true) and a low or no current at all represents 0 (or false).

 Watch the logic gates animation on Cambridge Elevate

Logic gates are switches that perform a logical function on one or more logical inputs and produce an output if the conditions are true or false.

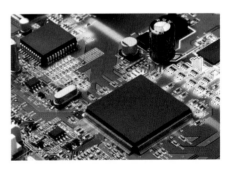

 Key term

logic gate: an electronic device which either produces or does not produce an output depending on the inputs it receives and the logic rule it is designed to apply.

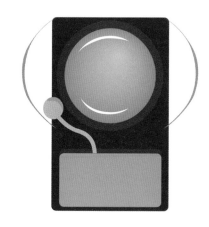

AND gate

This AND gate has two inputs, A and B and one output, Q. It has the same results as the truth table for the 'AND' operator above. Here is the truth table for this AND gate:

Inputs		Outputs
A	B	Q
0	0	0
1	0	0
0	1	0
1	1	1

An AND gate would be used in alarm systems to ensure that the alarm would sound only if the alarm was switched on AND the door was open.

OR gate

This OR gate has two inputs, A and B and one output, Q. Here is the truth table for this OR gate:

Inputs		Outputs
A	B	Q
0	0	0
1	0	1
0	1	1
1	1	1

In order for the gate to produce an output, there must be a current at **either** input.

OR gates would be used in a fire alarm system so that anyone could trigger the alarm, e.g. the one in the hall OR the one in the kitchen OR the one in the living room.

NOT gate

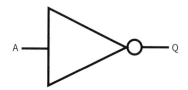

Tip

In the truth table we are using the digits 1 and 0. The digit 1 indicates that there is an electric current and 0 that there is no current. So 1 is used to represent 'on' and 0 to represent 'off'.

This NOT gate has one input A, and one output, Q. Here is the truth table for this NOT gate:

Inputs	Outputs
A	Q
0	1
1	0

If there is an input then there is no output, and vice versa.

A NOT gate would be used in a microwave. If the door is open then the microwave will not turn on. If the first is true then the second condition will be false.

 Download Worksheet 3.1 from Cambridge Elevate

Logic circuits

Logic gates can be combined to produce logic circuits. A logic circuit is designed with multiple logic gates so that it can take a variety of inputs (sometimes many hundreds) and process them to allow decisions to be made according to the various inputs. The inputs might be, for example, sensors on a motor car, or a plane, or at different points in a production line in a factory.

WORKED EXAMPLE

A student is setting up an automatic watering system for the greenhouse while she and her family are on holiday. She has a light sensor that is on and will emit a signal during the day, and a moisture sensor that is on and will emit a signal when the soil is wet. But she only wants the watering system to turn on at night and then only when the soil is dry, i.e. when there is NO light and when there is NO moisture. She chooses to use two NOT and one AND gates.

We can use letters to represent the inputs and outputs:

A = light (1) or dark (0) condition.

B = wet (1) or dry (0) condition.

Q = output to indicate whether the control system is to be active (1) or inactive (0).

So we can write:

Q = NOT(A) AND NOT(B)

So the watering system will turn on only if both conditions are false, i.e. it must be dark AND the soil must be dry. The following gates will be required.

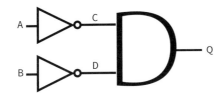

Tip

The numbers in brackets indicate whether 0 or 1 applies to a particular status (light, dark, wet, dry etc.).

Tip

The NOT gate is not negating the result of the AND gate.

The inputs from the two sensors (A and B) feed into NOT gates, which then feed into an AND gate. The outputs from NOT gates (C and D) provide the inputs for the AND gate. If there are inputs into the NOT gates there will be no outputs at C and D. So if the light and moisture sensors are supplying electric currents, they will be stopped by the NOT gates. And if they are not supplying a current then the NOT gates will transmit a current at C and D.

The truth table will be as follows:

Inputs		Outputs		
A	B	C	D	Q
0	0	1	1	1
1	0	0	1	0
0	1	1	0	0
1	1	0	0	0

The watering system will be turned on only if it is dark AND there is no moisture.

 Download Worksheet 3.2 from Cambridge Elevate

ACTIVITY 3.2

Give the logic gate and the truth table for the following statement:

Q = NOT (A OR B)

WORKED EXAMPLE

An alarm system uses 3 switches: A, B and C. The following combination of switches determines whether an alarm, X, sounds:

> If switch A OR switch B are in the ON position AND if switch C is in the OFF position then a signal to sound an alarm, X is produced.

This can be written as:

```
if (A == 1 OR B == 1) AND NOT (C == 1) then

    X = 1

endif
```

This can be represented by the following logic circuit:

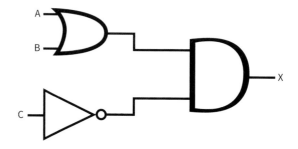

The truth table for this logic circuit would be:

Inputs			Outputs
A	B	C	X
0	0	0	0
0	0	1	0
0	1	0	1
0	1	1	0
1	0	0	1
1	0	1	0
1	1	0	1
1	1	1	0

 Complete Interactive Activity 3b on Cambridge Elevate

 Download Worksheet 3.3 from Cambridge Elevate

 Remember

1. Logic gates are switches which perform a logical function on one or more logical inputs and produce a single logical output.
2. There are logic gates for AND, OR and NOT logical functions:
   a. To produce an output in an AND gate, both inputs must have an electrical current.
   b. To produce an output in an OR gate either or both of the inputs must have an electrical current.
   c. In a NOT gate an output is produced if there is no input and vice versa.
3. Logic gates can be combined into logic circuits.
4. Truth tables can be used to compute the values of logical expressions.

 Complete Interactive Activity 3c on Cambridge Elevate

 Practice questions

1. The following logic circuit can be written as **P = (NOT A) AND B**:

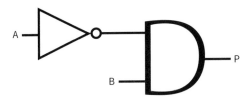

Complete the following Truth table for the circuit given below.

Inputs		Outputs
A	B	P
0	0	0
0	1	

2. Complete the following logic circuits by filling in the blanks.

The first one has been done for you.

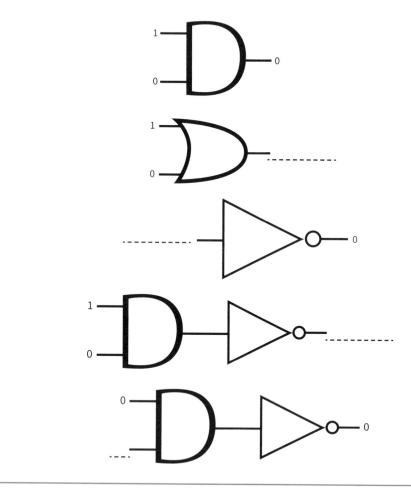

**Download
Self-assessment 3
worksheet from
Cambridge Elevate**

Your final challenge

- A healthy drinks company uses a conveyor belt in the factory.
- Before use, the bottles must be sterilised. They are moved along a conveyor belt which can be switched on by two switches, A and B, but only after the supervisor operates the master switch C.
- Draw the logic circuit and truth table to demonstrate to the designers for the system how it should work.

4 Data types and structures

Learning outcomes

By the end of this chapter you should be able to:

- explain what is meant by 'data type' and list some common types
- use the correct data types in algorithms
- carry out various manipulations such as finding the length of and slicing and concatenating 'string' data types
- create and work with simple array data structures
- create and work with two dimensional arrays
- describe other data structures.

Challenge: encode and decode messages with an encryption key

- Throughout history people have sent secret messages using invisible ink and by using cyphers and codes.
- Computers have enabled people to quickly encode and transmit messages using public and private keys.
- Your challenge is to create an algorithm to encode and decode messages using an encryption key!

Why data types and structures?

- We saw in Chapter 1 that data is stored in variables. There are different types of data and therefore the computer must be told what type each variable is storing. This process is called 'declaring' the variable.
- Data can take many different forms, depending on the type of information that is being stored, e.g. the data might be different kinds of numbers, text data or logical data.
- Data is held electronically all around us. This makes it easier for us to access. If we are ill whilst on holiday, a doctor can access our medical notes almost instantly.
- It is important to organise data. Dictionaries are organised alphabetically so that we can find the word we need. Digital data is the same: we need to put the data into categories in databases.
- Websites combine data from different databases all the time. An online bookshop will have data about books and data about customers – and each time you buy a book, a link will be made.

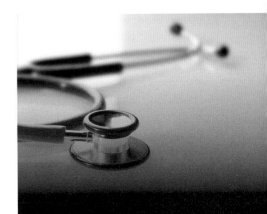

When you go to the doctor, information about what's wrong with you and the treatment you need is stored as data on computers.

Different data types

Examples of the different data types can be seen in this screenshot from a video game. The image shows the information page of a computer game displaying the user's progress.

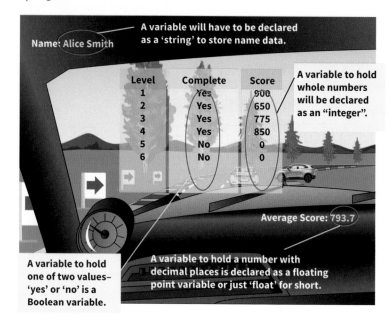

A variable will have to be declared as a 'string' to store name data.

A variable to hold whole numbers will be declared as an "integer".

A variable to hold one of two values– 'yes' or 'no' is a Boolean variable.

A variable to hold a number with decimal places is declared as a floating point variable or just 'float' for short.

In a computer program, a variable is used to hold data that can be used or manipulated in certain ways.

Computers need to be told what type of data it is, so they know how it can be manipulated and represented.

For example:

- A student created a variable called 'firstName' to hold the letters of a person's first name and declared it as a string variable, so that the computer would interpret the 1s and 0s as letters. It then won't try to use it in a mathematical equation because you can't multiply text.
- Similarly, a variable called 'length' is declared as a numeric variable, and can be multiplied by another number variable, e.g. 'width', to give the area.

Data type	Description of data type	Example
Integer	An integer is a numeric variable without a decimal. Integers are whole numbers and can be positive or negative. Sometimes a distinction is made between short and long integers, referring to how much data storage is used for the number. In most programming languages the word 'int' is used to designate an integer type but in some the word integer must be used.	3

Real	Real numbers include all of the integer numbers that exist to infinity plus all of their fractions and decimals. Therefore 3, 6,000,001 and 3.124569 are all real numbers.	3.25
	They do this using a data type called 'floating point', float or real.	
Character	A character data type is used to store a single, alphanumeric character: a character representing a letter, number or symbol.	C 3 *
String	A string is more useful than the character data type as it can hold a list of characters of any length. It represents alphanumeric data and symbols. When data is entered in a string variable it is enclosed with single or double quote marks e.g. firstName = "David".	"David" "2015" "April 1"

Boolean	Recall from Chapter 3 that Boolean data types can only represent two values: True or False.	This type of data type is very useful in loops, e.g.
		
		`correct = False`
		`while correct == False`
		`    guess = input("Please enter a number.")`
		`        if guess == mysteryNumber then`
		`            correct = True`
		`        endif`
		`endwhile`
		`print("You guessed the number.")`

🔑 **Key terms**

integer: a whole number without decimals (can be positive or negative)

real: a numeric variable with a fractional value; it will have digits on either side of a decimal point. Commonly used to store currency values, e.g. 1.50 for £1.50

character (often abbreviated to 'char'): a variable that holds one letter, number or symbol

Download Worksheet 4.1 from Cambridge Elevate

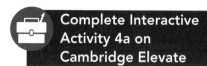

Complete Interactive Activity 4a on Cambridge Elevate

Programming languages can be divided into two types: 'strongly typed' and 'weakly typed'.

In a strongly typed language, you have to explicitly state the data type of a variable, e.g. `int age`. In this strongly typed language, the data type is specified: 'int', meaning 'integer'.

In a weakly typed language, the programming language assumes what the data type should be from the data that is input or stored, e.g.

Code
```
variable = 5 + 5
```

A weakly typed language would assume that this was an integer, even though it is not specified, because the variable is made up of integers.

Code
```
print(variable)
```

would return '10'.

And

Code
```
variable = "5+5"
```

A weakly typed language would assume this was a string, because of the quote marks.

Code
```
print(variable)
```

would return '5+5'.

Tip

Real numbers include integers, and a variable declared as a float could therefore hold an integer. More memory is used to store a float, so there is a separate data type for integers.

ACTIVITY 4.1

Shown below is part of the pseudocode for a program designed to enrol new members to a club.

```
firstName = input("Please enter your first name.")
lastName = input("Please enter your last name.")
initial = input("Please enter the initial of your middle name.")
age = input("Please enter your age in years.")
if age < 18 then
      print ("Sorry you are not old enough to join the club.")
else
      print ("Welcome to the club.")
endif
```

List the variables used in this code and suggest suitable data types for them.

Working with strings

If a variable is a string data type, the computer knows to interpret the 1s and 0s that make up the data as characters and the ways in which the data can be manipulated.

There are lots of useful operations that can be performed on strings. Here are a few.

The length of a string

One of the most important properties of a string is its length. All programming languages have a method of finding the length of a string. In pseudocode it is written as:

Code ————————————————————————————————

```
stringName.length
```

Here is an example of its use:

Code ————————————————————————————————

```
name = "Freda Smith"

print(name.length)
```

This would output the number 11 (don't forget to count the space!)

Here is the string with the index positions of the characters.

0	1	2	3	4	5	6	7	8	9	10
F	R	E	D	A		S	M	I	T	H

Although there are 11 characters, in many languages they are numbered 0 to 10.

Tip

Text assigned to a string is enclosed in speech marks.

Key terms

property: one of the characteristics or attributes of a data type; for example one of the properties of a string variable is its length, or the number of characters it contains

index: a number that indicates where a piece of data occurs in a string

Watch out

Always remember that computers start numbering at 0 and not at 1.

Key term

string traversal: moving through a string, one item of data at a time; sometimes this might just mean counting

WORKED EXAMPLE

In the following example, we will work out the number of times that a particular character occurs in a string.

The algorithm needs to use a loop to go through the string a letter at a time looking for the character. This is called string traversal. It will therefore need to know the length of the string.

In this example, the string is stored in a variable named 'myString' and the letter 'c' is being searched for.

Code

Code	Explanation
`times = 0`	A variable is assigned the value 0. This variable will be used to count the number of occurrences.
`for index = 0 to myString.length -1`	A for loop is started. The for loop will go through the string starting at index 0. It will run until it reaches the last index, which is equal to the length of the string minus 1, e.g. if the length of the string is 13 then it will have to run from index 0 to index 12 (12 is the length minus 1).
`    if myString(index) == "c" then` `        times = times + 1`	If the character is a letter 'c' then the variable 'times' is incremented by 1.
`    endif`	This ends the if block. </LABEL>
`next index`	This is the end of the loop. Processing will be directed to the start until the condition is met.
`print(times)`	This will display the value of the variable 'times'.

 Download Worksheet 4.2 from Cambridge Elevate

ACTIVITY 4.2

Create an algorithm that will count the number of times that a particular character, entered by a user, occurs in a string also entered by the user.

Splitting up strings

A string may need to be split up into substrings. In the following example, we are using a variable that contains the full name:

0	1	2	3	4	5	6	7	8	9	10
F	R	E	D	A		S	M	I	T	H

If this variable is being used to display information to the user, printing 'Hello Freda' would be far more friendly than printing 'Hello Freda Smith'.

WORKED EXAMPLE

Create an algorithm that will create two strings, one containing the first name and one containing the surname, from a string that contains the full name.

What we need to do is to find the space. Anything before that is the first name and everything after that will be the surname. A loop is needed. In this example the variable 'fullName' contains the whole name.

Code	Explanation
```firstName = ""``` ```lastName = ""```	Two variables are declared and given the values of empty strings so that they can be added to later.
```for index = 0 to fullName.``` ```length -1```	This for loop will traverse the string …

```   if fullName(index) == " "```
```   then```
```   position = index```
```   endif```
	… to find the index position of the space. This index position is stored in the variable 'position'. This ends the if loop.

```next index```	This is the end of the loop. Processing will be directed to the start until the condition is met.

```for index = 0 to position-1```
```   firstName = firstName +```
```   fullname(index)```
```next index```
	This loop traverses the fullName string up to the character before the string and adds them to the firstName string.

```for index = position + 1 to```
```fullName.length -1```
```   lastName = lastName +```
```   fullName(index)```
```next index```
	This loop traverses the fullName string from the character after the space up to the last character and adds them to the firstName string.

Key term

traverse: go through a string item by item

Tip

Note that the inverted commas contain a space, which is the character found between 'Freda' and 'Smith' in the string.

There will now be two new strings:

firstName	Freda
lastName	Smith

Finding substrings

An instance of one or more characters in a string is known as a substring: a string within a string.

In the examples above we have traversed a string looking for a single character. But what if we needed to find a substring that consisted of more than one character? This can again be found by using a loop. But it is more complicated!

Key term

substring: a smaller string which is part of the main string that you are using

WORKED EXAMPLE

This is our previous string example:

0	1	2	3	4	5	6	7	8	9	10
F	R	E	D	A		S	M	I	T	H

We could find if the substring 'RED' occurred and be notified of the index of its first letter.

We would have to start at index 0 and check if characters 0, 1 and 2 were equal to 'RED'. We would then start at index 1 and see if 1, 2 and 3 were equal to 'RED'. Then start at index 2 and so on.

But we cannot continue beyond index 8 as if we started at index 9, we would have to check indices 10 and 11. But there is no index 11 and we would get an error message!

```
myString = "FREDA SMITH"
```
The name is assigned to the variable myString.

```
testString = ""
```
This variable is given the value of an empty string so that it can be added to later.

```
for index = 0 to myString.Length -3
```
A for loop is set up to start from index 0 to 2 before the end of the string. We need to use -3 as the last item in the string is the length -1.

```
    testString = teststring + myString(index)
```
The character at this index position is added to testString.

```
    for test = 1 to 2
        teststring = testString + myString(index +
        test)
    next test
```
A loop is set up to add the next two characters to testString.

```
    If testString == "RED" then
        found = "Yes"
        position = index
```
If testString is equal to 'RED' then the variable 'found' is assigned the value 'Yes' and the variable 'position' is assigned the value of the start index.

```
    endif
    testString = ""
```
testString is changed back to an empty string for the next turn of the loop.

```
next index
If found == "Yes" then
    print("It was found at index " + position)
else
print("Sorry. Not found.")
endif
```
Messages are printed for the user informing them if the substring has been found.

ACTIVITY 4.3

A student has made a set of revision notes on her computer and would like to find ones containing the word 'variable'.

Create an algorithm that would notify her if the word appears and also the number of times it is used.

Concatenation: joining strings together

In addition to cutting strings up into substrings, strings can also be joined together, and this is called concatenation.

To concatenate two strings you would simply enter:

Code
```
stringOne + stringTwo
```

For example:

Code
```
firstName = "Freda"

lastName = "Smith"

fullName = firstName + lastName

Print(fullName)
```

The output would be:

Code
```
FredaSmith
```

They would be concatenated without a space: the computer doesn't know how we write names. But string variables can also be concatenated with literal text, as long as it is enclosed within speech marks. We could add a space as follows:

Code
```
firstName = "Freda"

lastName = "Smith"

fullName = firstName + " " + lastName

Print(lastName)
```

Tip

Investigate the string handling commands available in the OCR pseudocode and in the programming languages that you are studying.

Key term

concatenation: the placing together of two separate objects so that they can be treated as one, for example string variables can be joined end-to-end to produce a larger string

We could add any other literal text:

Code

```
fullName = firstName + " " + lastName + " is brilliant!"
```

Create an algorithm that would allow a user to enter their first name and their surname and would then print a message saying, 'Hello [first name surname]. How are you?'

Multiplying variables

Although we can't multiply string variables together, we can use the * symbol to generate multiple copies of the same string. For example:

Code

```
myString = "5"

print(myString * 3)
```

This would return:

```
555
```

Complete the Cambridge Computing Online activity
www.cambridge.org/links/kose4006

Converting strings to numbers and numbers to strings

This is referred to as casting.

Numeric data within a string may be needed for a mathematical calculation and must therefore be converted from string data type to a mathematical one, such as an integer or a real number.

This can be easily done.

Code

```
myNumber = int(myString)
```
would convert numeric data into an integer.

```
myNumber = float(myString)
```
would convert it into a real number.

Obviously, using the statement `myNumber = int(myString)` in an actual programming language would produce an error message if myString contained the data 5.3. It could only be a real number.

If you actually wanted an integer, you could do the following:

Code

```
myNumber = int(float(myString)).
```

Key term

casting: converting one data type to another

Watch out

Sometimes the computer can become confused as to whether a variable is a number or a string and produce an error message when one is used in a mathematical calculation. These problems can be solved by explicitly casting the variables.

Converting a number (integers and floating point numbers) to a string is far easier and uses the key word 'str()':

Code

```
myString = str(myNumber)
```

 Complete Interactive Activity 4b on Cambridge Elevate

 Remember

1. Data types include integer and real numbers, characters, strings and Boolean.
2. A real data type includes numbers with decimal places.
3. A string variable contains a list of characters.
4. Each character in a string has an index indicating its position.
5. Strings can be manipulated in many ways, e.g. they can be split up or concatenated.
6. Strings can be converted to integer and real numbers and vice versa.

 Tip

We have been manipulating strings using the commands available in the OCR pseudocode. Investigate the language that you are using for all of the methods available.

Storing multiple items of data

So far we have stored data in variables e.g.

Code

```
firstName = "David"

length = 13

answer = True
```

Each variable holds one, single item of information.

 Complete the Cambridge Computing Online activity www.cambridge.org/links/kose4007

 Watch out

In some languages, you cannot mix numbers, strings and literal text in print statements. The numbers would have to be converted into strings using this method.

If you were writing an algorithm to store the names of all your friends, you could do something like this:

Code

```
name_1 = "Catherine"

name_2 = "Jack"

name_3 = "Rosie"
```

or you could use the 'input' command:

Code

```
name_1 = input("Please enter a name.")

name_2 = input("Please enter a name.")

name_3 = input("Please enter a name.")
```

But when you start you may not know how many friends' names you have to enter. And what happens if you fall out with one of them?

Or what if you use the program again on another day and forget how many friends' names you have already stored and so don't know what number the next one will be.

Wouldn't it be great:

- if you could store all of the names in one list that you could add to?
- if when you had to enter another name it could just be appended to the end without having to remember what number it was?

And it would be even better if each item was indexed so that the items could be manipulated more easily.

Well, there is a solution! There are data structures called arrays that let you do some or all of these things.

Arrays

Watch the arrays animation on Cambridge Elevate

An array is a data structure that contains a group of linked elements that are usually of the same data type. They allow the storing of multiple pieces of data in one variable.

Arrays can be either static or dynamic. A static array has a fixed size and when it is declared the number of items it can hold must be stated. For example, **array friends [5]**.

In our pseudocode this will create an array with the identifier 'friends' that will hold 5 items.

Notice how square brackets are used with arrays.

Just as in a string the items will be numbered from 0 to 4. This is the item's index.

The data at a specific index can be printed, for example **print(friends[3])**.

Complete the Cambridge Computing Online activity
www.cambridge.org/links/kose4008

Key terms

array: a structure that contains many items of data of the same type. The data is indexed so that a particular item of data can be easily found

index: a number that identifies each element of an array

static array: an array that is of a set size

dynamic array: an array that has not had its size defined and can change as data is appended

Tip

Investigate the programming language you are using to see how to declare a dynamic array.

WORKED EXAMPLE

A teacher has set an online test with 10 questions. Create an algorithm that would store a student's answers to each question in an array.

```
array answers[10]
for index = 0 to 9
    response = input("Please enter your answer
    to question " + index + 1)

    answers[index] = response

next index
print("Test finished.")
```

The array is declared.
A loop is set up to store the 10 answers.
The student is asked to enter the answers.
As the loop runs from 0 to 9 each question is numbered as index + 1.
The student's answer is stored in the array.

The student is informed that the test is over.

ACTIVITY 4.5

Create an algorithm that will declare a static array identified as 'cars' with a length of 5 items and which will then ask a user to input data for all 5.

Whenever data is added to a static array the index must be stipulated, for example `cars[3] = "Hyundai"`.

If this was in a programming language and not pseudocode, and a user tried to add data to index `cars [6]` in the above example an error message would be generated as it has been declared as having only 5 items at indexes 0 to 4.

If an array is declared as a dynamic array in a programming language, then an item cannot be inserted at a particular index position as there aren't any index positions until items have already been inserted. There has to be a method to add one to the end. This can be the 'append' keyword.

Code

```
array cars []

cars.append("Hyundai")
```

Therefore "Hyundai" will be at the index position 0.

The append command will be available in the programming language that you are studying but it is not included in the OCR pseudocode.

Array length

Like a string, arrays have a length property indicating the number of items they contain.

Using the example of the static array above

Code

```
cars.length
```

would return the value 5.

Once the length is known, a loop can be used to traverse the array. The loop could be used to see if a value was present in the array and also return its index.

Code

```
for index = 0 to array.length -1
```
A for loop is set up to run from the first index (0) to the last (the length -1). Remember the last item in the array is 1 less than the length of the array.

```
    if cars[index] == "Renault" then
```
The user is looking for all items with the value 'Renault'.

```
        print("Renault is in the list at index " + index)
```
If it is at the index, a message is printed along with the index number.

```
    endif
next index
```

Tip

The length method for an array is not listed under arrays in the OCR pseudocode but as it is listed for strings, we are using it in this book.

ACTIVITY 4.6

Create an algorithm that would print all of the items stored in an array named 'cars'. (Remember that the numbering starts at 0 and that you can use the 'length' method.)

ACTIVITY 4.7

An array called 'sales' is used to store the name of each ice cream when it is sold at a shop. Create an algorithm that would find the number of '99' type ice creams that were sold.

ACTIVITY 4.8

An array contains all of the lower-case letters of the alphabet in alphabetical order. Create an algorithm that would return the array indexes of all the letters in the following string: 'computer'.

Tip

You will have to go through the string a character at a time and then search for that character in the array.

Max, min and mean

If you have an array of number values you can traverse it to find the maximum or minimum value.

Here is an algorithm that will find the maximum value. The values are stored in an array called 'results'.

Code

```
max = 0
```
A variable called max is assigned a value of 0.

```
for index = 0 to results.length -1
```
This loop will go through each item in the array.

```
    if results[index] > max then
        max = results[index]
    endif
```
If the data item has a value greater than is currently stored in 'max' then 'max' is assigned this value. So if any item is greater than currently stored then it replaces it.

```
next index

print(max)
```

ACTIVITY 4.9

A student has all of her computer science marks stored in an array. Create an algorithm that would allow her to find:

a. the minimum value

b. the mean of the marks.

Slicing an array

An array can be cut up – or sliced into smaller arrays in the same way as a string.

WORKED EXAMPLE

Here is an array that contains 7 data items:

```
colours = ["red", "orange", "yellow", "green", "blue", "indigo", "violet"]
```

If we wanted to create a smaller array with just the first 3 items, we could use the following algorithm.

```
colours = ["red", "orange", "yellow", "green",
"blue", "indigo", "violet"]
array someColours[3]
for index = 0 to 2

        someColours[index] = colours[index]

next index
```

Here is the original array named colours.

The new array is declared.
A loop is set up which will run from 0 to 2, i.e. the first 3 items.
The items are copied from the colour array to the someColours array.

The new array will contain the colours red, orange and yellow.

ACTIVITY 4.10

A student has an array that stores all of his computer science marks:

[6, 9, 2, 5, 8, 3, 9, 9, 10, 9, 5, 7, 10]

Create an algorithm, using pseudocode, which would create a new array called 'pass' and copy all the marks of 5 and over into this new array.

Tip

Before you create the array, you will have to find how many marks are 5 or over so that you can declare the new array.

Complete Interactive Activity 4c on Cambridge Elevate

Most programming languages have a 'slice' command and so you do not need to use a loop to copy the items to a new array. The slice command will slice the array between the items.

When an array is sliced the index positions given in the command are taken as being the gap before the data item. Here is the array containing the 7 colours:

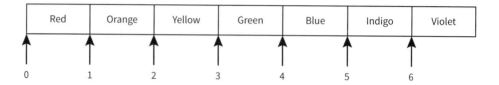

Red	Orange	Yellow	Green	Blue	Indigo	Violet

0   1   2   3   4   5   6

Therefore the following will achieve the same result as above:

Code

```
someColours = colours.slice(0, 3)
```

This would produce an array called someColours with the data items red, orange and yellow as the array would be sliced at index 0 and index 3 and everything between would be included.

Tip

When declaring the new array, you can use a variable instead of an actual number.

ACTIVITY 4.11

What data items would be included in the following:

a. `someColours = colours.slice(1, 4)`

b. `someColours = colours.slice(2, 5)`

c. `someColours = colours.slice(3, 3)`

Changing data items in an array

Changing a data item in an array is quite straightforward. The method is to create a loop to find the data item and then assign a new value at that index.

WORKED EXAMPLE

A student has been carrying out a survey of cars passing the school between certain times. The make of each car has been stored in an array called 'cars' but the student realises that he has misspelt 'Vauxhall', and has entered 'Vauxall' instead. The spelling mistakes can be corrected by using a loop:

```
for index = 0 to cars.length -1

        if cars[index] == "Vauxall" then

            cars[index] = "Vauxhall"

        endif

next index
```

A loop is set up to search through the indexes of the array. The 'length' method has been used to find the length of the array. If 'Vauxall' is found it is changed to 'Vauxhall'.

ACTIVITY 4.12

A teacher has created an array called 'exam1' to store the student marks for an exam. He discovered he had made a mistake in the mark scheme and results under 50 should be increased by 5 marks and results over 50 by 10 marks. Create an algorithm that would amend all of the results.

 Complete Interactive Activity 4d on Cambridge Elevate

Multidimensional arrays

In this array, `cars = ["Ford", "Renault", "Vauxhall"]`, there is only one item of information at each index position; the name of the manufacturer.

Wouldn't it be great if we could store several bits of information about the data item at each index position and access them using the index? We can do this by using a multidimensional array.

A multidimensional array is an 'array of arrays': each item at an index is another array.

We declared an array using this statement, `array cars[3]`.

If we wanted to create a two-dimensional array we could declare it as `array cars[3, 2]` if we wanted an array at each index to store two items of information.

In addition to the make of the car, we could store another item of data, such as the colour.

index 0		index 1		index 2	
Ford	Blue	Renault	Red	Vauxhall	Silver
index 0,0	index 0,1	index 1,0	index 1,1	index 2,0	index 2,1

Each item of information has two indexes. The value of `cars[2, 1]` is 'Silver'.

ACTIVITY 4.13

State the values at the following indexes.

a. `cars [0, 1]`

b. `cars [1, 1]`

Entering data into a two dimensional array

Here is how a user could be asked to enter data into a two-dimensional array to store the first names and surnames of their friends.

Code ───

```
array friends[5,2]
```
The array is declared.

```
for index = 0 to 4
```
A loop is set up running from 0 to 4 so that 5 entries can be made.

```
    friends[index, 0] = input("Please enter first
    name.")
```
The entries are made at index 'index', which will run from 0 to 4. The first one will be at 0,0 and the second at 0,1.

```
    friends[index, 1] = input("Please enter
    surname.")

next index
print("Thank you. You have entered all five
friends.")
```
This will be printed after all have been entered.

Rows and columns

We can visualise a two-dimensional array as a matrix of rows and columns. The car array would look like this

Cars

	0	1
0	Ford	Blue
1	Renault	Red
2	Vauxhall	Silver

Just as in the example above, 'Silver' is at position 2,1, assuming we use row number and then column number.

We could store more than two data items in a two-dimensional array. Here is some data about the members of a club:

Member Id	Surname	FirstName	Age	PostCode
001	Smith	Fred	15	CB3 4FT
002	Jones	Alice	6	CB1 3ST
003	Cooper	Jack	13	CB2 7XY

This data could also be stored in a two-dimensional array.

	0	1	2	3	4
0	001	Smith	Fred	15	CB3 4FT
1	002	Jones	Alice	6	CB1 3ST
2	003	Cooper	Jack	13	CB2 7XY

The array would be declared as members[3,5] as the array at each index of the main array has to store five items of information.

It would look like this:

Code
```
members[[001, "Smith", "Fred", 15, "CB3 4FT"], [002,
"Jones", "Alice", 6, "CB1 3ST"], [003, "Cooper", "Jack", 13,
"CB2 7XY]]

members[2,3] would be 13.
```

Searching a two-dimensional array

Data items can be searched for in a two-dimensional array in the same way as in a simple, one-dimensional array.

WORKED EXAMPLE

A teacher has stored the surnames and test scores of a class of students in a two-dimensional array (e.g results ["Smith", 69], etc.).

Create an algorithm that would print out the names and test scores of all the students who have scored 50 or over in the test.

```
for index = 0 to results.length -1
```
A loop is set up to search through the indexes of the array. The 'length' method has been used to find the length of the array.

```
    if results[index, 1] >= 50 then
```
If the result is greater than or equal to 50, then the name and the score are printed.

```
        print(results[index, 0] + results[index, 1]

    endif

next index
```

⬇ **Download Worksheet 4.3 from Cambridge Elevate**

ACTIVITY 4.14

A teacher has stored the surnames and test scores of a class of students in a two dimensional array, e.g. results ["Smith", 69], etc.

Create an algorithm that would print out the mean score for the class and the name and score of the student with the highest mark.

Saving the arrays

Time is taken entering data into an array and then the computer is turned off and all that data is lost! All that time is wasted.

Wouldn't it be great if the arrays could be saved to a disk file and then read in again?

Well, they can. They can be saved as text files. This is covered in Chapter 6.

Other data structures

Programming languages use many other data structures; some are common but some are specific to each language. Examples include lists, tuples, namedtuples, records and dictionaries.

Records

A record is a collection of data elements about a particular subject.

For example, records could be created about cars. Each record could have data elements for make, model, maximum speed etc. These separate data elements are called fields. The elements can be of different data types.

Each record that is created has the same structure and is a collection of the same data elements.

The elements can be indexed using numbers, as in arrays but also by their field names.

Databases

When large amounts of linked data need to be stored, a database is usually created using database management software which structures and manages the storage of the data allowing users to edit and sort it but more importantly, to search or query it.

The records are stored in tables, as shown in the figure below.

Table Members

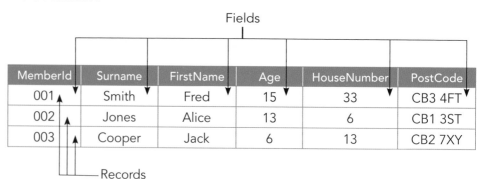

Fields

MemberId	Surname	FirstName	Age	HouseNumber	PostCode
001	Smith	Fred	15	33	CB3 4FT
002	Jones	Alice	13	6	CB1 3ST
003	Cooper	Jack	6	13	CB2 7XY

Records

Each record is a collection of data elements: MemberId, Surname, FirstName, etc. Each element is identified by a field name.

Structured Query Language (SQL)

Structured query language or SQL is a language for accessing and manipulating databases. It allows users to search for records which contain a particular item or items of data.

Key terms

field: is one item of information, e.g. in the example above, make, model and maximum speed are all fields

table: is a collection of rows and columns forming cells which are used to store data and user information in a structured and organised manner

Displaying records

If a user needed to display all of the records with all of their fields in the Members table above, they would write:

Code

```
SELECT * FROM Members;
```

SQL is not case sensitive, and so `select * from Members;` would work just as well.

To show only the Surname and FirstName fields the user would write:

Code

```
SELECT LastName, FirstName FROM Members;
```

Searching records

If the user wanted to query the database to find all members whose age was less than 10 they would write:

Code

```
SELECT * FROM Members

WHERE Age < 10;
```

This would display all of the fields for the record for Jack Cooper.

To show just the FirstName and Surname field the user would write:

Code

```
SELECT FirstName, LastName FROM Members

WHERE AGE < 10;
```

 Remember

1. An array is a data structure that contains a group of linked elements that are usually of the same data type.
2. They allow the storing of multiple pieces of data in one variable.
3. Arrays can be either static or dynamic.
4. Each data item stored in an array has an index.
5. The length of an array states the number of indexes used.
6. Arrays can be traversed and sliced.
7. Data items can be edited and deleted.
8. A multidimensional array stores more than one data item at each index.
9. Records allow data items to be referenced by field name as well as by index.
10. Databases allow users to structure large amounts of stored data.
11. Databases can be created, accessed and manipulated using structured query language (SQL).

Complete Interactive Activity 4e on Cambridge Elevate

 Practice questions

1. For a science experiment, Ann recorded the air temperature three times per day (morning, noon and evening) for a week. She stored the data in a two-dimensional array.

	0	1	2
0	6	13	5
1	5	12	6
2	9	17	8
3	9	20	9
4	7	15	6
5	6	13	6
6	7	13	6

a. If the array is named 'temperature', using pseudocode, state how Ann would declare this array.

b. State the data type Ann should use for this data.

c. If Ann wants to output the temperature at noon on Monday she would write the following code:

```
print(temperature[1, 1])
```

i. State the temperature that would be output.
ii. Write the code that she would use to output the temperature in the evening on Wednesday.

d. Ann needs to calculate the average temperature for each day and the average for the week.

Using a flow diagram or pseudocode, create an algorithm that would do this.

Your final challenge

Computers have enabled people to quickly encode and transmit messages using public and private keys. One method is to shift the letters of the alphabet to the right a set number of places. The number of 'shifts' that are made is called the key, for example with a key of 2, the alphabet would be changed to that shown on the bottom row:

A	B	C	D	E	F	G	H	I	J	K	L	M	N	O	P	Q	R	S	T	U	V	W	X	Y	Z
Y	Z	A	B	C	D	E	F	G	H	I	J	K	L	M	N	O	P	Q	R	S	T	U	V	W	X

Notice how the letters at the end move to the start of the alphabet.

So if the message was:

    PLEASE SEND MORE TROOPS

The encrypted version would be:

    NJCYQC QCLB KMPC RMMNQ

If the recipient knew the key used, they could decrypt the message.

What you have to do:

- Design an algorithm using a flow diagram or pseudocode to encode and decode messages in this way.
- You should then code and test the program using the programming language that you are studying.

Good luck!

Watch out

This is quite a difficult challenge, so here are some hints and tips:

- The message to be encoded or decoded will be in a string.

- All of the letters of the alphabet can be stored in a string or, if you are using upper- and lower-case, you could use two strings or even a two-dimensional string.

- When encrypting, each letter has to be moved to the left; the number to be moved depends on the key used and vice versa for decrypting.

- Each letter in the string can be searched for in the array(s) and the new encrypted version can be found according to the key.

- The most difficult part is at the ends of the alphabet, e.g. with a key of 2 an 'a' would be encrypted to a 'y'.

Download Self-assessment 4 worksheet from Cambridge Elevate

5 Searching and sorting algorithms

Learning outcomes

By the end of this chapter you should be able to:

- explain why sorted lists are of more value than unsorted lists
- describe the bubble sort, selection sort and merge sort algorithms
- use these algorithms to sort lists into ascending and descending order
- describe the linear and binary search algorithms
- use these algorithms to search sorted and unsorted lists
- write code for the implementation of these algorithms.

Challenge: write an algorithm to find the top ten!

- Every week the UK Top 40 is worked out by taking into account sales of CDs and vinyl, digital downloads and the number of times the music has been streamed.
- The total sales are collated and the final amounts sorted into order.
- At the end of this chapter, you will write a program to analyse the data to find the top ten!

Why search and sort?

Searching and sorting algorithms are used in lots of programs to make data easier to access and understand.

- Computer game leader boards are sorted from the *highest* score to the *lowest* score to make it easy to find the winner and your position in the list.
- Search engines like Google use special algorithms to help find us the most useful search results.
- Online shopping websites order their products by type, so that you can click straight to the department you're looking for, rather than searching through the whole site.

Key terms

searching: looking through a file to see if a particular piece of data is there

sorting: putting items of data into a precise order, for example alphabetical or numerical

If a train timetable wasn't sorted into order according to the times the trains left, you would have to read each one until you found the correct train and time.

Sorting

ACTIVITY 5.1

Sorting makes it easier to **search** for the data you need. Look at this football league table. The data hasn't been sorted. Time yourself to see how long it takes you to find the team in 13th position.

CompSci League 1				
	Played	Won	Drawn	Lost	Points
Naciri Orient	38	24	7	7	79
Walton Wanderers	38	10	8	20	38
Salisbury Hotspur	38	7	9	22	30
Whiscombefield	38	25	7	6	82
Axe Vans Albion	38	13	6	19	45
McGarvey Club Rovers	38	21	9	8	72
Campbell Palace	38	9	5	24	32
Valpy Harriers	38	10	7	21	37
St Smart Rangers	38	26	6	6	84
Fradford United	38	27	5	6	86
Watkins Athletic	38	19	7	12	64
Fayebury Town	38	15	4	19	49
Porterfield Green	38	8	9	21	33
Cunningham Town	38	15	11	12	56
Farr County	38	13	11	14	50
Stevens Town Park	38	10	8	20	38
Linghorn Lions	38	11	9	18	42
Mantovani United	38	21	6	11	69
Howardsmith Stanley	38	7	15	16	36
Walford Thistle	38	11	7	20	40

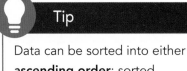

Tip

Data can be sorted into either **ascending order**: sorted from smallest to largest, e.g. 123456789 or ABCDEF

or

descending order: sorted from largest to smallest, e.g. 987654321 or FEDCBA

If data is *sorted* into a relevant order you can generally *search* it far more quickly.

Sorting algorithms

When sorting data items it is essential to compare them with each other so that they can be put into the correct order.

There may be millions of items of data to compare, so sorting algorithms must carry out the task as efficiently as possible so as not to cause a bottleneck – another part of the program may not be able to run until the sorting has been carried out.

Key term

compare: assess how items of data are similar or different to each other, to help decide which order they should go in

Key term

adjacent items: items of data that are next to each other

Watch the bubble sort algorithm animation on Cambridge Elevate

Bubble sort

This algorithm is used to sort an unordered list by comparing adjacent items. It works like this:

1. Start at the beginning of the list of values.

2. Compare the first and second values. Are they in order? If so, leave them; if not, swap them.

3. Compare the second and third values. Are they in order? If so, leave them; if not, swap them.

4. Now move on to the third and fourth values, then the fourth and fifth values. Continue in this way to the end of the list, comparing each pair of values. Working through the list once is called the first pass.

5. Go through the list of values for a second time (which will be the second pass) or even a third time (the third pass), repeating steps 1–4 until there are no more swaps to be made.

WORKED EXAMPLE

Sort this list into *ascending* order using the bubble sort algorithm.

6 3 1 2 7 4 5

In the following explanation, the swaps in each pass are shown.

First pass:

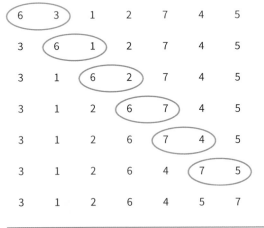

6	3	1	2	7	4	5	First and second values – wrong order – swap
3	6	1	2	7	4	5	Second and third values – wrong order – swap
3	1	6	2	7	4	5	Third and fourth values – wrong order – swap
3	1	2	6	7	4	5	Fourth and fifth values – correct order – leave
3	1	2	6	7	4	5	Fifth and sixth values – wrong order – swap
3	1	2	6	4	7	5	Sixth and seventh values – wrong order – swap
3	1	2	6	4	5	7	**End of first pass**

After the first pass the final number will be in the correct position, as it has been pushed along by comparing it with the other numbers. After the second pass, the second to last number will be in the correct position, and so on. So for each pass the number of comparisons needed is reduced by 1.

The **bubble sort** gets its name because the numbers move up into the correct order like **bubbles** rising to the surface.

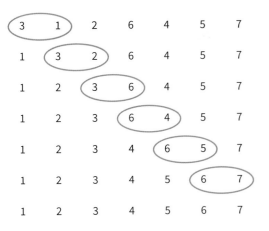

3	1	2	6	4	5	7	First and second values – wrong order – swap
1	3	2	6	4	5	7	Second and third values – wrong order – swap
1	2	3	6	4	5	7	Third and fourth values – correct order – leave
1	2	3	6	4	5	7	Fourth and fifth values – wrong order – swap
1	2	3	4	6	5	7	Fifth and sixth values – wrong order – swap
1	2	3	4	5	6	7	Sixth and seventh values – correct order – leave
1	2	3	4	5	6	7	**End of second pass**

Although the values are in the correct order after two passes, the algorithm would still have to do a third pass, as it repeats the comparisons until there are no swaps in the pass it has just completed.

ACTIVITY 5.2

Produce a table showing the results of the passes when sorting the following numbers into ascending order.

20 15 3 13 9 2 6

Complete Interactive Activity 5a on Cambridge Elevate

Coding the bubble sort algorithms

Now you know what bubble sort is and how to use it, but you need to write the code to be able to implement it.

Below is pseudocode for the bubble sort algorithm. The pseudocode is in the left column, with the explanations in the right column.

Watch out

If you are using Python, there is no term *array*. You should use the term *list*.

Code

Code	Explanation
`S = List of items`	The variable S is assigned to the array.
`N = length of list`	The variable N is needed to set the number of comparisons to be made.
`swapped = true`	A Boolean variable (swapped) is defined and is set to true.
`while  swapped = true`	This WHILE loop will run while swaps have occurred in the last pass.
`swapped = false`	Set the variable back to false ready for this pass.
`for X = 1 to N - 1`	Set up a loop to go through the list. N – 1 is used as the actual list numbering will start at 0 and not at 1 i.e. the first item on the list will be at position 0.
`If  S[X - 1] > S[X] then`	This compares two numbers next to each other. In the first run of the loop it will compare the number at position 0 with that at position 1. If it is larger, then the following stages will occur.
`temp = S[X - 1]`	A variable named temp is assigned the value of the first number.
`S[X - 1] = S[X]`	The second number is swapped to the position of the first number.
`S[X] = temp`	The second number is now assigned the original number of the first.
`swapped = true`	If a swap has occurred then the Boolean variable is set to 'true' so that the 'WHILE' loop will run again when the FOR loop is complete.
`endif`	End of IF selection.
`next x`	The 'FOR' loop will be repeated but the value of the variable x will be incremented by 1 each time it is run until it is equal to N – 1.
`endwhile`	The WHILE loop will run again as long as swapped is true.

Download Worksheet 5.1 from Cambridge Elevate

Remember

The bubble sort algorithm:

1. Compare the first two values. If they are not in the correct order, swap them.
2. Repeat for the second and third values.
3. Compare each pair until the end of the list and swap if necessary.
4. Repeat steps 1 to 3 until no swaps have been made.

Insertion sort

The insertion sort algorithm is used to sort an unordered list by examining each item in turn and inserting it in its correct position. It works like this:

1. If there is only one item in the list then stop.

2. Start with the second item and compare it with the first.

3. If it is larger than the first then leave it in place but if it is smaller swap the two numbers.

4. Now check the third number. If it is smaller than the second one then compare it with the first. If it is smaller than the first, place it in this position by moving the first two numbers along.

5. Repeat this procedure with all the numbers by comparing them with the numbers to the left until a smaller number is found. When it is, then place the number in the position to the right of it by moving the others along.

So, any number in the list that is out of place is moved towards the beginning of the list, until it fits.

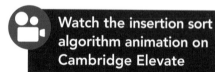

Watch the insertion sort algorithm animation on Cambridge Elevate

WORKED EXAMPLE

Using insertion sort, put this list in ascending order.

6 3 1 2 7 4 5

6	3	1	2	7	4	5	Second number – smaller than first – swap.
3	6	1	2	7	4	5	Third number – smaller than second, smaller than first: move third number to first position and move others to the right.
1	3	6	2	7	4	5	Fourth number – smaller than third, smaller than second, bigger than first: move fourth number to second position and move second and third to the right.
1	2	3	6	7	4	5	Now compare the next number with those to the left. As they are all smaller this number is left in position.
1	2	3	6	7	4	5	Repeat the procedure until the end of the list is reached and the numbers are in the correct order.
1	2	3	4	6	7	5	
1	2	3	4	5	6	7	

Complete Interactive Activity 5b on Cambridge Elevate

ACTIVITY 5.3

Produce a table showing the steps needed to sort the following numbers into ascending order using the insertion sort method.

20   15   3   13   9   2   6

ACTIVITY 5.4

A teacher has stored the test results for a particular class in an array.

Write the code that would sort the list into ascending order using the insertion sort algorithm.

Remember that the unsorted list decreases by one at each pass.

Run your program to check that it is working as you intended it to.

Tip

The difference between the insertion sort and the bubble sort is that the bubble sort keeps swapping pairs of numbers into the right order until the list is sorted whereas the insertion sort picks on one number and moves it along the list until it is in the best place for now.

Remember

The insertion sort algorithm:

1. If there is only one item in the list then stop.
2. Starting with the second item, check all items in the list with those to the left.
3. When a smaller number is found, place the item in the position to the right of it by moving all the other numbers along.
4. Repeat until the end of the list is reached and all the numbers are in the correct order.

Merge sort

The merge sort algorithm is used to sort an unordered list by repeatedly (recursively) dividing a list into two smaller lists until the size of each list becomes one. This is why it is called a 'divide and conquer' algorithm. The individual lists are then merged. It works like this:

1. If there is only one item in the list then stop.
2. Divide the list into two parts.
3. Recursively divide these lists until the size of each becomes one.
4. Recursively merge the lists with the items in the correct numerical order.

Watch the merge sort algorithm animation on Cambridge Elevate

Tip

A 'divide and conquer' algorithm works by dividing a problem into smaller and smaller sub-problems until they are easy to solve. The solutions to these are then combined to give a solution to the complete problem.

A 'brute force' algorithm does not include any techniques to improve performance, but instead relies on sheer computing power to try all possibilities until the solution to a problem is found.

WORKED EXAMPLE

Sort the following list into ascending order.

6 2 5 4 3 7 1

| 6 | 2 | 5 | 4 | 3 | 7 | 1 |

This is the original list.

| 6 | 2 | 5 | 4 | | 3 | 7 | 1 |

It is divided into two halves.

| 6 | 2 | | 5 | 4 | | 3 | 7 | | 1 |

And again.

| 6 | | 2 | | 5 | | 4 | | 3 | | 7 | | 1 |

Until the size of each list becomes one.

| 2 | 6 | | 4 | 5 | | 3 | 7 | | 1 |

The individual lists are now merged, with the items in the correct numerical order.

| 2 | 4 | 5 | 6 | | 1 | 3 | 7 |

| 1 | 2 | 3 | 4 | 5 | 6 | 7 |

Tip

The key thing to remember is that when the lists are merged, two at a time, they are merged with the items in the correct order.

Tip

It may seem that the merge sort is a complicated method but its advantage is shown below where the efficiency of the algorithms is compared. The answer can be seen below where the algorithms are compared.

ACTIVITY 5.5

Produce a table showing the swaps needed to sort the following numbers into ascending order using the merge sort method.

20 15 3 13 9 2 6

Complete Interactive Activity 5c on Cambridge Elevate

Remember

The merge sort algorithm:

1. If there is only one item in the list then stop.
2. Divide the list into two parts.
3. Recursively divide these lists until the size of each becomes one.
4. Recursively merge the lists with the items in the correct numerical order.

Download Worksheet 5.2 from Cambridge Elevate

Which algorithm should I use?

Choosing which sorting algorithm depends on what you want to do.

	Advantages	Disadvantages
Bubble sort	Simplest and easiest to code	Slowest
Insertion sort	Simple and easy to code	Twice as fast as the bubble sort but slower than the merge sort
Merge sort	Fastest. Faster to sort the list than the other two	More difficult to code than the other two

So if you have a very large list (more than 1000 items) and speed of execution is important, it is worth spending the extra time coding the merge sort algorithm. But if you have a list of less than 1000 items, then the time saved in execution is so tiny that it is negligible and so you could use an insertion or bubble sort, which is easier to code.

The following graph shows the times taken for the algorithms to sort lists of different lengths. As you can see, with small lists the differences are less than one second.

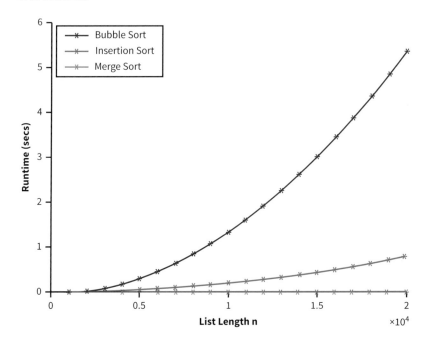

Searching algorithms

To find specific data, a list must be searched and the searching process will usually be far more efficient if the list has already been sorted into ascending or descending order.

Linear search

A linear search is a simple, sequential search. It starts at the beginning of the list and moves through the items, one by one, until it finds a matching value or reaches the end without finding one.

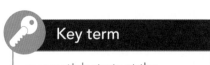

Key term

sequential: starts at the beginning and moves through the list one by one

Tip

Although a linear search doesn't need the list to be sorted, it takes far longer to find the required item. This could be a very serious problem when the amount of data being searched is very large. Users often search for data on Internet sites and they would not be prepared to wait for the slower linear sort.

Linear searches are easy to code and have one great advantage: they do not require the list to be sorted. They are frequently used by programmers as they are easy to code and code does not have to be written to sort the list first.

The linear search algorithm works like this:

1. Start at the first item in the list.

2. Compare the list item with the data you are looking for (the search criterion).

3. If they are the same then stop; if they are not the same then move to the next item.

4. Repeat steps 2 through 4 until then end of the list is reached.

ACTIVITY 5.6

An unsorted array contains the names of the 100 most popular names for children born last year.

Write code, in the programming language you are studying, that would inform a user if the name they had entered was, or was not, in the list.

Run your program to check that it is working as you intended it to.

Remember

The linear search algorithm:

1. Start at the first item in the list.
2. Compare the list item with the search criterion.
3. If they are the same then stop.
4. If they are not the same then move to the next item.
5. Repeat steps 2, 3 and 4.
6. If the end of the list is reached, then stop.

Tip

The median is the middle number e.g. if there are nine numbers then the 5th number is the median.

If there are an even number of items, choose the item to the right of the middle e.g. if there are eight numbers then chose the 5th as the median.

Binary search

The binary search algorithm searches an ordered list to find an item by looking at the middle (median) item and comparing it with the search value. It works like this:

You must first decide on the target value you are searching for (your search criterion) and ensure your list is ordered.

1. Select the middle item (median).

2. Compare this value with your search criterion. If they are equal then stop.

3. If your search criterion is lower, then repeat with the left-hand side of the list; if it is higher, repeat with the right-hand side of the list.

4. Repeat these steps until the search criterion is found (if it is not found, it is not on the list).

 Watch the binary search algorithm animation on Cambridge Elevate

WORKED EXAMPLE

Find the value 9 from the following list:

3 6 8 9 12 15 18 24 27

| 3 | 6 | 8 | 9 | (12) | 15 | 18 | 24 | 27 | Find the median of the sorted list. |

| 3 | 6 | (8) | 9 | | | | | | The target (9) is less than the median so select the sub-list to the left and find its median. |

The sub-list does not include the number you have just tried. It was the median of the list in the previous step in the algorithm so you know that it is not the number that you are searching for.

Note, if there are an even number of values select the one to the right of the middle.

| (9) | | | | | | | | | The target (9) is larger than the median so choose the sub-list to the right. |

There is only one number and so the target has been found.

ACTIVITY 5.7

Use the binary search algorithm to find the number 21 in the following list using a table as in the worked example.

3 15 21 27 33 39 42 48 56 60 66 67 69

ACTIVITY 5.8

A student wrote down the following list of numbers and asked a friend to think of one of the numbers without telling them which one.

3, 5, 6, 8, 9, 12, 15, 21, 23, 45, 56, 63, 69

The student then used the binary search algorithm to find the number.

Here are the results:

- The first guess was too low.
- The second guess was too high.
- The third guess was too high.
- The fourth guess was correct.

What was the number?

Before writing the code to perform a binary search of an array, a student wrote down a list of statements so that they understood exactly what they had to do.

Shown below are their statements but they are not all in the correct order.

Write out the statements so that they are in the correct order.

- Enter a number.
- If middle is less than number entered then start equals middle + 1.
- Inform the user that the number is not present.
- End of search items equals length of array - 1.
- End of while loop.
- Middle equals (start + end) / 2.
- Find the length of the array.
- If middle is greater than number entered then end equals middle - 1.
- While start is less than or equal to end.
- If middle is equal to number entered tell the user and stop the loop.
- Start (of search items) equals 0.

 Remember

The binary search algorithm (for a list in ascending order):

1. Select the median item of the list.
2. If the item is equal to the search criterion, then stop.
3. If the item is larger than the search criterion, then repeat steps 1 and 2 with the sub-list to the LEFT.
4. If the item is smaller than the search criterion, then repeat steps 1 and 2 with the sub-list to the RIGHT.
5. Repeat steps 3 and 4 until the search criterion is found or all items have been checked.

Linear search vs binary search
How efficient are the algorithms?

Suppose we have a sorted list of 100 items.

For a linear search, the *best case* would be for the search item to be the first item of the list and so require only one comparison. The *worst case* would be for the item to be at the end of the list and so it would have to examine all of them and 100 comparisons would be needed.

For a binary search, the *best case* would be for the search item to be the middle item of the list.

The *worst case* would be for the item to be the last possible division, i.e. the median items selected could be: 51, 26, 13, 7, 4, 2, 1.

Therefore in the worst case, the binary search would find the search item after only seven comparisons.

1. Check the median number:

1	51	100

2. Too large, so check the new median:

1	26	50

3. Still too large, so again use the sub-list to the left:

1	13	25

4. Still too large, so repeat the process:

1	7	12

5. Need to repeat again:

1	4	6

6. Still too large. So another comparison is needed.

1	2	3

7. If this one is too large, there is only one number left.

1	

Worst case for a search of 100 items	
Linear search	100
Binary search	7

Remember

Linear search vs binary search:

1. For a binary search the list must be sorted.
2. For a sorted list, the binary search will be more efficient with smaller, average search times.

Download Worksheet 5.3 from Cambridge Elevate

Practice questions

1. A student has stored the names of their friends in a file as shown below:

Jane	Stephen	Matthew	Mary	David	Catherine	Maureen	Francesca	Alice	Carol

    a. Show the stages of an insertion sort when applied to the data above.
        When the data was sorted it was in the following order:

Alice	Carol	Catherine	David	Francesca	Jane	Mary	Matthew	Maureen	Stephen

    b. Show the stages of a binary search to find the name 'Matthew' when applied to the data above.

 Download Worksheet 5.4 from Cambridge Elevate

 Complete Interactive Activity 5d on Cambridge Elevate

 Your final challenge

In the official charts list, the performers' names and their total sales have been saved in a two-dimensional array so that each index of the array stores a name and a total sales figure.

a. Write and test a program, using the language you are studying, that would sort the list into ascending order according to total sales.
b. The user would like to enter a performer's name and be given their chart position. Write and test a program that would do this.
c. Write and test a program that would allow the user to find out how many performers had total sales equal to or higher than the number entered and returns the result as a percentage of the total number of performers.

 Tip

Refer back to Chapter 4 for information on two-dimensional arrays. The final challenge uses a two-dimensional array. Check it out in the section on arrays.

 Download Self-assessment 5 worksheet from Cambridge Elevate

6 Input and output

Challenge: write a program to create and manage logins

- To use computer systems and social networking sites, users need to register for accounts, submit their details and create login names and passwords.
- They must then input their details to access the systems.
- Their names and passwords need to be authenticated each time they log in.
- Your challenge is to write a program in pseudocode or a programming language that will allow users to
  - create an account and password
  - change their password.

Why data input and output?

- Input and output devices are incredibly important as they allow us to interface with computer systems providing ease of use and security.

- The two most common methods are data input by keyboard and mouse, which enable us to create complex files quickly and easily.

- Data can be entered or browsed using a touchscreen.

- Users can enter data to prove their identities using their bodies, e.g. fingerprint characteristics, eye colour and size, or speech.

- Data about products can be entered automatically without users needing to type or point, using barcode scanners.

- Quick Response (QR) codes are barcodes that are machine readable, e.g. by smartphones. They contain information about the objects to which they are attached and can automatically connect the smartphone to websites, texts and emails.

 Watch the inventive use of input devices on mobile phones animation on Cambridge Elevate

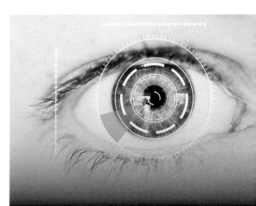

Eye gaze devices can be used by people with limited mobility to allow them to navigate and control their computer with only their eyes.

Tip

See Chapter 1 for information on designing algorithms that function correctly and efficiently and turning them into error-free executable code.

Key terms

logical error: a problem in the design of the algorithm

syntax error: a grammatical error in the source code of a program (this is covered in a later chapter)

validation: the process through which the program checks that data is sensible and reasonable and appropriate to be processed by the program

Input process output loop

In general, programs are created to process data. That's what they are for. The figure below shows how data is input, stored and processed into information which is output to the user.

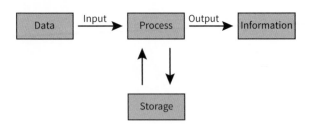

Data is input and is processed by the software running on the computer. The data that is input must be meaningful and correct – this is illustrated by the acronym GIGO, which stands for **G**arbage **I**n **G**arbage **O**ut. If the input data is incorrect, then so will any information that the program outputs to the user.

The computer program processes the data and it must function as expected: it must be free from logical and syntax errors. Designing algorithms free from logical errors was covered in Chapters 1 and 2 and syntax errors are covered in Chapter 7.

Complete Interactive Activity 6a on Cambridge Elevate

Validating data input

Validation routines are essential whenever data is input if the output is to be meaningful. For example, if a user has to enter a number into a variable called 'length' in a program to calculate the area of a rectangle, then entering a text string instead of a number is going to produce a strange result unless the data entry is validated. When data is validated, it is checked to ensure that it is sensible.

It does not check that it is *correct*, i.e. that the user did not enter the wrong data. That would be impossible. Only a person could check that, by checking the data they entered against the original. Even when data passes a validation test it may still be *incorrect*.

For example if a user enters '6' into a variable for the length of a rectangle, it could pass a validation check because it is a number, but the length may in fact be 5 and not 6. The validation check would not find this error.

Presence check

This is the most basic and obvious check. It ensures that the person who is using the program has made a choice so that some data has been entered. It should ensure that the program will not continue until the data has been entered. You can include it in your algorithms and programs.

For example, consider a series of multiple-choice questions that ask the user to enter a letter between A and D. If the user does not make a choice, the program will not show the next question.

Watch out

Take care with this kind of data entry. The choice from the user might be a letter rather than a number so it would need to be entered as a string variable.

Code

`letter = ""`	The variable letter is assigned the value of an empty string.
`while letter == ""`	A while loop is set up and it will run while the variable 'letter' contains an empty string.
`    letter = input("Please enter your selection.")`	The user is asked to input their selection. If they enter any text then the string will no longer be empty and the loop will stop.
`    If letter == "" then`	The variable 'letter' is checked to see if anything has been entered. If nothing has been entered it will still contain an empty string.
`        print("You have not entered anything.")`	This message will be output for the user.
`    endif`	
`endwhile`	This closes the while loop and sends processing back to the start if no entry has been made.

This output would be generated by the above code:

Code

`Please enter your selection:`
`You have not entered anything.`
`Please enter your selection:`
	Here is the error message displayed for the user. Notice how processing has moved back up to the start of the loop and the user is asked again to enter a selection.

Complete Interactive Activity 6b on Cambridge Elevate

Range check

Often when data is entered, it would be expected to fall within a certain range.

Looking again at the above example, the letter must be in the range A to D. This validation check can also be included in your programs.

Code

```
letter = ""

while letter != "A" AND letter != "B" AND letter != "C"
AND letter != "D"

    letter = input("Please enter your selection.")

    If letter != "A" AND letter != "B" AND letter
    != "C" AND letter != "D"

        print("The letter is not recognised.")

    endif

endwhile
```

The variable 'letter' is assigned the value of an empty string.

A while loop is set up and it will run while the variable 'letter' does not contain 'A', 'B', 'C' or 'D'.

The user is asked to input their name. If they enter an A or B or C or D the loop will stop.

The variable 'letter' is checked to see if an acceptable letter has been entered.

This message will be output for the user.

This closes the while loop and sends processing back to the start if a letter outside the range has been entered.

Tip

Computers haven't got a 'not equals' sign in the same way as mathematicians use it. 'Not equals' is written as != in computer programs

Tip

As the letter 'E' has been entered, the user is asked to make another entry.

Remember

1. If data that is input is incorrect, then the output will also be incorrect.
2. GIGO – **G**arbage **I**n **G**arbage **O**ut.
3. Validation checks that the data is sensible.
4. Validation checks include presence checks, range checks and length checks.
5. Data can pass validation checks but can still be incorrect.

This output would be generated by the above code:

Code

```
Please enter your selection: E
You have not entered anything.
Please enter your selection:
```

ACTIVITY 6.1

A student is applying for a driving licence, for which the minimum age is 17. Write a validation routine that would check that the age entered fell within the correct range. Use a programming language of your choice. Run your program to check that it is working as intended.

Length check

When we are asked to choose a password, we are often informed that it must have a certain number of characters. Obviously there must be a routine in the software to check the length of the text that is entered. Text is entered into a string variable (recall that in Chapter 4 we looked at the keyword used to find the length of a string).

ACTIVITY 6.2

A user is asked to enter a password of at least 9 characters and no more than 12. Write a routine that would validate their chosen password.

 Download Worksheet 6.1 from Cambridge Elevate

Modulus check digit

The most common errors are transcription errors, which occur when humans are entering precise data into a computer system. A user may have lists of numbers such as bank account or credit card numbers that they have to enter, but of course humans are prone to making mistakes.

The modulus check digit was invented to indicate when an input error has been made. The most used variety is the *modulus 11* check digit, which does a calculation on the digits and the total it finds must be divisible by 11.

Say, for example, that a bank account number needs seven digits. Calculations are then made and another (eighth) digit, based on a special calculation, is added onto the end of the main number. This last digit is the special check digit. Its job is not to be part of the required seven-digit number, but to be the digit used for checking the number later on. When the number is subsequently used, the check digit is checked and if the number has been entered correctly, it will be correct.

Watch the modulus check animation on Cambridge Elevate

WORKED EXAMPLE

This is Henry's bank account number: 14026937.

He telephones his bank and the bank advisor enters this number onto their system.

The system performs a modulus check:

1. The check digit is at the end of the number - 14026937. In this case it is 7.

2. Starting from the **right**, each number is given a weighting from 1 upwards.

Number	1	4	0	2	6	9	3	7
Weighting	8	7	6	5	4	3	2	1

3. Each digit is now multiplied by its weighting …

Number	1	4	0	2	6	9	3	7
Weighting	8	7	6	5	4	3	2	1
Multiplication	8	28	0	10	24	27	6	7

4. … and the total is found.

8 + 28 + 0 + 10 + 24 + 27 + 6 +7= 110

5. This number is divided by 11.

110/11 = 10

6. It is divisible by 11, therefore the number is accepted as an account number.

How to create the check digit

WORKED EXAMPLE

Henry's friend Simon wants to set up a new account. The system has to allocate him a new account number.

1. The system creates the first seven digits: **1468970**

   (Remember, the last digit – the check digit – hasn't been created yet.)

2. Starting from the right, each number is given a weighting from 2 upwards.

Number	1	4	6	8	9	7	0
Weighting	8	7	6	5	4	3	2

   (Note that there isn't a 1 weighting as the check digit still hasn't been created yet.)

3. Each digit is now multiplied by its weighting …

Number	1	4	6	8	9	7	0
Weighting	8	7	6	5	4	3	2
Multiplication	8	28	36	40	36	21	0

4. … and the total is found.

   $8 + 28 + 36 + 40 + 36 + 21 + 0 = 169$

5. This number is divided by 11.

   $169 / 11 = 15$ remainder 4

6. The remainder is subtracted from 11.

   $11 - 4 = 7$

   If the remainder is 1 then when it was deducted from 11 it would create a check digit of 10, which is two digits. Therefore an **X** is used as the check digit. If there is no remainder then a **0** is used.

7. The result becomes the check digit

   Account number = 14689707

8. We can do a quick check by weighting and multiplying as before …

Number	1	4	6	8	9	7	0	7
Weighting	8	7	6	5	4	3	2	1
Multiplication	8	28	36	40	36	21	0	7

9. … and dividing the total by 11 to check that there is no remainder.

   $8 + 28 + 36 + 40 + 36 + 21 + 0 + 7 = 176$

   $176 / 11 = 16$

10. Therefore the number is accepted as an account number.

 Download Worksheet 6.2 from Cambridge Elevate

 Complete Interactive Activity 6c on Cambridge Elevate

ACTIVITY 6.3

Create an algorithm that would allow a user to enter a 7-digit number and would then calculate the modulus 11 check digit. It should then show the complete 8-digit number to the user.

As an extension activity, you could create a second algorithm to check if the user enters the 8-digit number correctly. It should show an error message if they do not.

Authentication

The most common method for users to authenticate themselves (to prove they are who they say they are) is by entering a username and password, which are stored on the system.

Authentication is the process that a system uses to verify that a username with its associated password exist in the database. They are used to authenticate user identities for social networking sites, online banking and online ordering sites. They do not verify that the person entering the data is the actual person to whom they were issued.

The stealing of usernames and passwords is an example of 'identity theft'.

An authentication routine can be built into a program. It would require:

- a list of all the registered username and passwords
- data input for the username
- a routine to check that the user name is registered
- data input for the user's password
- a routine to check that the password is correct.

A list of user names with their passwords could be stored in an array (for more information on arrays, see Chapter 4).

The following algorithm assumes that they are stored in a two-dimensional array such as:

Code

```
users[["user1", "password1"], ["user2", "password2"], ["user3", "password3"]]

userEntry = ""                      The variable 'userEntry' is assigned the value of an
                                    empty string.

found_Name = 0                      This variable is used as a flag. It will be set to '1' if the
                                    username is found.

while userEntry == ""               A while loop is set up and it will run while the variable
                                    'userEntry' contains an empty string.
```

```
        userEntry = input("Please enter your
username.")
```

Please enter your username:

The user is asked to input their name. If they enter any text then the string will no longer be empty and the loop will stop.

```
        usersLen = users.length
```

The length of the array is stored in the variable 'usersLen'.

```
        for index = 0 to usersLen - 1
```

A for loop is set up to go through all of the indexes in the array.

```
            if userEntry == users[index, 0]
then
```

The first item at each index of the two-dimensional array is checked to see if it matches the one the user entered. If it is, then the password is checked.

```
                found_Name = 1
```

The flag is set to '1' if the username is found in the array.

```
                passwordEntry =
input("Please enter your password.")
```

The user is asked to enter a password.

```
                if passwordEntry == users
[index, 1] then
```

```
Please enter your username: David
Please enter your password:
```

It is checked with the second item at the index of the username (index) and if it is the same …

```
                    print("Username and
password are correct.")
```

```
Please enter your username: David
Please enter your password: Test
Username and password are correct.
```

… the user is informed that all is correct.

But if it is not the same …

```
                else
```

```
                    print("Sorry, the
password is incorrect.")
```

```
Please enter your username: David
Please enter your password:
Sorry, the password is incorrect.
please enter your username:
```

… the user is informed that the password is incorrect and processing goes back to the start of the while loop.

```
                    userEntry = ""
```

The variable 'userEntry' is set back to an empty string so that the while loop will run again.

```
                endif
```

The inner if block (for checking the password) is closed.

```
            endif
```

The outer if block for checking the user name is closed.

```
        next index
```

This re-runs the loop with index incremented by 1.

```
    if found_Name == 0 then
```
If the flag has not been set the user must be informed that the username has not been recognised.

```
        print("User name not recognised")
```

```
Please enter your username:
Incorrect Username
username not recognised.
please enter your username :
```

If the loop finishes and the user name entered does not match any of those in the array, then the user is informed and processing goes back to the start of the while loop.

```
        userEntry = ""
```
The variable 'userEntry' is set back to an empty string so that the while loop will run again.

```
    endif

endwhile
```
This closes the while loop and will send the processing back to the start if the username or the password are incorrect.

This is a simple solution and could be expanded to allow the user to input their password more than once.

ACTIVITY 6.4

Adapt the algorithm so that the user can enter their password up to three times before they receive the error message. Use a programming language of your choice. Run your program to check that it is working as you intended it to.

Tip

You could easily add code like this into your own programs to authenticate users.

Remember

1. A modulus check digit is used to check that a number, for example bank or credit card number, is valid.
2. Authentication is used to confirm the identity of a user.

Tip

You could use nested loops (for more on nested loops, see Chapter 2).

Output to screen

The program processes the data that has been entered and displays the results as information to the user. This data should be presented in as clear a way as possible. If a list of users and passwords is printed on screen, then it should be formatted.

If it is printed without any breaks, it will be confusing:

user1 password1 user2 password2 user3 password3 user4 password4 user5 password5

A line break could be inserted between each user:

user1 password1

user2 password2

user3 password3

user4 password4

user5 password5

It would be even better presented if tab stops were used to line up the different data:

user1   password1

user2   password2

user3   password3

user4   password4

user5   password5

Output to files

Data can be output to disk and stored in text files. These files of data can then be used to input data to programs when they need it.

Being able to do this is very useful because it means that data such as scores or usernames are not lost when a program is closed and can be loaded in again the next time it is run. To access a text file, you must first give it a file handle, e.g. 'myFile'.

Writing to a text file

When files are opened by programs, they can be opened in different ways. One of these ways is write mode. To write data to a file, it must be opened in write mode, for example:

Code

```
myFile = openWrite("samplefile.txt")
```

Writing data

Data can be written to the file using the following command:

Code

```
myFile.writeLine(Data to be written)
```

Watch out

If the file does not exist, then a file will be created but if it does exist then it will be overwritten. To prevent this, programming languages have an openAppend command. This is not available in the OCR pseudocode but check if it is used in the programming language that you are using.

Tip

Programming languages have commands that allow on-screen formatting. Have a look at the commands in the programming language you are using for on-screen formatting.

Key terms

file handle: a label that is assigned to a resource needed by the program. It can only access the file through the computer's operating system

write mode: the program can 'write' to the file, in other words, change the data in the file

overwritten: if a file exists on the computer and a new file is created with the same name, the new file is kept and the old file is written over and lost

Closing the file

When you have finished writing to the file it must be closed:

Code ————————————————————————————

```
myFile.close()
```

If it is not closed then data might be lost or it could become corrupted when the computer is switched off.

WORKED EXAMPLE

Anil is a student who has created a program that allows him to input his computer science test scores into an array which he declared as `scores[10]`.

He has now filled the array and wants to add code that will store the data in a text file called 'ComputerScienceScores'.

`myFile = openWrite("ComputerScienceScores.txt")`	This creates a text file on disk called 'ComputerScienceScores.txt". myFile is the variable representing it and is called its *file handle*.
`for index = 0 to 9`	This starts a 'for' loop to move through the ten indexes of the array.
`    myFile.writeLine(scores[index])`	The data at each index is written to the file.
`next index`	This closes the loop and will transfer processing back to the start until index = 9.
`myFile.close()`	This will close the text file.

 Download Worksheet 6.3 from Cambridge Elevate

Reading data from a file

Data can be read from a text file.

To read data from a file it must be opened in read mode i.e.

Code ————————————————————————————

```
myFile = openRead("samplefile.txt")
```

Reading the data

Each item of data can be read using the following command:

Code ————————————————————————————

```
myFile.readLine()
```

Closing the file

When you have finished reading from the file it must be closed:

Code ————————————————————————————

```
myFile.close()
```

Tip

The commands for file handling given here are the ones included in the OCR pseudocode. Your programming language will probably have a lot more so carry out research to find out other file handling commands and how they are written.

WORKED EXAMPLE

Anil now wants to add code to read the scores from the file 'ComputerScienceScores' back into the array declared as scores[10].

```
myFile = openRead("ComputerScienceScores.txt")
```
This opens the text file on disk called 'ComputerScienceScores.txt'. 'myFile' is the variable representing it and is its file handle.

```
for index = 0 to 9
```
This starts a for loop to move through the 10 indexes of the array.

```
    scores[index] = myFile.readLine()
```
Each line of data is input into the indexes of the array.

```
next index
```
This closes the loop and will transfer processing back to the start until index = 9.

```
myFile.close()
```
This will close the file.

What if you have forgotten the length of the file? In the above examples a for loop was used to write to and read from a file. That method can only be used if you know how many data items there are.

But what if you don't know or have forgotten? An example of this kind of situation is when other computers are writing data to the file and at certain times your program is processing the data. If your program was summing up the sales in a shop at the end of the day, then the data file might have had inputs from many different tills in the shop. At the close of business, your program can then collect all of that data and use it. Your program would not know the length of the file and would need to keep processing until it reaches the end of the file.

There is another command used to read in the data until it reaches the end of the file:

Code
```
myFile.endOfFile()
```

This command can also be used for printing out the data in a file.

Complete Interactive Activity 6d on Cambridge Elevate

WORKED EXAMPLE

Anil has lots of text files that his programs have created, but he has forgotten how many data items they each contain.

```
myFile = openRead("ComputerScienceScores.txt")
```
This opens the text file on disk called 'ComputerScienceScores.txt'. 'myFile' is the variable representing it and is its file handle.

```
while NOT myFile.endOfFile()
```
This starts a while loop, which will run until 'endOfFile' is reached so it doesn't have to be told how many loops to make.

```
    print(myFile.readLine)
```
Each line of data is printed.

```
endwhile
```
This closes the loop and will transfer processing back to the start until 'endOfFile' is reached.

```
myFile.close()
```
This will close the file.

ACTIVITY 6.5

A student has coded a computer game which stores the five highest scores in an array. She now wants to save those scores to a file and load them back in when the game is run again.

Write a program that will save the array of scores to a suitable text file and then load them back in again. Run your program to check that it is working as intended.

Remember

1. Data can be output to and stored in text files on storage media.
2. The file is accessed using a file handle.
3. Data can be written to the file and then read back in by a program running on the computer.
4. After writing to or reading from a file it must be closed.

Practice questions

1. a. Explain what is meant by validation.

   b. A school with years 7 to 13 use a computer program to enter student details. One of the items of data to be entered is the school year that the student is in. Using pseudocode or a flow diagram illustrate an algorithm that would carry out:
      i. a presence check
      ii. a range check
      when this data is entered.

Your final challenge

Your final challenge is to create algorithms to:

- Create a new username that is unique and hasn't been used before. The username is to be based on a person's name, gender, year of birth and postcode.
- Allow a user to enter a password of nine letters. This must be entered twice and be the same each time.

You do not need to create one program with all these features, but may write separate algorithms for each task. (We will be looking at linking these separate algorithms into one program in the next chapter.) The rules for creating a username are shown in the flow diagram.

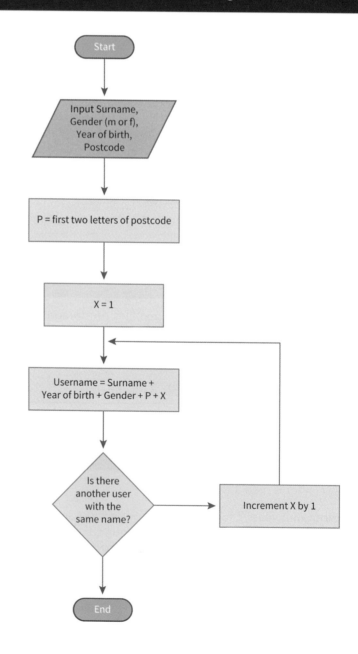

7 Problem solving

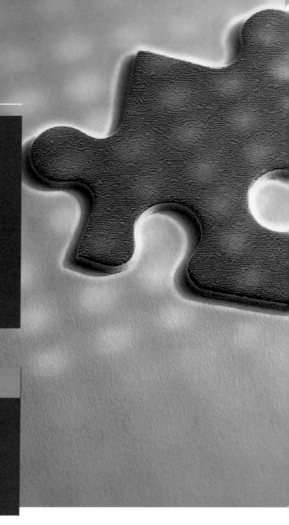

Learning outcomes

By the end of this chapter you should be able to:

- explain what is meant by computational thinking
- explain what is meant by *decomposition* and *abstraction* and use them to solve problems
- create algorithms to solve problems that you have analysed
- explain what is meant by top-down and bottom-up problem solving
- create structured programs using procedures
- follow the systems development cycle to analyse problems, design and implement solutions and test the outcomes.

 Challenge: write a program for ordering a pizza online

- Practically everything we need we can order online: clothes, food, music, cars and books.
- We can select the items we want in the comfort of our own homes and have them delivered.
- Your challenge is to write a program for ordering a pizza online.

Why problem solving?

- All our lives we have to solve problems. How to make a cup of coffee? How to tidy up our bedrooms? How to do our maths homework? Our lives are one long problem to solve!

- When you were creating algorithms in Chapter 1, you had to think about problems in a particular way. You had to think about:
  - inputs and outputs
  - data and processes
  - sequence, selection and iteration.

- In Chapter 5, you had to compare the efficiency of different algorithms and decide which one would be better in a particular circumstance. Thinking in this way is referred to as 'computational thinking'.

- Problem solving is essential for our survival, and the techniques used in computational thinking are being applied to solve world-wide problems.

 Watch the thinking logically animation on Cambridge Elevate

Problems such as global warming, pollution and the burning of fossil fuels are being tackled using computational thinking skills.

Problems and programming

A computer scientist's job can be divided into three areas:

1. defining and analysing problems

2. creating a structured solution or algorithm

3. coding the solution.

The first two parts contribute to what we think of as 'problem solving'. The third area, 'coding the solution' is what a computer scientist does after they have solved the problem.

Coding is not problem solving. It is translating the structured solution into a form that can be implemented by a computer. If the computer scientist has failed to solve the problem correctly, then no amount of advanced coding technique will produce a successful solution.

Computational thinking

The set of skills needed to solve problems is often referred to as 'computational thinking', a term coined by a computer scientist called Jeannette Wing at Carnegie Mellon University in the United States.

When you create an algorithm, you think in a computational way. For example, in Chapter 1, when you created an algorithm for making a cup of tea, you had to think about:

- the start state (empty kettle, cold water in tap, no tea bag in cup)

- the end state (what you had to end up with: hot water and tea bag in cup, milk in cup)

- the inputs needed (water, tea bag, milk, possibly sugar)

- the processes required and their correct sequence (fill kettle, turn on kettle, place tea bag into cup)

- selection (Is the kettle full? Is the water boiling?)

- iteration (checking and rechecking the water until it is boiling, pouring water into cup until it is full).

Four important skills included in computational thinking are:

1. decomposition

2. abstraction

3. pattern recognition

4. algorithm design (see Chapter 1).

Let's look at these now.

Tip

The terms 'programming' and 'coding' are often used to describe the same functions, but a programmer analyses the problem, creates an algorithm and then codes the solution, whilst a coder just codes the solution; the algorithm could be created by someone else.

Decomposition

Decomposition is the ability to break down a problem into smaller and smaller sub-problems or components. It is far easier trying to solve a small problem than a large one and decomposing a problem shows how its various components fit together.

We decomposed a problem when we looked at getting up in the morning and going to school. The sub-problems included:

Getting out of bed.

Showering.

Getting dressed.

Making breakfast.

These problems can be broken down even further. For example, to make breakfast:

Make tea.

Make toast.

And for each of these there are even more sub-tasks, such as boiling the water for the tea. Breaking down the problem into small parts allows greater focus on each one.

 Download Worksheet 7.1 from Cambridge Elevate

ACTIVITY 7.1

You have been asked to create a program that would allow a user to calculate the approximate cost of a car journey. List the sub-tasks involved in solving this problem.

Abstraction

Abstraction means ignoring or filtering out the unnecessary details that are not so important for the current purpose to get to the essential features of something.

We use abstraction all of the time so we are not constantly thinking about too many facts. If someone says that they have seen a 'car', we know what they mean because we have abstracted the essential features and have made a mental image of an object we call a car. We know that they mean something with four wheels, an engine and a steering wheel that uses fuel to travel to carry people along a road. Imagine trying to have a conversation without abstraction. We would have to describe the car in minute detail, giving dimensions, number of wheels, etc. Then we would have to explain what a wheel was, and so on.

Would the minute details for the following tasks really matter when describing a general solution that could be used by anybody?

 Key term

decomposition: means breaking a problem down into smaller, more manageable parts which are then easier to solve

 Key term

Abstraction: the process of removing unnecessary details so that only the main, important points remain

 Maths skills

The cost of the journey can be calculated using the following formula:

(Length of journey in miles / miles per gallon of the car) * cost of one gallon of petrol

- the way you remove a duvet cover

- the side of the bed you get out of

- putting on a pair of slippers

- how to get to the shower

- the colour of the mug that should be used

- the type of tea bag to be used.

These facts may be important to you, but what if a person following the algorithm doesn't have a duvet? Or doesn't wear slippers? Or has a different route to the shower? Or doesn't have the type of tea bag that you use? The minute details would be confusing. Only the essential features matter.

 Download Worksheet 7.2 from Cambridge Elevate

Pattern recognition

When you look at this picture what do you see? A young woman or an old one? How do you interpret the patterns?

We look at data and we can see patterns, often without thinking about it. For example, look at this sequence of numbers:

2, 4, 8, 16, 32, 64

Can you see a pattern? What would the next two numbers be?

We are always looking for patterns in human behaviour: if a person smiles at us, we assume they are going to be friendly.

When we see the patterns in the problem, we can use similar solutions. For example we could recognise that iteration will be required and so we immediately know that loops will be required.

3D pattern recognition is an essential skill needed by anyone hoping to solve the Rubik's cube.

Algorithm design

Algorithm design is the development of a step-by-step strategy for solving a problem and has been covered in Chapter 1.

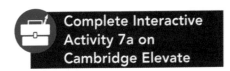

Complete Interactive Activity 7a on Cambridge Elevate

WORKED EXAMPLE

Look at this relatively simple problem about calculating the approximate cost of a car journey.

In order to solve the problem, we need to decompose the problem into sub-problems and then we need to identify the tasks required to solve them.

Create an algorithm that could be used to calculate the approximate cost of a car journey.

a. Decomposition

The following factors affect the cost and should be included in the algorithm:

- the length of the journey
- the efficiency of the car (how many miles the car travels on one gallon of petrol), i.e. the miles per gallon or mpg of the car (this value is given by the manufacturer or the user will know an average value from experience)
- the cost of one gallon of petrol
- the number of passengers
- the speed of the car
- the condition of the roads
- the amount of luggage carried
- the tyre pressure
- the use of the heater and air conditioning system
- the air temperature and air pressure.

b. Abstraction

We have identified lots of factors. The user will know some of the factors but not others. Before the journey, the user will not know:

- the speeds they will be travelling at
- the condition of the road
- whether they will be using the heater or air conditioning
- the air temperature and air pressure.

They will know:

- the number of passengers
- the tyre pressure.

But they probably will not know how this affects the efficiency of their particular car.

Because we are trying to find the *approximate* cost, we are going to have to do some abstraction.

The factors that will *most affect* the cost and which will most likely be *known* by the user are:

- the length of the journey

- the average miles per gallon for the car

- the cost of one gallon of petrol.

As we are trying to calculate the approximate cost of the journey, we will use these three factors.

We have abstracted the essential features and now we must represent them in an algorithm. We are in fact making a model of a car journey in an algorithm. We are converting a real-life event into a computer simulation of it.

c.   Algorithm design

We can illustrate the algorithm using a flow diagram.

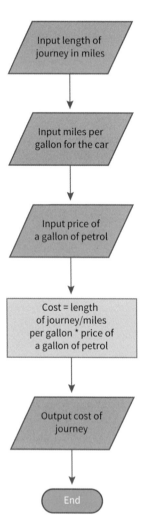

This algorithm will output the cost of the journey assuming that:

- Distance is input in miles.

- Price is given per gallon.

ACTIVITY 7.2

Adapt the flow diagram in the above Worked Example so that it if the price of petrol was entered as 'price per litre', the cost of the journey could still be calculated correctly.

Tip

You will have to research the conversion factor to calculate the number of litres in a gallon.

Top-down versus bottom-up problem solving

The solutions for the problems we have been looking at illustrate a *top-down* approach. This means that the problem has been broken down to gain an insight into the sub-problems that make it up. Each sub-problem has then been broken down into further problems that may have to be solved.

Bottom-up problem solving is the opposite of the top-down approach, and begins with specific details. These details are analysed and put into groups, which are grouped again into larger groups.

For example, a computer scientist might be asked to design a complete billing system for a company. They could start at the 'bottom', and look at all of the different kinds of bills that customers pay, such as full payment, part payment, discounts available, etc. They could design a solution for each one and then try to find similarities so that any code used to solve one could be used for the others. However, there is no certainty that all the solutions will fit together.

Tip

Top-down problem solving is said to be *strategic* because it starts with a larger problem and so gives an overview of the complete system, whilst bottom-up is *tactical*: work is started on sub-problems before there is any clear idea that they will fit together to solve the whole problem.

 Remember

1. Computational thinking involves decomposition, abstraction, pattern recognition and algorithm design.
2. Top-down problem solving starts with the main problem and breaks it down gradually into smaller sub-problems.
3. Bottom-up problem solving starts with a collection of small problems and tries to combine them together to form a larger system.

Structured programming

The top-down approach shows that any problem consists of sub-problems and so it follows that any solution can be built up of sub-solutions or modules. It is often helpful for modules to be designed and coded separately. They can be then be called and used in the program as many times as needed without having to rewrite the code each time. They can be reused in different programs.

This type of programming is called *structured* programming (or *modular* programming), and it makes a program more logical, easier to edit and far easier for another person to understand.

Login and password control

In Chapter 4, we looked at algorithms to allow users to create usernames and passwords and to change their passwords. Using a top-down approach, we can look at the tasks and sub-tasks involved:

 Key term

called: procedures are 'called' by the main program: this means that they are started up, given data, run and then the output is collected by the main program

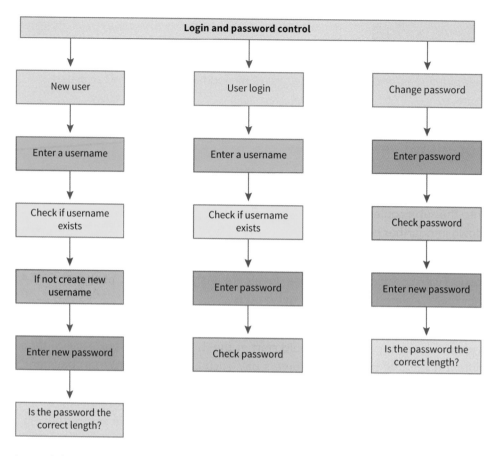

In total there are 16 sub-tasks that need to be coded, but many are used more than once. If we used a structured programming approach, we could use and reuse these modules. Each of these modules can be called and used when they are needed.

If a user wants to create a new login, the process is:

- call 'Enter a username' module
- call 'Check if username exists' module
- call 'If not create new username' module
- call 'Enter new password' module
- call 'Is the password the correct length?' module.

Four of the existing modules can be reused, and only 'If not create new username' is unique to this section.

Procedures and functions

In programming languages, these modules of code are called subroutines. There are two types of subroutine: *procedures* and *functions*.

Functions are called from an expression in the main program and return a value to it, e.g.:

Code —

```
area = findArea()
```

where 'area' is the name of the function.

Tip

To change their password, the user would have to use the modules for 'User login' and then the ones for 'Change password'.

Key term

subroutines: self-contained modules of code that can be 'called' by the main program when they are needed

Procedures are called from a statement in the main program but do not return any value to it. They just do something and then the main program continues, for example the statement:

Code

```
count()
```

would call the following procedure:

Code

```
procedure count()

    for x = 1 to 1000

    next x

endprocedure
```

The procedure would just count to 1000 and then return to the main program. Most programming languages have ready-made functions built-in.

Here is a list of functions in the Python programming language:

Built-in Functions			
abs()	divmod()	input()	staticmethod()
all()	enumerate()	int()	str()
any()	eval()	isinstance()	sum()
basestring()	execfile()	issubclass()	super()
bin()	file()	iter()	tuple()
bool()	filter()	len()	type()
bytearray()	float()	list()	unichr()
callable()	format()	locals()	unicode()
chr()	frozenset()	long()	vars()
classmethod()	getattr()	map()	xrange()
cmp()	globals()	max()	zip()
compile()	hasattr()	memoryview()	_import_()
complex()	hash()	min	
delattr()	help()	next()	
dict()	hex()	object()	
dir()	id()	oct()	

Tip

To find functions for other programming languages, search the Internet for 'programming language built-in functions'.

Watch out

Some programming languages such as Python just have functions and no procedures. Investigate the language that you are using to see how it handles functions and procedures.

Notice that each function is followed by open and close brackets for you to enter the data that you want the function to work on.

We have already used some of these functions in the pseudocode that we have been using.

For example `print()` and `input()`. When the print function is called, the item or items to be printed are enclosed within the brackets, e.g. `print("Hello")` would output the word "Hello".

Using these functions is another example of abstraction. They can be called to carry out an action without a programmer actually knowing how they do it.

Tip

When functions are created, they should be given meaningful names relating to the actions they perform. It is easier to remember what they are for if they are given meaningful names.

When the print function is used, the programmer does not need to know all of the commands used by the function to display the characters, encoded as binary, on the monitor.

We use this type of abstraction in our daily lives. For example, a car driver does not need to know how the engine and gears work or how the car starts when the key is turned. They can still drive the car without knowing or understanding these things.

Creating functions

In addition to using these built-in functions, programming languages allow us to write our own.

WORKED EXAMPLE

Kim is creating a game in which users have to throw two dice and add the results together to find the total score. This has to happen many times in the game and, without using functions, the code would have to be rewritten many times. But by using a function, the code only has to be written once and called when needed.

```
function dice()
```
This defines a function named 'dice'. This signals that a value will be returned as a result of this module.

```
    number1 = random(1, 6)
```
The variable 'number1' is assigned a single value of between 1 and 6 produced by the built-in random() function. The two numbers given to the function (1, 6) indicate the lower and upper limits of the number to be generated.

```
    number2 = random(1, 6)
```

```
    number = number1 + number2
```
The variable 'number' is assigned the value of the sum of number1 and number2.

```
    return(number)
```
The value of the variable 'number' is what the function has to return to the main program.

```
endfunction
```
This statement ends the function definition.

Kim has used her powers of abstraction to work out the essential features of a die - that it will return a random number between 1 and 6. Any other features such as colour or the material it is made of are unimportant. She has then represented them in pseudocode. She has made a computer model of a real-life event.

Watch out

The total of the two dice is stored in two different variables. In the main program which calls the function it is stored in the variable 'score' but in the actual function it is stored in a variable named 'number'.

ACTIVITY 7.3

In your chosen programming language, create and test a game, using a function, in which a user is asked to throw three dice to find the total. The game should keep the highest score and notify the user if they have beaten it. The user should be able to keep throwing the dice until they select an option to stop playing the game.

Arguments and parameters

In the dice example a value was returned to the main program by the function when it was called. In a similar way values, stored in the main program, can be passed to the function. These are called arguments.

 Watch the arguments and parameters animation on Cambridge Elevate

WORKED EXAMPLE

In this example, a user is asked to enter their first and surname. The procedure is used to print a message.

```
procedure message(one, two)
```

This defines the procedure. It uses two variables named 'one' and 'two'. These are called the parameters of the procedure. They signal that values will be passed from the main program.

```
        print("Hello " + one + " " + two)
```

The procedure then prints a welcome message using these two variables.

Until the procedure is run, the variables are empty: they have no value. The values for these variables have to be passed to it from the main program when it is called.

```
endprocedure
firstName = input("Please enter your first name.")
```

The user is asked to enter their first name.

```
secondName = input("Please enter your surname.")
```

The user is asked to enter their surname.

```
message(firstName, secondName)
```

The procedure is called and the values stored in these two variables (the arguments) are passed to the procedure's parameters. The procedure uses them in the order they are given, i.e. 'one' assumes it has to have the value of firstName and 'two' the value of 'secondName' as they are passed in that order.

Local and global variables

In the previous example, different variables have been used to hold the same data.

Data	Variable in the main program	Variable in the procedure
The user's first name	firstName	one
The user's surname	secondName	two

Key terms

local variable: a variable that is used only within a function. When the function has completed its work, the local variable is discarded

global variable: a variable that is used in the main program. It can be used by any of the commands or subroutines in the program

The variable in the procedure exists only within the procedure and is called a local variable. Any data stored in the local variable is only available for manipulation in the procedure. That's why it is called 'local'.

In the main program, the same data is stored in another variable and this can be used by other commands in the main program. It is available to all and is therefore said to be global.

If you added another statement to the main program, such as the one below shown in red:

Code

```
firstName = input("Please enter your first name.")
secondName = input("Please enter your surname.")
message(firstName, secondName)
fullName = firstName + " " + secondName
```

that would be fine as the two variables, firstName and secondName are global variables within the main program.

However, if the statement was

Code

```
fullName = one + " " + secondName
```

then an error message would be returned, because 'one' and 'two' have not been declared in the main program. They exist only in the procedure.

You could actually use the same variable names in a function or procedure as in the main program but it is easy to get into a muddle with the logic and mix them up.

ACTIVITY 7.4

Rewrite the message function and the calling program so that it prints the welcome message with surname before the first name.

Several arguments passed and several values returned

In the previous example, two arguments were passed to the procedure but nothing was returned.

Just as more than one argument can be sent to the function, more than one value can be returned.

In the following example, a function used to calculate the area and perimeter of a rectangle, there are two arguments and two values returned.

Code

```
function rectangle (length, width)

    area = length * width

    perimeter = (length * 2) + (width * 2)

    return(area, perimeter)
```

This function has two parameters, 'length' and 'width'.

The area of the rectangle is assigned to the variable 'area'.

The perimeter of the rectangle is assigned to the variable 'perimeter'.

The values of these local variables are returned to the main program.

```
endfunction
```

```
rectLength = int(input("Please enter the length."))
```

The user enters the length of the rectangle. The command 'int' is used to convert the input from a string to a number.

```
rectWidth = int(input("Please enter the width."))
```

And now the width.

```
rectArea, rectPerimeter = rectangle(rectLength, rectWidth)
```

Main program   **Function rectangle**

rectLength ⟶ length

rectWidth ⟶ width

rectArea ⟵ area

rectPerimeter ⟵ perimeter

The function 'rectangle' is now called in this statement and the values of the two global variables ('rectLength' and 'rectWidth') are passed to it as arguments.

The two variables, 'rectArea' and 'rectPerimeter' are declared and will be given the values of the two local variables (area and length) that are returned from the function.

Complete Interactive Activity 7b on Cambridge Elevate

ACTIVITY 7.5

Shown below is a function:

```
function calculate(input1, input2)

    solution = int((input1 * input2) / (input1 + input2))

    while solution < 3

        solution = int((input1 * input2) / (input1 + input2))

        input1 = input1 + 1

        input2 = input2 + 1

    endwhile

    return(input1, input2)

    endfunction
```

Complete a trace table for this function when it is called with the following arguments (Refer to Chapter 2):

```
Calculate(3, 6)
```

Download Worksheet 7.3 from Cambridge Elevate

Key term

menu: a set of options to help a user find information or use a program function

Subroutines and menus

Functions are useful when using menus in a program. When a user selects a menu option, they can be sent to a particular function or procedure.

WORKED EXAMPLE

For a system login and password control, the main program could have a menu system like this:

1. Register as a new user

2. Login

3. Change your password

4. Exit.

Now that we are using structured programming using procedures, it is relatively easy to direct a user to the part of the program they need.

The user enters a number between 1 and 4 and is directed to the correct section:

```
print ("1. Register as a new user.")
print ("2. Login.")
print ("3. Change your password.")
print ("4. Exit.")
choice = input ("Please select a menu option.")
if choice == "1"
        newUser()
elseif choice == "2"
        login()
elseif choice == "3"
        changePassword()
elseif choice == "4"
        exit()
else
        print("Incorrect option. Try again.")

endif
```

The on-screen menu is set up.

The user enters a menu number.

The user is directed to a different function depending on their choice.

This message will be displayed if the entry is not one of the above.

ACTIVITY 7.6

Owners often want to know the 'human equivalent' of their pet's age. Here are two rules for calculating this for dogs and cats:

- Assume that a 1-year-old dog is equal to a 12-year-old human and a 2-year-old dog is equal to a 24-year old human. Then add 4 years for every year after that.

- Assume that a 1-year-old cat is equal to a 15-year-old human and a 2-year-old cat is equal to a 24-year-old human. Then add 4 years for every year after that.

Your task is to design an algorithm for a program to allow a user to find the 'human equivalent age' of their dog or cat and then code it in the language you are studying.

It should have a menu system to allow them to select the type of animal and use functions for the calculations.

Extension: Allow the user to use the menu as many times as they want until they select an option to quit.

The benefits of using subroutines

Subroutines are a natural way of implementing 'top-down' design because some of the tasks identified can be allocated to a subroutine. They therefore assist with decomposition and abstraction.

Repeated sections of code need only be written once and called when necessary. This shortens the development time of a program and means that the finished program will occupy less memory space when it is run.

Subroutines also improve the structure of the code, making it easier to read through and follow what is happening. It's easier to check your code if you use subroutines because each subroutine can be coded and tested independently. The program is easier to debug as each subroutine can be inspected independently. If changes have to be made at a later date it is easier to change a small module than having to work through the whole program.

In large development teams different members can be working independently on different subroutines. They can use and develop standard libraries of subroutines that can be reused in other programs.

 Download Worksheet 7.4 from Cambridge Elevate

Software development

Software is developed for a purpose. There is a problem or someone thinks that something could be done more efficiently, and software or whole systems of software are developed to meet that need.

The problem is that lots of this development results in failure.

In order to maximise success, various schemes or methods have been developed detailing the way it should be done.

 Remember

1. In structured programming a program consists of distinct blocks of code that are linked together.
2. Functions are subroutines that can return a result to the command that called it.
3. Procedures do not return a result.
4. Subroutines can accept parameters or values that they can use.
5. Subroutines can be called from menus.

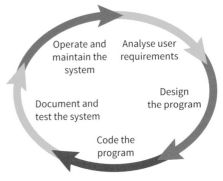

All of these schemes are variations of the systems development cycle, a step-by-step process for planning, creating and testing, deploying and maintaining a system.

We will look through these stages using the following problem.

You have been asked to create a system to assess and accept or reject passwords entered by users. Passwords should be at least 6, and no more than 12, characters long. If a password does not meet these criteria, the user should be told why and be allowed to re-enter a password. If it is acceptable, the user must be informed.

After the password has been accepted, the user should also be informed of the strength of the password based on the following rules:

Weak   if the password is all lower case or all upper case or all numeric characters.

Medium   if two of the above types are used.

Strong   if all three types are used.

Problem identification and analysis

The first thing any software developer needs to do is to fully understand the problem. They should read and re-read until they have identified all of the details about what is required.

The developer can then decompose the problem into tasks and sub-tasks. Note taking and identifying links (pattern recognition) is very important.

The following are some of the tasks and sub-tasks involved:

- Data entry for user's password.

- Check if it is 6 to 12 characters in length

    o   If it is not then inform user and allow them to re-enter.

    o   If it is then check password characters.

        –   Count lower case characters.

        –   Count upper case characters.

        –   Count numeric characters.

            •   If all are greater than 0 then inform user that password strength is strong.

            •   If one is 0 then inform user that password strength is medium.

            •   If two are 0 then inform user that password strength is weak.

As the developer is decomposing the problem into tasks and sub-tasks, they will be thinking ahead about how some of these can be solved. For example:

- How can I count the number of characters?

- How can I allow the user go back to re-enter if there are not sufficient characters?

- How can I count the number of lower case characters?

These are just three of many questions raised by the identification and analysis stage and in the next stage the developer plans how to solve them by doing what you are already brilliant at: creating algorithms.

Design

This is the creative section, where the developer can design solutions to the problems. Although developers will use the same tools (algorithms, flow diagrams, pseudocode) they will probably end up with different designs. There are always many different solutions to a problem!

The analysis identified the tasks and sub-tasks and showed how different modules or sub-routines can be used to contribute to the complete solution.

The following shows a flow diagram that could be used to illustrate an algorithm for password entry.

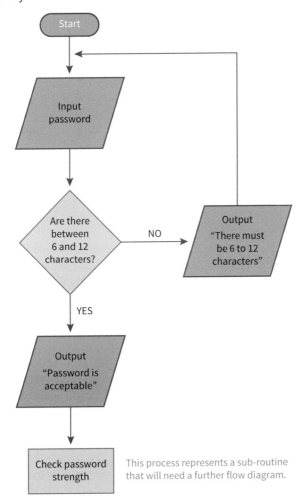

The flow diagrams show the logical structure and navigation of the algorithm, where selection, iteration, input and output will be used.

This can be refined using pseudocode.

Using pseudocode will enable the developer to identify the variables and functions that will be required and decide on suitable names and data types.

The following shows sample pseudocode for the flow diagram shown above:

Code ————————————————————————————————————

```
password = ""
```
The variable 'password' is assigned the value of an empty string.

```
while password == ""
```
A loop is set up which will run while 'password' contains an empty string.

```
    password = input("Please enter a
    password of between 6 and 12
    characters.")
```
The user is asked to enter a password, which is stored in the variable 'password'.

```
    if password.length <6 OR password.length
    > 12 then
```
If the length of the password entered is less than 6 characters or more than 12 then …

```
        print("The password must be between
        6 and 12 characters. Please enter a
        different password.")
```
… the user is given a message asking them to choose another password.

```
        password = ""
```
The variable 'password' is set back to an empty string so that the loop will run again.

```
    endif
endwhile
print("The password is acceptable.")
```
As the password entered 'passed the test' the user is informed.

Key terms

unambiguous: this means that the instruction cannot be misunderstood and the correct action will always be performed. All instructions given to a computer must be unambiguous or it won't do anything!

In the design phase, the developer will also:

- Design the interface. Will a graphical user interface be used with input boxes for password entry or will it be purely text based? If it is graphical then the complete input form will be designed.

- Design the output. The text for the user should be as unambiguous and clear as possible. Will different fonts be used? Will the text be in different colours?

Tip

Using pseudocode allows the programmer to concentrate on the logic of the solution without having to think about the way the actual programming language has to be written with its rules and syntax.

Watch out

Everyone is human and we can make errors in our design. It is important to check for logic errors (see Chapter 1) at this stage because they are easier to identify and correct than when the code has been written.

Implementation

This is the stage where the algorithm, either in a flow diagram or pseudocode, is translated into an actual programming language.

Now the developer has to produce a solution that works in a particular programming language on a computer with a specific operating system.

It is important that there are no syntax errors. Since computer programs must follow strict syntax to compile correctly, any aspects of the code that do not conform to the syntax of the programming language will produce a syntax error. Syntax errors are small grammatical mistakes, sometimes limited to a single character. For example, a missing semicolon at the end of a line or an extra bracket at the end of a function may produce a syntax error.

 Complete the Cambridge Computing Online activity www.cambridge.org/links/kose4009

 Key term

syntax error: a grammatical error in the source code of a program

 Complete Interactive Activity 7c on Cambridge Elevate

 Watch the debugging animation on Cambridge Elevate

Integrated development environments

If we make mistakes with our spelling, punctuation or grammar then the person reading our work will probably still be able to understand it. They can make allowances.

If you make one mistake in an essay your English teacher doesn't immediately refuse to read it and give you zero marks. But computers are not so forgiving. One mistake in a program and they will not be able to continue to run the program.

We have already looked at logical errors, but most errors causing programs to malfunction are syntax errors such as misspelling, missing brackets, statements not indented, missing colons or semi-colons. The list is endless.

Programmers therefore need all the help they can get. They get no help if they write their code in a word processor or text editor but thankfully IDEs (integrated development environments) have been developed. An IDE is a software application that provides facilities to computer programmers for software development. It typically consists of a source code editor, debugger, complier or interpreter and might well have a graphical user interface (GUI). Using an integrated development environment (IDE) will help to prevent syntax errors.

Source code editor

A source code editor is a text editor designed specifically for the writing and editing of source code for computer programs. It should provide facilities such as syntax highlighting, which displays source code in different colours and fonts according to the category of terms, for example commands, variables and strings enclosed in quotation marks. It improves the readability of the text and makes it easier to spot if a delimiter such as a bracket or quote mark has been omitted.

Here is an example of highlighting in a source code editor:

Code ───────────────────────

```
import random
mysteryNumber = random.randint(1, 100)
```

```
guess = 0
while (guess == 0):
    guess = int(input("Please enter a number between
1 and 100: "))
    if guess > mysteryNumber:
        guess = 0
        print("Your guess is too high.")
    elif guess < mysteryNumber:
        guess = 0
        print("Your guess is too low.")
print("well done. You guessed correctly.")
```

Tip

Different categories have different coloured fonts.

Autocomplete or word completion

This involves the source code editor predicting a word or phrase that the user wants to type in without the user actually typing it in completely, e.g. if the user types a 'p' the editor might suggest the word 'print'.

Bracket matching

Bracket matching is a syntax highlighting feature that highlights matching sets of delimiters such as brackets or quote marks. The purpose is to help the programmer navigate through the code and spot any opening brackets that do not have closing ones and vice versa.

Auto indentation

This feature will automatically indent the next line if it is required when the Return key is pressed. In some languages indentation is a requirement.

Debugger

This is used to test the code and highlight and remove programming errors. When an error is found, it will show its location in the code.

Step by step or single-stepping

Step by step or single-stepping is often referred to as 'animation'.

This allows the code to be run and inspected one line at a time. It allows the effects of that single statement or instruction to be evaluated in isolation.

Breakpoints or pauses

Breakpoints, or pauses, are the intentional stopping of the program at a specified place so that the programmer can inspect the code and see if the programme is functioning as expected up to that point. It is useful if there is an overall problem so that the code can be tested bit by bit.

Variable tracing

This feature allows the programmer to see the values of variables at any stage in the running of the program and check if they are as they intended.

Compiler or interpreter

There is a sort of virtual computer in the debugger that runs the program as if it was being executed by the actual computer.

Auto documentation

This feature allows the automatic documentation of all the variables and modules in a text file. This is especially useful when teams of programmers are working on the same project to ensure that they all understand the coding.

Complete the Cambridge Computing Online activity
www.cambridge.org/links/kose4010

As the solution is coded, extensive use should be made of comments, or explanations of the code.

Remember that these are used by the programmer to explain the code to other users or even to themselves at a later date. When the program is executed, these comments are ignored because they are enclosed within specific identifiers.

All programming languages allow comments but use different symbols to denote them. Often forward slashes are used (//) or the hash symbol (#).

In the following programming language, multiple line comments are enclosed with three quote marks (''') and a single line comment with a hash symbol.

Here is an example of a program with comments:

Key term

comment: information typed in the program which is for the programmers to read

Code

```
'''
This is part of a program developed
to demonstrate part of a
menu system
'''

def menu(): #This is the start of a function named menu.

    print ("1. Register as a new user.")
    print ("2. Login.")
    print ("3. Change your password.")
    print ("4. Exit.")
    response = input("Please select an option: ")
    if (response == "1"):
        newUser()
        run = True
        return(run)
    elif (response == "4"):
        run = False
        return(run)
```

Testing

The software is tested to ensure that:

- It is technically correct, it does not contain any bugs and it produces the expected results.

- It meets the needs of the user. It might function perfectly, but does it actually do what the user needed? Is it easy to use? Can data be input and output in a convenient way?

Alpha testing

The first phase of testing, called alpha testing, is carried out by the actual programmers. It is intended to find any errors or bugs in the program. Test data is used to ensure that the program produces expected results.

The testing plan should include the data to be used, the expected results, the actual results and the corrective action taken.

For example, part of a program might ask a user to enter a number between 1 and 10 and the square of that number is then output. Here is part of a test plan for this function.

Test number	Test data	Expected result	Actual result	Type of test
1	3	9	9	Valid or **in range** test
2	1	1	1	Boundary **test**
3	10	100	100	**Boundary test**
4	12	Message stating that the number should be between 1 and 10	The message was displayed as expected	Erroneous or **out of range** test.

 Complete the Cambridge Computing Online activity www.cambridge.org/links/kose4011

Beta testing

Beta testing is the second phase of testing, where a selected group of potential users are given a pre-release version to operate in a working situation and report bugs and improvements. They use their normal operating data. Their comments are used to correct and refine the software.

Evaluation

During the evaluation stage of software development, the developer writes an evaluation report comparing their finished software with the requirements identified in the problem analysis phase. It should include details of improvements made in the light of testing and user feedback.

Maintenance

The developer is then responsible for maintaining the system. Maintenance can be:

- **corrective**: rewriting the code when further bugs are found or if the program does not function as expected

- **adaptive**: developing new functions that the user identifies as they are using the program.

Key terms

alpha testing: testing done by the programmer

test data: carefully planned, sample data, used to try out programs to check that they give the correct outputs

testing plan: a plan for the way in which a program is to be tested

valid test: ensures that the correct result will be produced with the expected data (sometimes called an 'in-range test')

boundary test: where the highest or lowest acceptable numbers are entered; these check any logical errors that may have been introduced using the <= and >= operators. A boundary test can also be called a 'limit' test or an 'extreme' test

erroneous test: data that should be rejected is deliberately input to check that authentication routines are functioning as expected (sometimes called an 'out-of-range test')

beta testing: testing done by a selected group of individuals to receive their feedback about how well the program works

Practice questions

A student has been asked to design an algorithm to analyse any sentence that a user inputs.

The algorithm should analyse the sentence to find how many times each of the vowels (a, e, i, o, u) has been used.

Design the algorithm so that the analysis is carried out by a function and the main program then outputs the vowels and the number of times they have been used.

Your final challenge

A pizza shop offers the following ingredients for buyers to design their own pizza:

Bases

Small	£1.00
Medium	£1.50
Large	£2.00

All bases are supplied with tomato sauce.

Toppings

Pepperoni	Spicy minced beef
Chicken	Anchovies
Cajun chicken	Tuna
Mushrooms	Peppers
Red onions	Jalapeños
Sweetcorn	Cheese
Ham	Green chillies

All toppings cost 50p and a customer can order as many as they want.

Your task is to design and create a program that will allow a customer to:

- Select and order all the toppings that they want.

When they have finished ordering, the customer should be informed of the following:

- The type of base and all of the toppings they have ordered.
- The total cost of their pizza.

The customer should then be asked if they are going to collect the pizza or want it delivered.

If they are collecting the pizza there is a 10% discount and they should be informed of the new cost.

Remember

1. Software should be developed using the systems development cycle.

2. It has the following stages:

   a. problem identification and analysis

   b. design

   c. implementation

   d. testing

   e. evaluation

   f. maintenance.

**Download
Self-assessment 7
worksheet from
Cambridge Elevate**

8 Binary and hexadecimal

Learning outcomes

By the end of this chapter you should be able to:

- explain how data is represented by computer systems
- explain why the binary system is essential for computer processing
- convert binary numbers into denary and vice versa
- carry out addition, subtraction, multiplication and division on binary numbers
- use left and right shifts when multiplying or dividing binary numbers by powers of 2
- explain why hexadecimal numbers are used
- convert between binary, denary and hexadecimal.

Challenge: write a program that will convert between different number formats

- Computers can manipulate and use numbers only if they are in binary format. Trying to remember strings of 1s and 0s is very difficult for humans. We are used to our denary numbering system.
- We can shorten the strings by using hexadecimal but it is still difficult for us.
- Your challenge is to write a program that will allow users to enter numbers in denary, binary or hexadecimal and convert them into the other number formats.

All computer programs and the data that computers store have to be converted into billions of 1s and 0s as that is all that computers can work with.

Why binary?

- The microprocessor contains the central processing unit, which carries out all of the program instructions by carrying out millions of calculations each second.

- These calculations are performed by billions of transistors acting as switches. They are either on or off. They have only two states: they either transmit an electric current or they do not.

- Any system involving two states is called a binary system.

- As there are only two states (off or on), they can be represented by the two digits of the binary system: 0 and 1.

- All computer programs are lists of instructions switching transistors off or on and therefore they can be represented by the digits 0 and 1.

Binary data

The digits 0 and 1 are known as binary digits or *bits* for short. These are used because computers are digital so the inputs and outputs to devices can only be either electrically 'on' or 'off'. If the input or output is 'on' then we represent that by a 1 and we represent 'off' by a 0.

Series of combinations of 'on' and 'off', i.e. 0s and 1s, are used to represent numbers in the binary number system.

If there are only two digits then how can we communicate complex data and commands to a computer?

We are able to communicate complex concepts and ideas using only the 26 letters of our alphabet.

We do this by combining the letters into words and the words into phrases and sentences.

In a similar way, the two bits, 0 and 1, can be combined to represent different meanings.

If each 'word' consisted of two bits there could be four different 'words': 00, 11, 01 and 10.

With 3 bits there are eight possible 'words': 000, 001, 010, 011, 100, 110, 101, 111.

Can you use your pattern recognition skills to see the relationship?

Number of bits used	Number of combinations
2	4
3	8
4	16
5	32
6	64
7	128
8	256

Yes. It is 2 (the number of different bits - 0 and 1) to the power of the number used in combination. This results in the number of combinations doubling.

Number of bits used	Number of combinations
2	2^2
3	2^3
4	2^4
5	2^5
6	2^6
7	2^7
8	2^8

Therefore to communicate with a computer we must 'talk' to it in words made up of strings of 0s and 1s.

Key term

binary digits: computers can only communicate directly in 0s and 1s; series of 0s and 1s represent the codes for instructions and data

ACTIVITY 8.1

Write down all of the possible combinations if the bits were arranged in groups of 4, e.g. 0000, 0001, 0010, etc.

Maths skills

$2^2 = 2 \times 2$

$2^3 = 2 \times 2 \times 2$

Tip

All commands and data processed by a computer, including text, images and sound are represented by strings of 0s and 1s; often billions of them.

For a computer to print 'hello', you would have to input the following:

0110100001100101011011000110110001101111

Quite a mouthful!

Complete the Cambridge Computing Online activity
www.cambridge.org/links/kose4012

An image as it would appear to us.

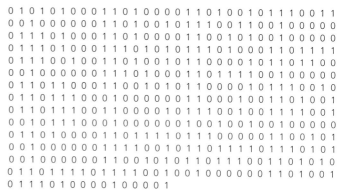

Part of the image as it would appear to a computer.

Tip

Humans use the denary or decimal system, which comprises 10 digits - 0, 1, 2, 3, 4, 5, 6, 7, 8 and 9. This originated because we learnt to count on our 10 fingers.

Humans are not very good at communicating using the binary system. We use a different number system.

Number systems

Watch the number systems animation on Cambridge Elevate

In most numbering systems, the position of a digit determines the value associated with it.

Denary system

Our denary system is said to be base 10 because the position assigns a value that is *ten times the value of the position to the right*.

For example, here is a number:

369

Reading from the right, the '9' is in the first position and has a value of 9 x 1.

The '6' directly to its left has a value of 6 x 10.

The '3' therefore has a value of 3 x 100.

The total number is therefore 300 + 60 + 9, which is equal to 369.

The values of the digits are called their place values.

Key terms

base 10: each place value is ten times bigger than the place to its right

place value: the value that a digit's position in a number gives it, for example (for decimal) in the number 356, the digit 5 has a value of 50 whereas in the number 3560, the digit 5 has a value of 500

The following table shows some of these place values:

Place values of the denary system					
100000	10000	1000	100	10	1

The place value is ten times the value of the place value to the right.

These place values are equal to powers of 10.

Place values of the denary system					
10^5	10^4	10^3	10^2	10^1	10^0
100000	10000	1000	100	10	1

Therefore 369 is equal to:

10^2	10^1	10^0
100	10	1
3	6	9

$(3 \times 10^2) + (6 \times 10^1) + (9 \times 10^0) = 300 + 60 + 9$

Binary system

The binary system also has place values and the value at any position will be *two times the value at the position to the right*: it is base 2. In the same way as in the denary system, the place values increase, but as powers of 2.

Remember that bits are combined into groups to represent data. The basic group is one of eight bits and is called a byte.

The following table shows the place values and the denary equivalents for each bit in a byte.

Place	2^7	2^6	2^5	2^4	2^3	2^2	2^1	2^0
Denary equivalent	128	64	32	16	8	4	2	1

To aid our understanding, we can translate binary into denary.

WORKED EXAMPLE

The following is a byte of bits:

10011010

This has meaning for the microprocessor but we need it to be translated into our denary system.

We can use the above table to do this:

Place	2^7	2^6	2^5	2^4	2^3	2^2	2^1	2^0
Denary equivalent	128	64	32	16	8	4	2	1
Byte	1	0	0	1	1	0	1	0

Just as we did for the denary system above, we can work out the overall value of this byte by using the place values of each bit.

Maths skills

Any number to the power of 0, e.g. 10^0 or 2^0, is equal to 1.

Key terms

base 2: each place value is two times bigger than the place to its right

byte: a group of eight bits

1×2^7	128
0×2^6	0
0×2^5	0
1×2^4	16
1×2^3	8
0×2^2	0
1×2^1	2
0×2^0	0
	154

Therefore **10011010** in binary is equivalent to **154** in denary.

Complete the Cambridge Computing Online activity
www.cambridge.org/links/kose4013

ACTIVITY 8.2

Convert the following 8 bit binary numbers into denary ones.

a. 11001101   b. 01000100   c. 10101010   d. 11110000   e. 10111100

Complete the Cambridge Computing Online activity
www.cambridge.org/links/kose4014

Converting denary numbers to binary

Denary numbers up to 255 can be converted into 8-bit binary ones.

WORKED EXAMPLE

Convert the denary number 113 to binary.

Method 1

Use a table to make your conversion clear.

- Start at the left (here with 2^7 or 128) and ask if the number is equal to or greater than this place value.

- If the number is less than the place value, place a 0 at that position.

- If the number is greater than or equal to the place value, place a 1 and subtract that value from the place value to find the remainder.

Place	2^7	2^6	2^5	2^4	2^3	2^2	2^1	2^0
Denary equivalent	128	64	32	16	8	4	2	1
Byte	0							
Byte	0	1						
Remainders		49						
Byte	0	1	1					
Remainders		49	17					
Byte	0	1	1	1				
Remainders		49	17	1				
Byte	0	1	1	1	0	0	0	
Remainders		49	17	1	1	1	1	
Byte	0	1	1	1	0	0	0	1
Remainders		49	17	1	1	1	1	0

113 < 128, so place a 0 in the place value.

113 > 64, so place a 1
Remainder is 113 − 64 = 49

49 > 32, so place a 1
49 − 32 = 17

17 > 16, so place a 1
17 − 16 = 1

The remainder is now 1 and that is less than 8, 4 and 2.

1 = 1, so place a 1

Therefore 113 in denary is equivalent to 01110001 in binary.

Method 2

Using this method the number is continually divided by 2 and the remainders are found.

Number	Result of division by 2	Remainder
113	56	1
56	28	0
28	14	0
14	7	0
7	3	1
3	1	1
1	0	1

Now add these remainders to the table but in reverse order starting at 2^0.

Place	2^7	2^6	2^5	2^4	2^3	2^2	2^1	2^0
Denary equivalent	128	64	32	16	8	4	2	1
Byte	0	1	1	1	0	0	0	1

As this position has been left out and doesn't have a remainder, a 0 is placed in it.

Brilliant! Both methods have returned the same binary equivalent!

Complete Interactive Activity 8a on Cambridge Elevate

 Download Worksheet 8.1 from Cambridge Elevate

 Complete the Cambridge Computing Online activity www.cambridge.org/links/kose4015

 Complete the Cambridge Computing Online activity www.cambridge.org/links/kose4016

ACTIVITY 8.3

Convert the following denary numbers into 8-bit binary ones.

a. 13   b. 69   c. 131   d. 199   e. 245

Counting in binary

The following shows the sequence in binary of counting up to 15 in denary.

Denary	0	1	2	3	4	5	6	7	8	9	10	11	12	13	14	15
Binary	0	1	10	11	100	101	110	111	1000	1001	1010	1011	1100	1101	1110	1111

ACTIVITY 8.4

Try counting up to 31 in binary using the fingers of one hand. The raised fingers represent a 1 and the lowered fingers a 0. Here is how to start: look how the pattern of fingers is the same as the binary underneath:

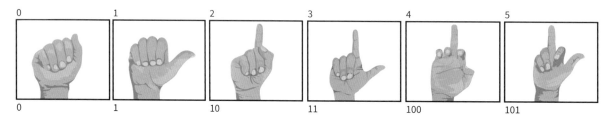

Groups of bits

A byte is a group of 8 bits. The word 'byte' can be represented by upper-case B and 'bit' by lower-case b.

Obviously lots of bytes are needed to represent programs and data and so larger units are needed.

The next in size is the kilobyte, or KB. This is actually 1024 bytes but as the prefix 'kilo' is usually used to represent 1000, a KB is usually taken to mean 1000 bytes.

Then in order of magnitude:

1 megabyte (MB) is 1000 kilobytes

1 gigabyte (GB) is 1000 megabytes

1 terabyte (TB) is 1000 gigabytes

1 petabyte (PB) is 1000 terabytes

 Watch out

A byte is represented by an upper-case B and a bit is represented by a lower-case b. People are often confused by claims made by Internet service providers as they quote bandwidth in kb or mb (kilo**bits** and mega**bits**), which are a lot less than KB or MB!

ACTIVITY 8.5

a.   Calculate how many bits there are in a gigabyte.

b.   Express 2048MB in gigabytes.

c.   Express 1 terabyte in kilobytes.

 Complete the Cambridge Computing Online activity
www.cambridge.org/links/kose4017

 Download Worksheet 8.2 from Cambridge Elevate

 Remember

1.   Bits are **BI**nary digi**T**s – they have single binary values of either 0 or 1.
2.   The bits can be combined into groups as letters are combined into words.
3.   All commands and data processed by a computer consist of groups of bits.
4.   In any number system the value of a digit is determined by its place value.
5.   Binary is a base 2 number system.
6.   Binary numbers can be converted to denary and vice versa.

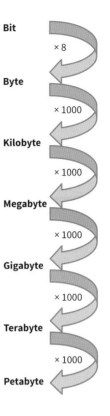

Binary sums

Calculations can be made with binary numbers in the same way as with denary ones.

Addition

Here is a simple denary addition - 965 + 328.

Carry over	1		1	
		9	6	5
		3	2	8
Total	**1**	**2**	**9**	**3**

If the total of one column is greater than 9, for example 13, then the 10 is carried over to the next column and the remainder, 3, is written as the total in this column.

WORKED EXAMPLE

Carry out the following binary addition:

01011 + 00111

Carry over	1	1	1	1	
	0	1	0	1	1
	0	0	1	1	1
Total	1	0	0	1	0

In the same way that a 10 is carried in denary, a 2 is carried in binary.

In binary, 1 + 1 = 10 (2 in denary). The 1 is carried and the 0 is placed in this column.

In binary, 1 + 1 + 1 = 11 (3 in denary). The 1 on the left is carried and the other 1 is placed in this column.

 Complete the Cambridge Computing Online activity
www.cambridge.org/links/kose4018

When computers are processing binary, they may only be able to cope with a fixed number of bits.

Look at this addition being performed by an 8-bit processor.

Carry over	1	1	1	1	1	1		1	
		1	0	0	1	1	1	0	1
		1	1	1	1	0	1	0	1
Total		1	0	0	1	0	0	1	0

Key term

overflow error: when a calculation produces a result that is greater than the computer can deal with or store

But there is a problem. All eight bits have been used and the 1 that was carried over in the last column has nowhere to go: it has been *carried out*. Therefore the result of the calculation would be wrong! This is called an overflow error.

This condition occurs when a calculation produces a result that is greater than the computer can deal with or store. When this occurs, the microprocessor is informed that an error has occurred.

⬇ Download Worksheet 8.3 from Cambridge Elevate

💼 Complete Interactive Activity 8b on Cambridge Elevate

ACTIVITY 8.6

Complete the following binary additions.

a.　0　0　1　1　1　0　1　1
　　0　1　0　1　0　0　0　1

b.　0　1　0　0　1　1　1　1
　　0　1　0　1　0　1　1　1

c.　1　1　0　1　0　0　1　1
　　1　1　1　0　1　1　1　1

The most famous disaster caused by an overflow error was the crash of the Ariane 5 space rocket launched by the European Space Agency in 1996.

Complete the Cambridge Computing Online activity
www.cambridge.org/links/kose4019

Binary shifts

Multiplication

In denary, when we want to multiply by 10 we add a 0, e.g.

$15 \times 10 = 150$

We have done a *left shift*: we have shifted the digits to the place values to their left.

10^2	10^1	10^0
100	10	1
	1	5

Will become:

10^2	10^1	10^0
100	10	1
1	5	0

If we multiplied by 100, then we would shift them two places to the left, and multiplying by 1000 would result in a shift three places to the left. A left shift is used when multiplying by powers of ten. Similarly, we can also use a left shift in binary when we are multiplying by powers of 2. If we multiply the 8-bit binary number 00001011 (denary 11) by the binary number 10 (denary 2) we could do one left shift.

2^7	2^6	2^5	2^4	2^3	2^2	2^1	2^0
128	64	32	16	8	4	2	1
0	0	0	0	1	0	1	1
0	0	0	1	0	1	1	0

Therefore 00001011 x 10 = 00010110.

We can check this in denary: 11 x 2 = 22.

Division

Division of a binary number by powers of 2 is very easy. You just shift the bits to the right. So if the binary number 10011011 is divided by 2, the bits are shifted to the right one place and the one at the right end drops off and is removed. The result would be 01001101. We can test this:

2^7	2^6	2^5	2^4	2^3	2^2	2^1	2^0
128	64	32	16	8	4	2	1
1	0	0	1	1	0	1	1
0	1	0	0	1	1	0	1

If you convert the numbers to denary you can see that 10011011 (155) divided by 2 gives the result 77 using the right shift method. The result is not precise as it should be 77.5. Using right shift leads to a loss of accuracy.

ACTIVITY 8.7

State the results of the following binary left shifts:

a. 00101101 left shift by 3.
    This means that 00101101 is being multiplied by 8 or 2 to the power of 3.

b. 10001101 left shift by 4.
    This means that 00101101 is being multiplied by 4 or 2 to the power of 2.

c. 10110111 left shift by 2.
    This means that 00101101 is being multiplied by 2 or 2 to the power of 1.

This method can also be used for any number that is a power of 2. For example, if the number is divided by 16 (which is 2^4), there should be a shift of 4 places to the right.

2^7	2^6	2^5	2^4	2^3	2^2	2^1	2^0
128	64	32	16	8	4	2	1
1	0	0	1	1	0	1	1
0	0	0	0	1	0	0	1

The result in denary is 9 and 16 multiplied by 9 is equal to 144 and not 155.

Therefore the result given is the nearest, lower integer.

 Complete Interactive Activity 8c on Cambridge Elevate

ACTIVITY 8.8

State the results of the following binary right shifts.

a. 00101101 right shift by 3.

b. 10001101 right shift by 4.

c. 10110111 right shift by 2.

Hexadecimal

Hexadecimal is a base 16 number system: there are 16 digits, 0 to 15.

As we only have 10 single digits (0 to 9), we use upper-case letters A to F for the remaining 5 digits.

Therefore hexadecimal digits are represented as:

0 1 2 3 4 5 6 7 8 9 A B C D E F

Why do we need hexadecimal numbers?

We need hexadecimal numbers because of our human limitations. Computers do not understand or use hexadecimal, only binary. Hexadecimal is used because we get confused with large binary numbers, so we simplify them by representing them in hexadecimal notation.

Here is a byte (8 bits):

1	1	0	1	0	0	1	1

Saying that is quite a mouthful but it is easier if it is represented as hexadecimal.

To convert the binary to hexadecimal the byte is split into two halves of 4 bits each. These are called nibbles.

 **Key term**

nibble: half a byte

1	1	0	1

Nibbles

0	0	1	1

Each nibble is now converted into its denary number. Here are the nibbles with their place values.

8	4	2	1
1	1	0	1

8	4	2	1
0	0	1	1

The denary numbers are 13 and 3

Therefore the hexadecimal representation is D3

It is far easier to say and remember 'D3' than '11010011'.

As we will see later, hexadecimal numbers are used to simplify colour codes, which consist of 24 bits. It is far easier to represent colour codes as 6 hexadecimal digits rather than 24 binary ones.

Here are some colours with their hexadecimal codes.

#FF66FF		#CC66FF		#9966FF	
#FF66CC		#CC66CC		#9966CC	
#FF6699		#CC6699		#996699	
#FF6666		#CC6666		#996666	
#FF6633		#CC6633		#996633	
#FF6600		#CC6600		#996600	
#FF33FF		#CC33FF		#9933FF	
#FF33CC		#CC33CC		#9933CC	
#FF3399		#CC3399		#993399	
#FF3366		#CC3366		#993366	

ACTIVITY 8.9

Investigate the hexadecimal codes for the different colours that can be used.

Hexadecimal is also used in assembly language programming and also in error messages. When anything is represented by a hexadecimal number, a # sign is used, e.g. #FF0000 is the hexadecimal for red.

Using hexadecimal raises another problem. We have to be able to convert from binary and denary into hexadecimal and vice versa. Converting from binary to hexadecimal has been shown above but we will now look at the other conversions.

Converting denary to hexadecimal
Here is a denary number: 213.

To convert to hexadecimal, we must progressively divide by 16 until the result is 0 and remember the remainders.

Number	Result of dividing by 16	Remainder
213	13	5
13	0	13

D 5

Therefore '213' in denary in hexadecimal is 'D5'.

We can check this if we create a table showing place values for base 16.

16^3	16^2	16^1	16^0
4096	256	16	1
		D	5

Therefore, D5 is equal to (13 x 16) + 5, which is 213.

Converting hexadecimal to denary

Here is a hexadecimal number: CD. We can convert it to denary using the table.

16^3	16^2	16^1	16^0
4096	256	16	1
		C	D

Therefore the denary is equal to: (12 x 16) + (13 x 1), which is equal to 192 + 13.

Therefore 'CD' in hexadecimal equals '205' in denary.

Converting hexadecimal to binary

We will use the same hexadecimal number: CD.

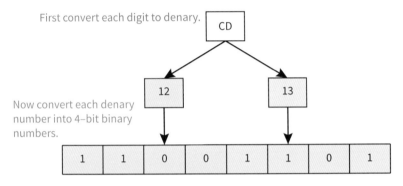

First convert each digit to denary.

Now convert each denary number into 4–bit binary numbers.

Therefore 'CD' in hexadecimal is '11001101' in binary.

Complete Interactive Activity 8d on Cambridge Elevate

Download Worksheet 8.4 from Cambridge Elevate

Remember

1. Addition, subtraction, multiplication and division can be carried out on binary numbers in the same way as denary ones.
2. When multiplying or dividing binary numbers by powers of 2, a left or right shift can be used.
3. Hexadecimal numbers are used to represent binary ones because they are easier for humans to remember and use.

ACTIVITY 8.10

Convert the following hexadecimal numbers to denary and binary:

a. C4   b. 46   c. FA

Convert the following denary numbers to hexadecimal:

d. 96   e. 201   f. 141

Complete the Cambridge Computing Online activity
www.cambridge.org/links/kose4020

Practice questions

1. Convert the binary number 01101101 to denary.

2. Carry out the following binary addition.

0	0	1	0	1	0	1	1
0	1	1	1	0	1	0	1

3. Convert the denary number 213 to

   a. binary

   b. hexadecimal.

Your final challenge

You have been asked to create a program to help people who are struggling with binary and hexadecimal representations of numbers.

- The user should be able to enter a number in hexadecimal, binary or denary.
- The number should be between 0 and 255.
- You will need some validation to ensure the numbers fall within the required range.
- The program should then display that number in the other two number systems.
- You could use a menu system to allow the user to select the number system for entering the number.
- The user should be able to keep using the converter until they select an option to quit.

Download
Self-assessment 8
worksheet from
Cambridge Elevate

9 Binary representations

Learning outcomes

By the end of this chapter you should be able to:

- explain how characters are represented in binary
- calculate the ASCII code for any character
- calculate the size of a text file
- explain how images are represented in binary
- calculate the size of an image file
- explain how sound is represented in binary
- calculate the size of an audio file
- explain the disadvantages of large image and audio files
- explain how file compression reduces the size of files
- explain the differences between lossless and lossy file compression.

 Challenge: create a program to compress and decompress image files for a social media site

- Millions of image, video and sound files are uploaded and downloaded each day.
- On Facebook alone more than 200 million images are thought to be uploaded each day! It is in everyone's interest to compress these files as much as possible.
- Your challenge is to create a program to compress and decompress image files.

Why binary representation?

- Computers operate and communicate using binary.

- All instructions and data have to be represented by strings of 1s and 0s.

- All text, images and sound have to be reduced to combinations of 1s and 0s: they have to be represented by binary.

- To the computers on which this book was written edited and produced, it is nothing more than billions of bits: 1s and 0s.

- The bits have to be arranged so that they can be interpreted as text, images or sound.

Representations of text

All data processed by a computer is represented as binary digits. When we enter a letter from the keyboard, a stream of bits is transmitted to the processor. It cannot recognise the letter 'A' or an exclamation mark, only a set of 1s and 0s. The list of these binary codes that can be recognised by the computer hardware and software is known as its character set.

Digital sound recording has allowed anyone to record and distribute their music from their homes without needing to use expensive studios.

ASCII code

At first, different manufacturers used their own codes for their computers. However, they soon realised that if computers wanted to share information, they needed to also share a common encoding system for text. The first character-encoding scheme to be used as a common standard for all computers was called ASCII (which stands for 'American Standard Code for Information Interchange').

ASCII was originally a 7-bit code, and the 128 possible code sequences represent English characters and control actions such backspace, shift on, shift off and carriage return. The following table shows the printable characters of the ASCII code with their 8-bit binary and denary values.

Key term

character set: the list of binary codes that can be recognised by computers as being usable characters

ASCII	8-bit binary	Denary
32	00100000	space
33	00100001	!
34	00100010	"
35	00100011	#
36	00100100	$
37	00100101	%
38	00100110	&
39	00100111	'
40	00101000	(
41	00101001	)
42	00101010	*
43	00101011	+
44	00101100	,
45	00101101	-
46	00101110	.
47	00101111	/
48	00110000	0
49	00110001	1
50	00110010	2
51	00110011	3
52	00110100	4
53	00110101	5
54	00110110	6
55	00110111	7
56	00111000	8
57	00111001	9
58	00111010	:
59	00111011	;
60	00111100	<
61	00111101	=
62	00111110	>
63	00111111	?

ASCII	8-bit binary	Denary
64	01000000	@
65	01000001	A
66	01000010	B
67	01000011	C
68	01000100	D
69	01000101	E
70	01000110	F
71	01000111	G
72	01001000	H
73	01001001	I
74	01001010	J
75	01001011	K
76	01001100	L
77	01001101	M
78	01001110	N
79	01001111	O
80	01010000	P
81	01010001	Q
82	01010010	R
83	01010011	S
84	01010100	T
85	01010101	U
86	01010110	V
87	01010111	W
88	01011000	X
89	01011001	Y
90	01011010	Z
91	01011011	[
92	01011100	\
93	01011101	]
94	01011110	^
95	01011111	_

ASCII	8-bit binary	Denary
96	01100000	`
97	01100001	a
98	01100010	b
99	01100011	c
100	01100100	d
101	01100101	e
102	01100110	f
103	01100111	g
104	01101000	h
105	01101001	i
106	01101010	j
107	01101011	k
108	01101100	l
109	01101101	m
110	01101110	n
111	01101111	o
112	01110000	p
113	01110001	q
114	01110010	r
115	01110011	s
116	01110100	t
117	01110101	u
118	01110110	v
119	01110111	w
120	01111000	x
121	01111001	y
122	01111010	z
123	01111011	{
124	01111100		
125	01111101	}
126	01111110	~
127	01111111	DEL

Tip

As the codes are grouped we do not need to remember the code for each upper and lower case letter. We only need to remember that A = 65 and a = 97 and from those we can easily work out the codes of all the other letters.

The codes are grouped according to function:

0–32	Control codes (non-printing)
33–47	Printable symbols such as ! / \ &
48–57	**The digits 0 to 9**
58–64	Printable symbols such as < > =
65–90	**Upper case characters A to Z**
91–96	Printable characters including [ ]
97–122	**Lower case characters a to z**
123–127	Printable characters including { }

ACTIVITY 9.1

Translate this ASCII code message into English. The denary codes of the characters have been used. So 65 would be upper case 'A' and 97 would be lower case 'a'.

84 104 101 32 65 83 67 73 73 32 99 111 100 101 32 114 101 112 114 101 115 101 110 116 115 32 99 104 97 114 97 99 116 101 114 115 46

Tip

Investigate the language that you are using to see how it is done.

Converting string characters to ASCII code and vice versa

To a computer, a character in a string is just a number; a number representing one of the characters in the ASCII code. An algorithm might need to find the ASCII code for a character. All programming languages have commands for doing this.

For the following examples we will use the following pseudocode functions:

Code

```
CHR() to return a character from a number.

ASC() to return a number from a character.
```

Therefore:

```
myString = CHR (67)

print(myString)
```

would return the letter upper case C as 67 is the ASCII code for that letter.

Entering:

```
ASC ('D')
```

would return the number 68 as that is its number in the ASCII code.

ACTIVITY 9.2

Create an algorithm asking a user to input a sentence and then print the codes (in denary) for each of the characters or symbols with each one printed on a new line. Code and test it in your programming language.

Complete the
Cambridge Computing
Online activity
www.cambridge.org/
links/kose4021

The extended ASCII code

In the ASCII code there are 96 printable characters but there was always a need for more in order to accommodate foreign languages, mathematical symbols and special symbols for drawing pictures.

As computers process data in 8-bit bytes, it was sensible to extend ASCII to an 8-bit code, which allows 256 codes. Unfortunately there was no standardisation and different manufacturers such as IBM and Apple created their own versions with different characters represented by the same codes. With the huge popularity of home computing in the 1980s and the proliferation of manufacturers such as Atari and Commodore, each creating their own operating systems, there were many different versions of extended ASCII.

Unicode

To overcome the problems of multiple versions of ASCII, the Unicode Consortium was founded to develop and promote a Unicode standard to represent and handle text in most of the world's writing systems. Unicode has become the universal standard recognised and used by the major hardware and software manufacturers such as IBM, Apple, Microsoft, Oracle and Sun.

Unicode can represent the characters in all known languages. For compatibility and because ASCII was the previously recognised standard, Unicode characters 0 to 127 are the same as ASCII. In English-language documents, Unicode is represented using the same codes as it was in 8-bit ASCII.

Size of ASCII files

Because one byte is used for each character, the size of a plain text file in bytes should be equal to the number of characters.

Here is a picture of a text file:

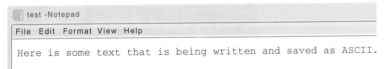

This file consists of 59 characters, including spaces, and so the size should be 59 bytes.

The file size is shown as 59 bytes.

Download Worksheet 9.1 from Cambridge Elevate

ACTIVITY 9.3

Create an algorithm that will allow a user to enter a sentence or phrase and will then inform them of the size of the text file (in bytes) created.

Remember

1. A character set is a defined list of characters recognised by the computer hardware and software.

2. The ASCII code is a 7-bit code and the 128 possible code sequences represent English characters and control actions.

3. Extended ASCII uses 8 bits and was developed to cater for foreign language and graphics characters.

4. Unicode can represent characters in all known languages and writing systems.

Complete Interactive Activity 9a on Cambridge Elevate

Key term

pixel: the smallest possible dot on a computer screen; images are made up of pixels

Tip

Each pixel has its own individual colour and therefore the greater the number of pixels, the greater the detail that can be shown as with fewer pixels a larger area of the image has to be reduced to only one colour. The following images are made up of different numbers of pixels.

Representations of images

Computers also represent and store images as binary code.

Complete the Cambridge Computing Online activity www.cambridge.org/links/kose4022

A digital image is composed of many small points of colour or picture elements, pixels for short. Each pixel is represented by a number of bits. Programs can indicate where each pixel is placed on the screen and what colour it is to be.

The size of the image is given as the number of pixels in the width and then the number of pixels in the height, for example 640 x 480 or 2048 x 1536.

Therefore an image described as 640 x 480 is made up of 307,200 pixels and one described as 2048 x 1536 contains 3,145,728 pixels.

As the number of pixels used to represent the image falls, then so does the resolution (the amount of detail that can be seen).

Key term

resolution: the number of pixels per square inch on the computer screen: the higher the resolution, the better the picture

640 x 420

320 x 210

160 x 110

80 x 60

Colour depth

The colour depth is important for the quality of the colours in an image. Colour depth is the number of bits used to encode the colour of each pixel.

If one bit is used to encode each pixel, then only two colours can be used (2^1). The 0 represents black and the 1 represents white.

Here is a file encoding a 1-bit graphic. This would encode the following graphic on an 8-bit grid.

11000011	11011111
11011111	11011111
11011111	11011111
11000111	11000011

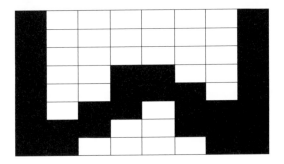

Key term

colour depth: the number of bits used to encode the colour of each pixel

Complete the Cambridge Computing Online activity
www.cambridge.org/links/kose4023

ACTIVITY 9.4

Write the file to encode the following 1-bit graphic.

A colour depth of 3 allows eight colours to be used: 2^3.

Black is encoded as 000 and white as 111. The palette contains red, green and blue and their complimentary colours cyan, magenta and yellow.

The present standard most widely used is 24-bit representation. This means that the colour data for each pixel is encoded in 24 bits with 8 bits used for each of the primary colours: red, green and blue. Each colour in the palette is a combination of each of these in different proportions.

Using 8 bits allows 256 different levels of each of red, green and blue. Therefore 256 x 256 x 256 or 16,777,216 different colour variations are possible. This number of bits produces such a realistic image it is described as being 'true colour'.

Complete the Cambridge Computing Online activity
www.cambridge.org/links/kose4024

Hexadecimal

Entering a colour code in binary for a 24-bit number is very laborious. e.g.

The code for black is 000000000000000000000000

Red is 111111110000000000000000

These are very easy ones to enter but the binary code for this shade of purple is more complex.

110001100011000011110100

That string would be far more difficult to enter without making a mistake, which is where hexadecimal comes to the rescue of us error-prone humans. The hexadecimal code for that number is 'C630F4'. It is far easier to remember and enter. That is why programming languages allow users to enter colour codes in hexadecimal.

Remember that hexadecimal codes should have a hash sign in front. Therefore the code entered would be #C630F4.

Complete the Cambridge Computing Online activity
www.cambridge.org/links/kose4025

The following screenshot shows the denary and hexadecimal codes for the green colour shown.

These are the denary values for the red, green and blue channels.

Convert them to hexadecimal to check if the value shown below is correct.

The hexadecimal code for this colour.

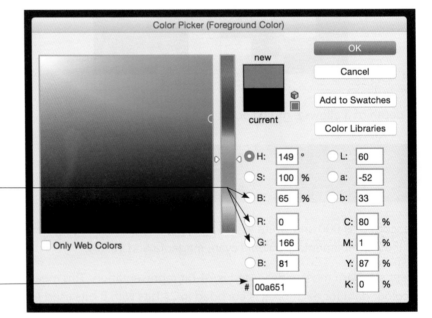

Maths skills

The number of bits is divided by 8 to find the number of bytes.

This is divided by 1000 to find the number in kilobytes.

File sizes

As the number of pixels and the colour depth increases, then so will the size of the image file. For a modern camera a digital image of around 2048 x 1536 pixels is a standard size. This gives a total of 2048 x 1536 = 3,145,728 pixels. Because 24 bits are used to encode each pixel, the file size will be 3,145,728 x 24 = 75, 497, 472 bits. This is equal to 75, 497, 472 / 8 = 9,437,184 bytes or almost 9.5 megabytes.

The file size in bits can be calculated using the following formula:

W x H x D

Where 'W' is width, 'H' is height and 'D' is the colour depth used.

ACTIVITY 9.5

Calculate the file sizes of the following digital images.

a. 4220 x 2641 with a colour depth of 24 bits.

b. 640 x 480 using a 256 colour palette.

The better the image quality, the larger the file size. This can be a problem if the image needs to be transmitted electronically, because it will take a long while to download. In many instances (e.g. sending a holiday photograph to a friend) the image quality will be reduced in order to reduce the file size and therefore the download speed. There is always a compromise between file size and image quality.

Image metadata

Metadata is 'data about data'. Included in many files, in addition to the stored data, is information about the file. For example in a Microsoft Word document there is information about the person who created the file and when it was saved.

The metadata included in a digital image file contains technical and descriptive information and it is stored in a format called *Exif*, which stands for **Ex**changeable **i**mage **f**ile format. Exif is able to record camera information in an image file at the point of capture.

It can include technical items such as:

*   make and model number of the camera

*   aperture setting

*   speed settings

*   dimensions of the image and the file size.

The metadata can also store the location where the image was taken. If the camera has GPS facilities then it is recorded automatically or the user can edit the data and enter the location manually. Image editing software will show the location on a digital map or using a service such as Google Earth.

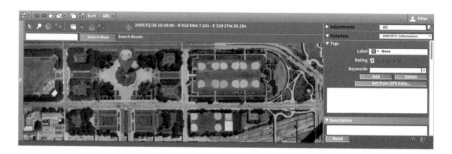

The user can insert other descriptive data such as:

- captions

- headlines

- titles

- comments about the location or the people in the image.

Watch out

There could be a privacy or security risk if images are displayed on social network sites with the metadata included.

Complete the Cambridge Computing Online activity
www.cambridge.org/links/kose4026

Remember

1. A digital image is made up of picture elements, or pixels.
2. The greater the number of pixels, the greater the clarity of the image.
3. The colour data of a pixel is encoded in binary.
4. In modern applications 24 bits are used to encode each pixel.
5. There are 8 bits for each of the red, green and blue elements (channels) of the pixel.
6. The file size of an image can be found using the formula W x H x D.
7. Because file sizes can become large, there is always a compromise between the quality of the image and the needs for storage and transmission of the image.
8. Metadata is information about the image.

Complete Interactive Activity 9b on Cambridge Elevate

Representations of sound

Sound is caused by vibrations travelling through a medium such as air, water or metal. These vibrations compress and then pull apart the air molecules so causing changes in air pressure.

If these vibrations enter our ears and cause tiny sensory hairs to vibrate, then we can hear the sound.

When we speak, our vocal cords vibrate and cause the air to vibrate. Musical instruments function in the same way: the strings of a guitar, the reed in a clarinet or the air in a flute are all made to vibrate. Vibrations travel out in waves; these are called sound waves.

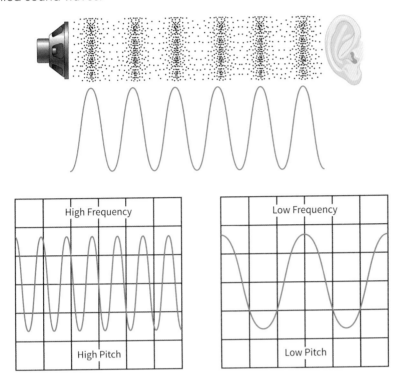

The waves of vibrations produced by the loudspeaker can be represented by the graph plotting the changes in air pressure.

These graphs show the differences between high and low pitched sounds. For the high pitched sound there are more waves of vibrations every second. They have a high frequency.

The graphs show that there are continuous changes in the air pressure and recording methods that try to capture this continuous change by trying to convert all of the changes in air pressure to analogous changes in voltage are called analogue recordings. Analogue recordings such as vinyl albums and audio cassette capture completely the continuous changes in air pressure as continuous minute changes in voltage.

Computers are digital. They cannot represent continuous, minute changes in voltage; each transistor is either on or off, with nothing in between.

Because the sound wave cannot be represented as a series of continuous changes on computer, snapshots of it must be taken and then fitted together. This is called sampling.

A digital sound file therefore doesn't contain all of the total available information that an analogue one does. But there are benefits to digital recordings such as:

* It can be edited and manipulated easily by computer equipment.

* It is more portable; it can be carried on a memory stick or SD card while a vinyl record or tape are not as portable.

 Key terms

analogue: data which can use any value in a continuous range

sampling: making a physical measurement at set time intervals and then converting the measurements to digital values

149

Maths skills

File size (in bits) = sample rate x bit depth x number of channels x length (in seconds)

Tip

Sampling is similar to creating a visual animation from lots of still images (snapshots), each slightly different to the next. The smaller the changes between each one and the greater the number used each second, the more realistic will be the animation.

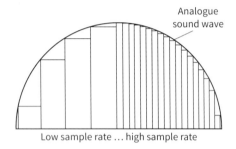

Low sample rate ... high sample rate

- It can be played over and over again without deterioration. LPs and tapes deteriorate.

- It can be easily copied on a computer. Expensive equipment is needed to copy a vinyl record.

- Digital audio files can be easily emailed, downloaded and streamed by users.

- Equipment to record and process digital sound is relatively cheap.

- It has allowed people to produce their own commercial music at home.

There are two factors that will determine how accurately the digital recording matches the original sound: sample rate and bit depth.

Sample rate

The sample rate is the number of samples taken each second. The higher the sample rate, the more accurately the sound will be represented. For CDs, a sampling rate of 44,100 samples per second (44.1 KHz) is used and 96,000 is used for Blu-ray audio.

Bit depth

By increasing the number of bits used to encode each sample, the amount of detail contained in each sample is increased.

Using more bits enables the range of the sound to be more accurately represented.

The dynamic range is the range of volume of sound in the music. Using 8 bits allows 256 gradations to be measured; 16 bits allows 65,536 and 24 bits allows 16.7 million. Using more bits allows for much smaller gradations in the volume. For CD recordings a bit depth of 16 bits is used.

Digital audio file sizes

To calculate the file size the following need to be considered:

- sample rate

- bit depth

- number of channels (mono or stereo)

- length of the recording.

The size of a 3 minute stereo audio file with a sample rate of 44,100 per second and a bit depth of 16 bits would be: 44,100(sample rate) x 16 (bit depth) x 2 (stereo) x 180 (3 minutes in seconds) = 254,016,000 bits. This equals 31,752,000 bytes or 31.752 megabytes.

ACTIVITY 9.6

Calculate the size of an audio file of a song lasting five minutes which is sampled in stereo at a rate of 41,100 samples per second and a bit depth of 24 bits.

Audio file sizes can become very large and, as with image files, there is always a compromise between file size and the quality of the recording.

If there is unlimited storage space and powerful computers for processing the audio then file size isn't a problem but if the audio files have to be transmitted electronically or stored on portable devices then the files need to be as small as possible and this results in a loss of quality.

 Complete Interactive Activity 9c on Cambridge Elevate

 Remember

1. Sound is caused by waves of vibrations travelling through a medium, usually air.
2. These vibrations cause continuous changes to air pressure.
3. Recording methods that capture the continuous change are called analogue.
4. Recording techniques that sample the changes at fixed periods are called digital.
5. The quality of a digital recording is determined by the rate of sampling and the number of bits used to encode the data in each sample.
6. Digital file sizes can be calculated by the formula: Sample rate x bit depth x number of channels x length in seconds
7. There is always a compromise between the sound quality and the storage and transmission requirements.

Compression

Files, especially graphic and audio files can become very large.

On Facebook more than 200 million images are thought to be uploaded each day. On Snapchat, almost 100,000 are apparently uploaded each minute. It has been estimated that in total over 1.8 billion images are uploaded to social media sites each day! Millions of audio and video files are also being downloaded every day.

It is therefore in everyone's interest to make these files as small as possible. Users need upload and download times to be short and social media sites want to store them in as small a space as possible.

That is why file compression is important. It reduces the file size and gives the following benefits:

- it uses less internet bandwidth when they are downloaded

- transfer speed is quicker

- it takes up less storage space on the servers of storage providers

- smaller files reduce congestion on the Internet, which is good for everyone

- it makes audio and video files suitable for streaming.

 Download Worksheet 9.2 from Cambridge Elevate

 Key term

compression: reducing the size of a file so that it takes up less storage space or bandwidth when it is transmitted

Compression algorithms are used to ensure that the file size is as small as possible. If the compressed file can be decompressed to the original without any loss of data, it is called lossless compression. But if the file is compressed by removing some of the data, the original cannot be recovered and it is called lossy compression.

Lossless compression

If a lossless compression algorithm is used to compress the file, then the original can be reconstituted when it is decompressed. Nothing is lost.

The algorithm checks for redundancy: items that don't need to be there.

Look at the following short paragraph:

> The size of an image file depends on the colour depth and dimensions. The size of an audio file depends on the sample rate and bit depth. The size of an image file and an audio file can be very large.

This paragraph has 41 words and 200 characters including spaces. Therefore the file size would be 200 bytes.

But in the paragraph there is lots of redundancy: some words are used more than once.

Here is a list of words that appear more than once:

1	the
2	size
3	of
4	an
5	image
6	file
7	depends
8	on
9	and
10	depth
11	audio

This list is a numbered dictionary that can be referred to when the file is being decompressed.

Using the dictionary, the file can be written as:

1 2 3 4 5 6 7 8 1 colour 10 9 dimensions. 1 2 3 4 11 6 7 8 1 sample rate 9 bit 10. 1 size 3 4 5 6 9 4 11 6 c4 be very large.

This version has only 124 characters. The dictionary that would have to be included with the file has 55. The total is 179 and so would have a size of 179 bytes, a saving of 21 bytes.

This saving has been made in only a small file and with a very simple algorithm – checking word redundancy. But imagine if this was done to this book: the same words could be referenced many times and there would be a greater saving of bytes.

Using this method, nothing is lost; the whole paragraph can be rewritten from the compressed file.

Text files are relatively easy to compress in this way as they have lots of repeated items (words) and compression rates of 50% are relatively easy to achieve.

Run-length encoding (RLE)

RLE works by reducing the physical size of a repeating string of characters. This repeating string, called a run, is encoded into two bytes. The first byte represents the number of characters in the run and the second gives the character.

For example the following string:

aaabbbbbbbccccccccc

has a length of 18 bytes.

Using run-length encoding, this could be compressed to:

3a6b9c

It could be reduced to 6 bytes.

Run-length encoding provides very good compression ratios when there are long runs of a particular character or value. A black-and-white image where there are long runs of either black or white will encode very well but a colour photograph where there are short runs of many different colours will not encode as well.

We have already looked at this 1-bit graphic:

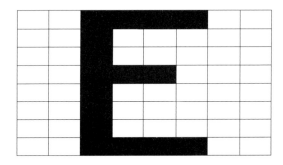

The code for this graphic is:

11000011

11011111

11011111

11000111

11011111

11011111

11011111

11000011

Which represents the colours:

wwbbbbww

wwbwwwww

wwbwwwww

wwbbbwww

wwbwwwww

wwbwwwww

wwbwwwww

wwbbbbww

When represented by a letter, the size of the file is 64 bytes: 8 bytes per line. Using run-length encoding, this size could be reduced.

		Bytes
wwbbbbww	2w4b2w	6
wwbwwwww	2w1b5w	6
wwbwwwww	2w1b5w	6
wwbbbwww	2w3b3w	6
wwbwwwww	2w1b5w	6
wwbwwwww	2w1b5w	6
wwbwwwww	2w1b5w	6
wwbbbbww	2w4b2w	6
		48

Therefore the file size of this one character can be reduced from 64 bytes to 48 bytes.

ACTIVITY 9.7

Show the result of applying a run-length encoding algorithm to the following 1-bit graphic.

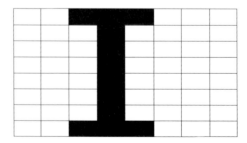

Lossy compression

Lossy compression decreases the file size by throwing out some of the data. Unlike lossless compression, the original can never be reconstituted. It has been irreversibly changed.

That is why it cannot be used for text files or program files: a book with lots of missing words would be unreadable!

But it can be used for graphic and audio files as they contain lots of data that can be discarded.

A high-resolution image with a 24-bit colour depth has a very large file size. Images that have not been compressed and which contain all of the colour data are called RAW files. (RAW is not an acronym, it just means that the file is as it was when produced by the camera sensor. It has not been compressed in any way.)

During lossy compression, the algorithm analyses the image and finds areas where there are only slight differences that we might not be able to distinguish. It will then give these the same value and so can rewrite the file using fewer bits.

The most commonly used compression technique was developed by the Joint Photographic Experts Group and produces JPEG files with the extension 'jpg' (or 'jpeg').

Here are three images all made from the same RAW image, which had a size of 10.7 megabytes. All have the dimensions of 4288 x 2848. The number of pixels has not been reduced but pixels with similar colour values have been made the same so that the number of bits needed has been reduced.

There are some differences in detail and colour variations but even the one with the greatest compression would be acceptable for a web page.

Audio files can be compressed in a similar way. Digital audio files that contain all of the sound data are saved in Waveform Audio (WAV) format. Typically, a 3 minute recording will have a file size of 30 megabytes. There are frequencies and tones that we cannot hear and slight differences in volume and frequency that we cannot distinguish. These are removed to reduce the size and an MP3 file is usually about a tenth the size of a WAV file. Therefore the 30-megabyte WAV file can be reduced to a 3-megabyte MP3 file.

The Original (RAW) Image

4.25 megabytes

740 kilobytes

193 kilobytes

 Remember

1. Files are compressed to reduce transfer speeds and storage space.
2. With lossless compression, the data in the original file is not changed.
3. With lossy compression, original data is permanently deleted.
4. Lossy compression is used to reduce the size of media files so that they can be more easily be uploaded, downloaded and streamed and the loss in quality is not usually perceived by human senses.

 Practice questions

1. Calculate the files sizes (in megabytes) of the following:
   a. a digital image of 2120 x 1320 pixels with a colour depth of 24 bits
   b. a 4 minute stereo sound file with a sample rate of 44,100 and a bit depth of 16 bits.

 Complete Interactive Activity 9d on Cambridge Elevate

 Download Worksheet 9.3 from Cambridge Elevate

2. For the following 1-bit graphic

   a. show the result of applying a run-length encoding algorithm
   b. state the original file size and the size after applying run-length encoding.

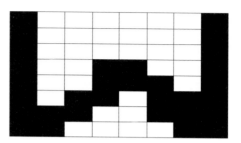

3. Explain, using an example for each, the difference between lossy and lossless compression.

 Your final challenge

Your challenge is to create algorithms and code programs to compress and decompress files using run-length encoding.

a. The first part of the challenge is to create and test a program that will perform run-length encoding on a 1-bit image file where the bits are given as one continuous string, for example.

bbwwwbbbbbbbwwwwwwwwwwwwwwbbbbbbbbbbbbbbwwbb
bbbbbbbbbbwwwwwwwww

It should take the above string and print:
2b3w7b14w14b2w13b9w.

b. Now create and test a program that will return the original string from the run-length encoded data.

 Tip

Two-dimensional arrays may help to solve this problem.

 Download Self-assessment 9 worksheet from Cambridge Elevate

10 Programming languages

Learning outcomes

By the end of this chapter you should be able to:

- describe the difference between low and high level languages
- explain the advantages of using high level languages
- explain how program instructions are encoded in low level languages
- explain why high level languages need to be translated
- explain the characteristics and use of
  - an assembler
  - a compiler
  - an interpreter.

Challenge: write programs using a low level language

- Programs may be written in assembly language.
- They can be checked with a program called a computer simulator.
- Computer simulators mimic the actions of a real computer.
- Your challenge is to write programs in assembly language and check them using a computer simulator.

Why programming languages?

- Programming languages are used to give instructions to computers: to tell them what to do.

- Programming languages evolve over time (just like living organisms) as users make improvements or add new features and gradually they become so different to the original that they are a new language.

- Just like evolution in the living world, changes to the environment stimulate the evolution of new types. For example, Java was created to develop applets for the World Wide Web and portable electronic devices. Without the WWW or tablets there would probably be no Java.

- Different languages have strengths and weaknesses in different areas. For example, Fortran and Algol are orientated to solving mathematical and statistical problems, Cobol is better for business data processing and JavaScript for building web-based applications.

- But whatever the language used it still has to be converted into strings of 1s and 0s: the only language that computers can understand.

Ada Lovelace, the daughter of the poet Lord Byron, is credited with writing the first computer program in 1842.

Popular programming languages

Programming languages such as Python, Java, C and Visual Basic all provide instructions for the microprocessor to carry out or execute.

For example, the following simple program written in the Python programming language will instruct the microprocessor to ask for two inputs and then calculate the area and perimeter of a rectangle.

Code

```
def rectangle(leng, wid):

        ar = leng * wid

        per = (leng*2) + (wid*2)

        return(ar, per)

length = int(input("Please enter the length."))

width = int(input("Please enter the width."))

area, perimeter = rectangle(length, width)

print(area, perimeter)
```

It uses words and symbols like '=' and '*' that we can easily understand. But, unfortunately, written in this way, the microprocessor would not be able to understand it.

A microprocessor cannot understand English. It can only understand binary (strings of 1s and 0s).

Machine code

The commands that the microprocessor executes, represented as strings of 1s and 0s, are called machine code or machine language.

Just as combinations of 1s and 0s are used to encode characters in the ASCII code, similar combinations are used to encode the instructions that have to be carried out. The microprocessor interprets the strings of binary digits as instructions.

Each type of microprocessor has a fixed number of commands that it can understand. These make up its instruction set and they are different for the different types of microprocessor.

For example the string '0010' could be used as an instruction in one type of microprocessor to add one number to another.

The instructions for the microprocessor have two parts, or 'fields'. The two fields are the opcode and the operand.

- The *opcode* specifies the operation that is to be performed, e.g. add numbers or store data in a memory location.

- The *operand* represents the data that is to be used or the memory location in which the data can be found or has to be stored, e.g.

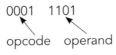

0001   1101

opcode   operand

Assembly language

As it is difficult for humans to think and write programs in pure machine code using 1s and 0s (just imagine trying to debug a program consisting of millions of 1s and 0s), we program in 'higher' languages. They are called 'higher' as they resemble our spoken languages more closely.

Instead of writing opcodes in binary, in assembly language mnemonics are used.

In assembly language, the mnemonics are English-like words used to represent the binary opcodes of machine language, for example the mnemonic ADD could be used in assembly language for the binary opcode to add one number to another.

SUB, MUL and DIV are other mnemonics used in assembly language to represent the binary opcode commands to subtract, multiply and divide numbers. Although assembly language makes programming easier for humans, the microprocessor cannot understand it. Therefore the commands need to be translated into machine code.

Translation

An assembler translates the mnemonics of assembly language programs into machine language instructions for the microprocessor to execute. As assembly language is very similar to machine code there is one assembly language instruction for each machine language one.

Because the assembly language instructions are very similar to those in machine language, assembly language is referred to as a 'low level' language.

Key terms

mnemonic: a tool or technique designed to help a person's memory (e.g. 'Richard of York gave battle in vain' used to help remember the order of the colours of the spectrum: red, orange, yellow, green, blue, indigo and violet)

assembler: a program which translates assembly language into machine code

ACTIVITY 10.1

The following table shows part of the instruction set of a particular microprocessor that uses 4 bits for opcode and 8 bits for the operand.

Opcode	Mnemonic	Explanation
0000	STO	Store data at memory location indicated by the operand
0001	LOAD	Load the number located in the operand
0010	LOAD	Load the number found at the memory location indicated by the operand
0100	ADD	Add the number located in the operand
1000	ADD	Add the number found at the memory location indicated by the operand

The opcode and operand for the command 'Load the number 13' would be 000100001101.

As 0001 is the opcode for 'Load' and 00001101 is 13 in binary.

Give the opcodes and operands for the following:

a. Load the number found at memory location 6.

b. Add the number 113.

c. i. Load the number 10, add the number 21 and store the result at memory location 30.

   ii. State the data that would be found at memory location 30.

Download Worksheet 10.1 from Cambridge Elevate

ACTIVITY 10.2

For a taste of programming in assembly language, investigate The Little Man Computer, which can be accessed at www.cambridge.org/links/kose4060. This 'computer' has a limited instruction set and the site provides some tutorials for you to work through.

High level languages

Programming in assembly language is more user-friendly than using machine code but it is still more difficult than writing programs in our natural language using statements like 'if … then', 'do … until' and 'while'.

The commands will still need to be translated into machine language before they can be executed by the microprocessor. There are two ways of doing this: using a compiler or an interpreter.

Compiler

A compiler reads the whole high level code (the source code) and, if there are no errors, translates it into a complete machine code program (the object code), which is output as a new file and can be saved.

Key terms

compiler: a program that converts high level programming languages into low level languages

interpreter: a program that will run a high level program directly, interpreting the instructions and converting them to machine code as the program is executed

Advantages	Disadvantages
The translation is done once only and as a separate process.	If it encounters any error it carries on trying to compile the program and reports the errors at the end. The programmers then have to use the error messages to identify and remove the bugs.
The program that is run is already translated into machine code so is much faster in execution.	You cannot change the program without going back to the original source code, editing that and recompiling.

Interpreter

An interpreter reads the source code one instruction or line at a time, converts this line into machine code and executes it. The next line is read and translated and so on. This has to be done each time the program is run.

Advantages	Disadvantages
When an error is found the interpreter reports it and stops so the programmer knows where the error has occurred.	Every line has to be translated every time it is executed and because of this it is slower.
The program can be easily edited as it always exists as source code.	

Advantages of using high level languages

The advantages of using high level languages are:

* Faster program development: it is less time consuming to write and then test the program.

* It is not necessary to remember the registers of the CPU and mnemonic instructions.

* Portability of a program from one machine to other. Each assembly language is specific to a particular type of CPU, but most high level languages are generally portable across different CPUs.

Advantages of using low level languages

The advantages of using low level languages are:

* They require less memory and execution time.

* They allow the programmer to directly control system hardware.

 Complete the Cambridge Computing Online activity www.cambridge.org/links/kose4028

 Practice questions

1. A developer is writing a program.

   a. The program is written in a high level code and is then translated into machine code. Describe two differences between high level code and machine code.

   b. One type of translator is an interpreter.

      i. Describe how an interpreter translates high level code into machine code.

      ii. State the name of a different type of translator that can be used to translate high level code into machine code.

 Your final challenge

Your final challenge is to write and test programs using the Little Man Computer simulator at www.cambridge.org/links/kose4060 to carry out the following:

* input two numbers and output them in numerical order
* input two numbers and multiply them together.

 Download Self-assessment 10 worksheet from Cambridge Elevate

 Remember

1. The microprocessor can only execute commands given in machine code (machine language).

2. Each instruction consists of an opcode and an operand.

3. Assembly language uses mnemonics to make it easier for humans to remember and write the opcodes.

4. An assembler converts the assembly instructions into machine code.

5. High level languages are more like human languages.

6. High level languages have to be converted to machine code by compilers or interpreters.

 Download Worksheet 10.2 from Cambridge Elevate

 Complete Interactive Activity 10a on Cambridge Elevate

 Watch the Branches and Little Man Computer animation on Cambridge Elevate

11 Computer systems: hardware

Learning outcomes

By the end of this chapter you should be able to:

- explain what is meant by a computer system
- explain what is meant by an embedded system
- describe the structure of the central processing unit and the functions of its components
- describe the fetch-decode-execute cycle
- explain the need for and role of multiple cores and cache and virtual memory
- describe secondary storage media and the advantages and disadvantages of each.

 Challenge: create a learning resource

- Many learning resources are created and used on computers by students.
- Your challenge is to create a multiple-choice quiz to test a pupil's knowledge of the items in this chapter.

ENIAC, the first computer, was 8 feet high and 100 feet long and far less powerful than today's laptops.

Why computer systems?

- The microprocessor is responsible for executing the instructions given to it in a program.

- It follows the instructions in order to do something useful.

- The microprocessor relies on other devices

  - To allow users to input the instructions

  - To store the instructions

  - To transfer the instructions to it so that it can carry them out

  - To carry out the commands it issues e.g. to print an essay or display an image.

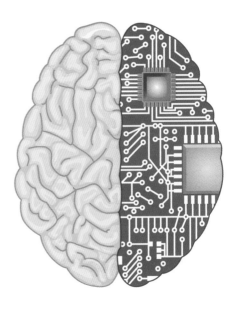

Computer systems

The microprocessor is often called the 'brain' of a computer because it is where data is processed, decisions are made and actions are initiated.

However the brain cannot function independently. It needs things like:

- sensors, e.g. eyes and ears, to provide it with data

- memory, to store data and information

- muscles, to carry out the actions it decides are necessary

- bundles of nerves to transmit messages to and from the muscles and sensors.

The input devices for a human central nervous system are shown in the diagram below.

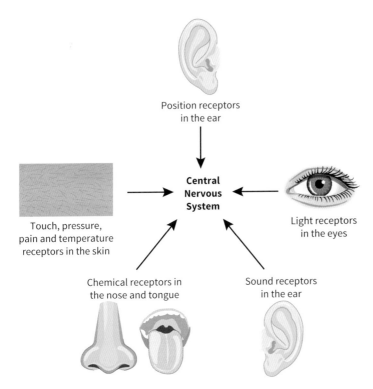

In a similar way, the microprocessor needs other components:

- input devices such as keyboards, mice and light sensors to provide it with data

- memory to store the instructions and the results of its processing

- permanent, long-term memory devices such as hard disk drives

- output devices like monitors, printers and motors to carry out the results of its processing

- bundles of wires, called buses, through which data is transmitted from one component to another.

 Key term

bus: a bundle of wires carrying data from one component to another or a number of tracks on a printed circuit board (PCB) fulfilling the same function

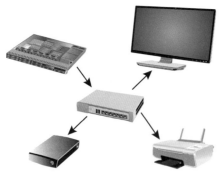

Some input and output devices for a computer system.

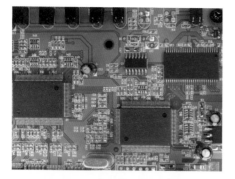

Download Worksheet 11.1 from Cambridge Elevate

The components mentioned above are all physical devices and are referred to as hardware.

But there is another vital component, called *software*, which consists of all the programs that a computer system needs to function.

Even before a computer system can do anything useful, it needs software called system software to 'wake it up' and tell it how to operate. For example, the system software tells the microprocessor how to communicate with all of the other devices.

It can then use the application software such as word processors, spreadsheets and integrated development environments to do something useful.

Embedded systems

An embedded system is a computer system built within a larger device such as:

- Washing machines

- Digital cameras

The computer systems in these devices have been built for a range of specific tasks.

Embedded devices are limited to a certain number of tasks, unlike desktop and laptop computers, which are general purpose computer systems capable of carrying out many different tasks.

All of the components in an embedded system including microprocessor, memory and input and output interfaces are on a single printed circuit board. The memory contains the program. The board is a component built into a larger device, hence the name 'embedded'.

ACTIVITY 11.1

Many modern electronic devices contain embedded systems.

a. Explain what is meant by an 'embedded system'

b. List three devices that contain embedded systems.

Remember

1. A computer is a machine that can be programmed.
2. All computers contain a microprocessor.
3. A computer system consists of hardware and software.
4. An embedded system is built into a larger device and carries out a limited number of functions.

The central processing unit

The microprocessor is the central processing unit (CPU) of the computer. It is here that the data processing takes place.

The way the CPU is designed and executes (carries out) the program instructions is known as 'von Neumann architecture'. In 1945, John von Neumann (shown in the photo below) proposed his design for a 'stored program' computer where both the program and data were stored in the memory. Previously, computers had to be rebuilt for each new program that was needed!

The diagram below shows how this is put together. Take a look at the components; their functions will be described when we look at the way in which program instructions are executed.

Key term

central processing unit (CPU): this is the component of the computer that controls the other devices, executes the instructions and processes the data

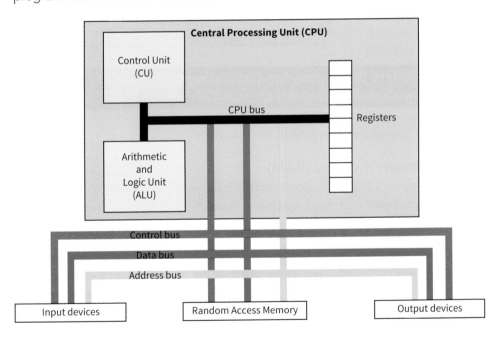

Executing the instructions: the fetch-decode-execute cycle

The way in which the 'von Neumann architecture' executes the program instructions is through the fetch-decode-execute cycle.

Before the cycle starts, the program instructions are copied from a storage device such as a hard disk drive or DVD to the random access memory (RAM).

Fetch

In the fetch part of the cycle, instructions and data are moved from the random access memory to the central processing unit.

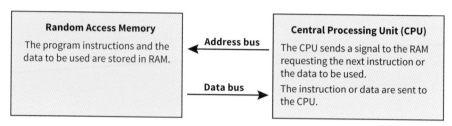

Random Access Memory		Central Processing Unit (CPU)
The program instructions and the data to be used are stored in RAM.	← Address bus Data bus →	The CPU sends a signal to the RAM requesting the next instruction or the data to be used. The instruction or data are sent to the CPU.

Decode and execute

In the decode part of the cycle, the control unit interprets the instructions and decides what action to perform. During the execute phase, these instructions are carried out.

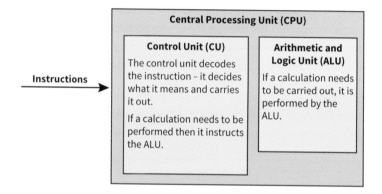

Central Processing Unit (CPU)

Instructions →

Control Unit (CU)	Arithmetic and Logic Unit (ALU)
The control unit decodes the instruction – it decides what it means and carries it out. If a calculation needs to be performed then it instructs the ALU.	If a calculation needs to be carried out, it is performed by the ALU.

Complete the Cambridge Computing Online activity
www.cambridge.org/links/kose4029

We will now look at the components in more detail.

Random access memory (RAM)

If you are making a meal, you don't want to have to go all the way to the shop every time you need each new ingredient. Instead you buy all the ingredients and put them in the fridge; it's much quicker to go there than to the supermarket!

It's the same for computers. It can take a long time to fetch data and program instructions from the hard drive. Therefore they are stored in the random access memory (RAM), a temporary store of data, so that information can be retrieved quickly by the CPU when required for the program it is running.'

Memory can be thought of as consisting of billions of pigeon-holes or storage locations. Each one can hold a byte of data and each one has an address so that the CPU knows where to store and retrieve the instructions and data.

Location 0
Location 1
Location 2
Location 3
Location 4
Location 5

Key terms

storage location: a place in RAM where a single piece of data can be kept until it is needed

address: a number assigned to the storage location so that it can be accessed

RAM is said to be 'random access' because each memory location can be accessed in any order if the 'address' of that location is specified. This speeds up data retrieval as the CPU can go to any location and does not have to start each time at the first location and go through them in order until it finds the correct one. That method is called 'serial access'.

RAM is said to be volatile because if there is no electrical power then the RAM will lose all of its data.

There are different types of RAM: Dynamic RAM (DRAM) and Static RAM (SRAM). DRAM is slower than SRAM but it is used as the main memory store because it is cheaper.

Key term

volatile: data is permanently lost when power is switched off

ACTIVITY 11.2

Carry out research to find out why DRAM is slower than SRAM.

Read-only memory (ROM)

Although it is not directly involved in the fetch-decode-execute, read-only memory is also used in computer systems. Read-only memory (ROM) is an integrated circuit on a chip. It is programmed with specific data to perform a particular function when it is manufactured.

The BIOS (basic input/output system) is stored in ROM. The BIOS controls what happens when the computer is first switched on. The BIOS checks the hardware devices to ensure there are no errors and loads basic software so that it can communicate with them. It then locates and passes control to the operating system.

The data can be read but it cannot be changed: the computer cannot write to the chip, unlike RAM.

Where RAM is volatile, ROM is not and the data is not lost when power is removed.

ACTIVITY 11.3

a. Describe the functions of random access memory (RAM) and read-only memory (ROM) in the operation of a computer.

b. List two basic differences between RAM and ROM.

Remember

1. Random access memory (RAM) acts as a temporary store of program instructions and data.
2. RAM consists of billions of memory locations with unique addresses.
3. The addresses can be accessed in any order.
4. RAM is volatile and can be written to.
5. Dynamic RAM (DRAM) is slower than static RAM (SRAM) but is far cheaper.
6. Read-only memory is used to store basic information and instructions that a computer needs when it is starting up (booting).
7. Read-only memory (ROM) is non-volatile but cannot be written to.

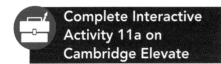
Complete Interactive Activity 11a on Cambridge Elevate

Buses

A bus is a collection of wires that carry signals or communications between the various components of the computer system. The control bus connects the control unit (CU) with the other components of the CPU and devices in the computer system. The control unit uses it to send instructions to other components of the computer. The components use it to send information back to the CPU as well.

Components of the central processing unit (CPU)

Registers

Registers are storage locations within the CPU itself. They can be accessed even more quickly than the RAM described above. The functions of these registers will be explained in a later section.

Some of the registers, such as:

- the accumulator (A or ACC),

- the program counter (PC),

- the memory address register (MAR),

- the instruction register (IR) and

- the memory data register (MDR) or memory buffer register (MBR)

serve specific functions, but some of them are general purpose registers used for the quick storage of data items that will be required later.

The arithmetic and logic unit

The ALU performs arithmetic and logical operations. It carries out activities such as:

- addition and subtraction

- multiplication and division

- logical tests using logic gates (explained in Chapter 3)

- comparisons, such as whether one number is greater than another.

The control unit

The control unit coordinates the actions of the computer by sending out control signals to the other parts of the CPU such as the ALU and registers and also to the other components of the computer system such as the input and output devices. Control signals make everything happen inside a CPU.

The two main elements of the control unit are the clock and the decoder.

The clock

Pulses are sent out to the other components to coordinate their activities and ensure instructions are carried out and completed. The timing is controlled by a vibrating quartz crystal.

One instruction can be carried out with each pulse of the clock, and therefore the higher the clock speed, the faster the CPU will be able to carry out the program instructions.

Key term

register: a storage location that is inside the CPU itself

Key term

control signals: electrical signals that are sent out to all of the devices to check their status and give them instructions

The clock speed is measured in cycles per second. 1 cycle per second is a rate of 1 Hertz. 1 megahertz (MHz) equals 1 million cycles per second and 1 gigahertz (GHz) is 1,000,000,000 cycles per second. Rates of 1 to 3 GHz are common in most home computers.

The decoder

This part of the control unit decodes the program instructions (works out what they mean) that have been brought from the memory and decides what actions should be taken. It then sends control signals to the other components to carry them out.

 Complete Interactive Activity 11b on Cambridge Elevate

ACTIVITY 11.4

Name the parts of the CPU that perform the following functions:

a. carries out arithmetic and logical computations

b. stores data within the CPU itself

c. coordinates the activities of the CPU and computer.

 Complete the Cambridge Computing Online activity www.cambridge.org/links/kose4030

An example of the fetch-decode-execute cycle in operation

The following section illustrates how the fetch-decode-execute cycle carries out the instructions of a simple program stored in RAM.

This table shows the instructions and data of a simple program to add two numbers together. It is stored in RAM at the following locations.

Address	Contents
0	LOAD 4
1	ADD 5
2	STORE 6
3	
4	3
5	6
6	

Get the data stored at memory location 4
Add the data stored at memory location 5
Store the result at memory location 6

The following table shows the registers that were mentioned above. At the moment all are empty.

Program counter	
Memory address register	
Memory data register	
Instruction register	
Accumulator	

The fetch cycle

In the fetch cycle, instructions and data are transferred from the random access memory to the central processing unit.

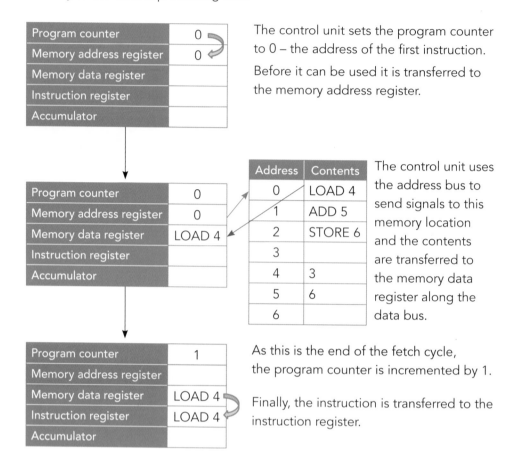

The control unit sets the program counter to 0 – the address of the first instruction.

Before it can be used it is transferred to the memory address register.

The control unit uses the address bus to send signals to this memory location and the contents are transferred to the memory data register along the data bus.

As this is the end of the fetch cycle, the program counter is incremented by 1.

Finally, the instruction is transferred to the instruction register.

The decode cycle

The control unit now decodes this message. It checks it against its instruction set and works out that it has to get the contents of memory location 4 and put them into the accumulator (one of the registers).

The execute cycle

The control unit now executes this instruction by doing another fetch. It transfers the contents of memory location 4 (the number 3) to the accumulator.

Program counter	1
Memory address register	
Memory data register	LOAD 4
Instruction register	LOAD 4
Accumulator	3

Address	Contents
0	LOAD 4
1	ADD 5
2	STORE 6
3	
4	3
5	6
6	

Using the address and data buses the contents of location 4 are transferred to the accumulator.

The fetch cycle

The cycle then begins again using the new address in the program counter.

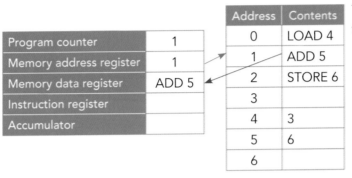

Program counter	1
Memory address register	1
Memory data register	
Instruction register	
Accumulator	3

The address of the instruction is transferred to the memory address register.

Program counter	1
Memory address register	1
Memory data register	ADD 5
Instruction register	
Accumulator	

Address	Contents
0	LOAD 4
1	ADD 5
2	STORE 6
3	
4	3
5	6
6	

The instruction is fetched.

Program counter	2
Memory address register	
Memory data register	ADD 5
Instruction register	ADD 5
Accumulator	3

As this is the end of the fetch cycle, the program counter is incremented by 1.

The instruction is transferred to the instruction register.

The decode cycle

The control unit now decodes this message; it checks it against its instruction set and works out that it has to get the contents of memory location 5 and add them to whatever is in the accumulator.

The execute cycle

The control unit now executes this instruction by doing another fetch. It adds the contents of memory location 5 (the number 6) to the number already in the accumulator (3) to give a total of 9.

Program counter	2
Memory address register	
Memory data register	ADD 5
Instruction register	ADD 5
Accumulator	9

Address	Contents
0	LOAD 4
1	ADD 5
2	STORE 6
3	
4	3
5	6
6	

The fetch-decode-execute cycle will turn again. The instruction is fetched.

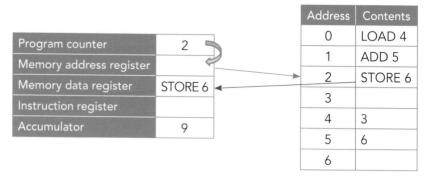

Program counter	2
Memory address register	
Memory data register	STORE 6
Instruction register	
Accumulator	9

Address	Contents
0	LOAD 4
1	ADD 5
2	STORE 6
3	
4	3
5	6
6	

The instruction is decoded. The data in the accumulator has to be stored in memory location 6. It is then executed.

Program counter	2
Memory address register	
Memory data register	STORE 6
Instruction register	
Accumulator	9

Address	Contents
0	LOAD 4
1	ADD 5
2	STORE 6
3	
4	3
5	6
6	9

The contents of the accumulator (the number 9) are stored in memory location 6.

Complete the Cambridge Computing Online activity
www.cambridge.org/links/kose4031

Pipelining

In the above example, only one instruction can be fetched, decoded and executed at once. Modern processors can use a technique called pipelining which allows them to process more than one instruction at a time.

While the first instruction is being decoded, the second instruction can be fetched. While the first instruction is being executed, the second can be decoded and third can be fetched. And so on.

This process speeds up the execution of the program but there can be problems as each stage may not take the same time to implement and this makes coordination difficult.

 Key term

pipelining: the process of allowing many instructions to be processed at the same time. As one instruction is being decoded the next one can be fetched.

ACTIVITY 11.5

With the aid of diagrams, describe the events that take place during the fetch-decode-execute cycle.

 Remember

The CPU processes data by carrying out three steps:

1. Fetch: an instruction is transferred from the memory to the CPU.
   a. The program counter supplies the address of the instruction to be fetched.
   b. The program counter is a register (also referred to as memory location) in the CPU.
2. Decode: the CPU works out what the instructions mean.
3. Execute: the control unit carries out the instructions using the ALU for instructions involving logical or mathematical operations.

172

Microprocessor performance

Everyone wants their computers to work faster and faster and so manufacturers have continued to increase the speeds at which they work.

Clock speed

The rate at which instructions are processed is controlled by the clock speed. The faster the clock speed, the faster the rate of processing. Clock speeds have increased and a rate of 3 GHz is common in modern computer processors. But increasing the clock speed to increase processing speed has limitations:

- The instructions are processed by transistors. The rate at which they work has not become faster.

- The microprocessor generates a large amount of heat and this increases with the clock speed. Although the heat is dissipated by a fan and heat sink to prevent it from malfunctioning or even melting, there are limits to the rate of cooling.

- Microprocessors with clock speeds of 9 GHz require cooling by liquid nitrogen!

Key term

heat sink: a metal device, glued to the CPU chip with thermally conducting paste, to transfer the heat away from the chip

ACTIVITY 11.6

In order to increase the speed of their computers, users often increase the clock frequency.

a. What is this process called?

b. A user who increased the clock frequency noticed that his computer was now far noisier.

Explain why this could be caused by increasing the clock frequency.

Tip

Overclocking is the process of increasing the clock speed to a higher level than that recommended by the manufacturer. It causes an increase in heat and can result in instability and permanent damage to the processor.

Multi-core processors

Manufacturers introduced multi-core processors in 2006 to increase processing speed. A multi-core processor has more than one CPU. The following diagram illustrates the structure of a dual-core processor.

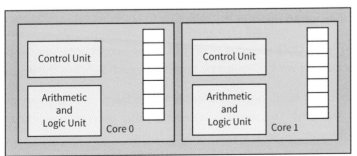

Complete the Cambridge Computing Online activity www.cambridge.org/ links/kose4032

The following table shows the names given to processors having different numbers of cores.

Number of cores	Common name
1	Single-core
2	Dual-core
4	Quad-core
5	Penta-core
8	Octa(o)-core
10	Deca-core

Key terms

parallel processing: when the processor cores work on different parts of the same program

multitasking: when the processor cores work on different programs at the same time

Complete the Cambridge Computing Online activity www.cambridge.org/ links/kose4033

The advantages of multiple core processors over single core processors are:

- the cores can work together on the same program; this is called parallel processing

- the cores can work on different programs at the same time; this is called multitasking.

However, not all programs will run at twice the speed with a dual-core processor. The tasks required might not be able to be carried out in parallel. They might be sequential so that one task requires output from a previous task and so the second task cannot start until the first has finished.

Cache memory

Bottlenecks occur when one component cannot work as fast as the others and so hinders progress.

In the fetch-decode-execute cycle, this bottleneck is caused by the dynamic RAM (DRAM) that is used to store the instructions and data.

Watch the Von Neumann bottleneck animation on Cambridge Elevate

Although it is far quicker to fetch the instructions from the DRAM than from a hard disk drive, the RAM is still far slower than the CPU and then the instructions have to be transferred through the data bus.

However much the clock speed is increased or the number of cores used, the speed of processing will be limited by the RAM, which supplies the instructions.

Key term

cache: a temporary data store so that it can be accessed very quickly when needed

The solution to this bottleneck problem is to use faster memory very close to, or even within, the CPU. This memory is used to store recently used data and data likely to be frequently used, and is called a cache.

This allows the CPU to check the fast cache for the data it needs. If it finds it, it doesn't have to wait for it to be fetched from the much slower DRAM. The faster static RAM (SRAM) is used for the cache.

The larger the cache memory, the slower it is to access the instructions and data in it. To overcome this constraint, there are different levels of cache memory.

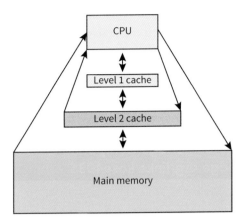

The fastest, Level 1 cache is the smallest and closest to the CPU. It stores the most frequently accessed data and is checked first.

The Level 2 cache is larger, further from the CPU and slower than Level 1 but still much quicker than the main memory. It is checked after the Level 1 cache. Some processors may have three or more levels of cache memory.

The sizes and positions of the caches are shown in the following diagram.

The cache sizes can be found in the BIOS setup screen of a computer.

Virtual memory

When a computer is running the operating system and several applications at the same time, the random access memory (RAM) often becomes full.

Instead of closing some programs the 'memory manager' program of the operating system will use 'pretend' or virtual memory to store some of the data, usually on the hard disk drive.

It works like this:

- A process running on the computer may need to store data in the physical memory.

- If there is no free memory, the memory manager will 'swap out' some of the data stored in RAM to the swap area on the hard disk drive and 'swap in' the requested data into the now free area.

- Usually the least recently used stored data is swapped out.

- If data is swapped out and then is needed again, it is swapped back in, from the swap area, at the expense of other data.

There are disadvantages of using virtual memory:

- The read/write speed of a hard drive is much slower than RAM, and the technology of a hard drive is not geared towards accessing small pieces of data at a time.

- If the system has to rely too heavily on virtual memory, there will be a significant performance drop.

Complete the Cambridge Computing Online activity www.cambridge.org/ links/kose4034

Download Worksheet 11.3 from Cambridge Elevate

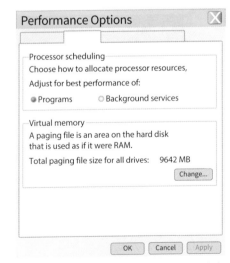

The size of the area on the hard disk drive to be used for virtual memory can be set by the user.

- Often the operating system has to constantly swap information back and forth between RAM and the hard disk drive, which operates all of the time. You can hear the disk drive operating continuously. This is called 'disk thrashing' and significantly slows down the execution of the programs.

The more RAM a computer has then the less virtual memory will be needed. That is why inserting more RAM will significantly improve the performance of a computer.

 Complete the Cambridge Computing Online activity
www.cambridge.org/links/kose4035

ACTIVITY 11.7

A computer is advertised as being 'quad-core'.

a. Explain what is meant by 'quad-core' and how it improves the performance of the computer.

b. Explain how using cache memory also improves the performance.

 Remember

1. The clock speed cannot be increased indefinitely because of the extra heat generated.
2. A processor with several CPUs is said to be multi-core.
3. The processing speed of the CPU is limited by the speed that data can be supplied by the slower RAM.
4. Cache memory stores regularly used items of data so that they can be accessed more quickly
5. When the main memory (RAM) is full, the operating system will store data on an area of the hard disk drive (the virtual memory).
6. The least used data items are swapped out to the virtual memory and moved back when needed.

 Complete Interactive Activity 11c on Cambridge Elevate

Key terms

secondary storage devices: devices that store information but which do not lose the data when they are switched off; usually not on the main circuit board (motherboard)

magnetic storage: storing data using magnetic media such as a hard disk drive

optical storage: storing data using optical devices such as CDs and DVDs

electrical storage: storing data using devices such as flash memory. This is sometimes called 'solid state'

Secondary storage devices

Because RAM is volatile, data must be stored on other devices called secondary storage devices so it is not lost when the computer is switched off.

Storage devices store data in three different ways: magnetically, optically and electrically (solid state).

Magnetic storage

- Magnetic storage devices include hard disk drives and magnetic tape.

- Hard disk drives consist of stacks of non-removable disks coated with magnetic materials.

- The discs spin and read-write heads move across the disks. Electro-magnets in the read-write heads read and write the data.

Hard disk drives are suitable for the storage and backup of large amounts of data that do not have to be transported.

Advantages	Disadvantages
Very fast access speeds.	Not very portable.
Random access: data can be read instantly from any part of the disc.	Susceptible to physical knocks that might cause the read-write heads to hit the discs and corrupt data.
Store large amounts of data: hard disk drives that store terabytes of data are common in most home computers.	
Low cost.	

Optical storage

Optical storage uses light from lasers to read and write data on discs.

Here are some examples:

- compact discs (CDs) typically store 700MB

- digital versatile discs (DVDs) typically store 4.7 GB

- Blu-ray discs typically store 128GB.

Optical disks are useful for distributing program files and images and backing up data, which can then be stored at another site.

Advantages	Disadvantages
Cheap.	Do not store as much as hard disk drives.
Easy to transport from one site to another.	Slow access speeds.
	Stored data degrades over time.
	Data cannot be written over as it can on hard disk drives.

Solid state storage

Data can be stored electrically using flash memory.

Flash memory was developed from a type of ROM called 'electrically erasable programmable read-only memory' (EEPROM) and was introduced in 1984.

EEPROMs had to be completely erased before they could be written to, but flash memory can be written to and read in small blocks.

- Flash memory is used in

- SD (secure digital) cards (4–32GB)

- Micro SD cards (4–32GB)

- SDXC (extended capacity) cards (2TB)

- USB flash drives (256GB but can be up to 1TB).

Key term

flash memory: this is memory which can be programmed electrically but then keeps its data when the power is turned off

Flash memory is used for data storage in cameras, mobile phones and embedded devices and increasingly as the main secondary storage device in computers, especially in laptops as solid state drives (SSDs).

The MacBook Air uses a flash memory solid state drive (SSD) for its main secondary storage.

Flash memory devices are ideal for transporting data as they are light and being solid state have no moving parts which could be damaged.

Advantages	Disadvantages
Very fast access speed; far faster than discs.	More expensive than a hard disk drive or DVD.
Small, light and easily portable.	The storage capacity is less than a hard disk drive.
Quiet.	There is a limited number of erase/write cycles, up to 100,000 for high quality SSDs and so it cannot be used indefinitely.
Flash memory is said to be 'solid state' as it has no moving parts that could be damaged if the device was knocked or dropped and therefore there is less chance of losing data.	

Secondary storage media compared

	Hard disk drive	Optical drive	Solid state
Capacity	Very large. 1–2TB common in home computers.	Low. Compact discs (CDs) typically store 700MB. Digital versatile discs (DVDs) typically store 4.7GB. Blu-ray discs typically store 128GB.	Solid state drives are usually about 1TB.
Speed	Fast.	Slow.	Very fast.
Portability	Not very portable as physical knocks may cause the read-write heads to hit the discs and corrupt data.	More portable than a hard disk drive but discs are relatively large.	Very portable. Small solid state storage devices can be fitted inside cameras and mobile phones.
Durability	Very durable.	Easily scratched and data can be damaged. Data cannot be overwritten.	Lower than a hard disk drive. Limited number of erase/write cycles.
Reliability	Very reliable.	Very reliable if not scratched.	Very reliable and data is not affected by magnetic fields as it is in hard disk drives.
Cost	Very low.	Very low.	More expensive than hard disk drives and optical devices.

 Download Worksheet 11.4 from Cambridge Elevate

Cloud storage

Cloud storage is off-site storage. Users store and back up their data on storage devices, usually hard disk drives, somewhere that they can access over the Internet. Where in the world that 'somewhere' is, they do not know.

There are vast data centres around the world that store all the data that users upload such as their photographs and images.

Advantages	Disadvantages
Data will be secure if there is a fire or other problem at the site.	Needs an Internet connection.
The data can be accessed from anywhere in the world with an Internet connection.	Download and upload speeds can be affected by the Internet connection.
No need to buy an expensive storage device.	The hosting company could be targeted by online hackers.
Many users can access the data and collaborate with each other from anywhere in the world.	You have less control if the data is held by another company.
	Storing some data online may breach the Data Protection Act as it should be kept secure and confidential.

Complete Interactive Activity 11d on Cambridge Elevate

ACTIVITY 11.8

Suggest, with explanations, suitable storage solutions for the following people:

a. A gap-year student is travelling around the world. She would like to be able to back up the photographs from her camera so that friends at home will be able to see them.

b. The owner of a mail-order company has constantly changing order and customer information as orders are being processed throughout the day. What would be the best backup medium for this company?

c. A school student needs a method to back up his schoolwork and transfer documents between school and home.

d. The owner of a small business with only one computer and no Internet access would like to back up the business data once a week.

Remember

1. Magnetic media: electromagnets in read-write heads read and write data on discs coated with magnetic materials.
2. Optical media: light from lasers read and write data on specially prepared discs.
3. Electrical or solid state storage: data is stored electrically using flash memory.
4. Cloud storage: off-site storage accessed over the Internet.

Practice questions

1. Catherine has bought a new laptop computer which was advertised as having a 1.6GHz dual-core central processing unit (CPU) and 512KB Level 1 cache.
   a. State the purpose of the CPU.
   b. Describe what is meant by
      i. 1.6GHz CPU
      ii. dual-core CPU
      iii. L1 cache.

Download Self-assessment 11 worksheet from Cambridge Elevate

Your final challenge

Your challenge is to design and code a multiple-choice quiz based on the contents of this chapter.

The design brief
- There should be at least five questions.
- Each question should have four possible answers, only one of which is correct.
- After taking the quiz the user should be
  - informed of their score
  - told the correct answers for those that they got wrong.
- You should create and then test your quiz.

Extension
- Ask the users to enter their names and then save the users and their scores in a text file.

12 Computer systems: systems software

Learning outcomes

By the end of this chapter you should be able to:

- explain what is meant by systems software
- explain what is meant by an operating system
- describe the functions of the operating system
- explain what is meant by utility systems software
- list some examples of utility systems software and their functions.

Challenge: create a program to clean up a hard disk drive

- Over time, the hard disk drive in a computer becomes very messy with parts of files spread around in different locations. This is called 'fragmentation' and leads to a loss of performance as it takes far longer to load and save the files.
- Your challenge is to write a program to put the files back together again.

Why systems software?

- Computer hardware needs to be told what to do! This is the role of the systems software.

- The CPU can't communicate with the other devices without the help of systems software.

- The systems software gets the instructions from memory when the CPU needs them.

- If a word processing or spreadsheet program needs something to be printed on screen or on paper, the systems software communicates with the monitor and the printer.

- If several programs are running at the same time, the systems software keeps them all running smoothly.

- Utility systems software helps with maintenance jobs such as defragmenting the hard disk drive, compressing files and improving security.

Systems software manages all the actions of the computer and helps users to organise their programs and data and tell the computer what they want it to do.

Key terms

systems software: software that runs the computer, tells it what to do, tells it which programs to run, controls what the users see on screen, etc.

applications: programs that are called up by the systems software and which perform specific tasks

BIOS: the **B**asic **I**nput/**O**utput **S**ystem controls the computer when it is first switched on. It tests the system hardware and loads the operating system. It is specially written for each motherboard and performs any other operations that are needed by that particular motherboard

motherboard: the main printed circuit board of the computer; it has connectors that other circuit boards can be slotted into

Systems software and applications

A computer system consists of hardware and software, which includes systems software and applications.

The systems software includes the BIOS and also the *operating system* and *system utilities*.

Operating system

An operating system is a set of programs that controls how the user interacts with the hardware and software of a computer system. It has programs that:

- manage all of the hardware devices and software
- control all of the processes running on the computer
- ensure that all hardware and software interact correctly.

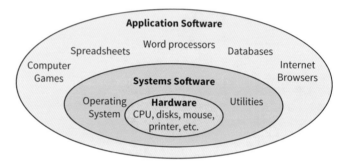

There are many different operating systems in use today including:

- Windows
- OS X
- Linux
- Ubuntu
- Unix
- Android
- iOS.

The operating systems all have four basic managers:

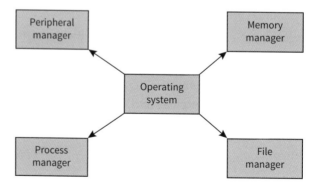

Memory management

The memory manager is in charge of the RAM. Programs often need to use the RAM throughout their operation. Some programs will be large and complex and will use the RAM extensively whereas some very small programs won't need to use it much. The memory manager checks that all requests from programs for memory space are valid and allocates accordingly. It will also de-allocate space and swap out data to the swap file as mentioned in Chapter 11.

Process management

In a computer system, many programs will be running at the same time (this is called multitasking) and the activities they are performing are called processes. They all require the use of the CPU and the process manager prioritises the tasks and allocates time to each process.

The software makes its requests to the operating system through application program interfaces (APIs), which are standard software routines that developers can build into their software for this purpose.

Peripheral management

The peripheral manager manages all of the computer input and output by managing requests from programs to use devices such as printers, speakers, keyboards, hard disk drives.

It communicates with the devices through software called drivers, which translate the instructions sent by the device manager into ones that the devices can understand.

File management

The file manager controls all of the different files on the system, e.g. text files, graphic files, program files. It controls file permissions such as a user's ability to see or open a file, write to a file or delete it. It is therefore important for the security of the system.

File management also helps to organise and control files so that they are as easy to use as possible for the user. It can help to protect the user from accidental mistakes too.

Complete Interactive Activity 12a on Cambridge Elevate

User interfaces

Users interact with the operating system through a user interface. The user interface is a system which converts what the user inputs to a form that the computer can understand and vice-versa.

Key terms

RAM: (also known as random access memory) memory that can be used by computer programs to store data and instructions, but all of its data is lost when the computer is switched off

swap file: this is a file, kept on the hard drive or other storage device, used to store data and instructions while a program is running but when the RAM is full; it is not as quick as RAM

multitasking: when a computer is running several programs at the same time

process: an activity that a computer program is performing

driver: a program which is called by a peripheral manager to operate any devices for example printers, the screen, mouse, when they are called by the main program

permission: a rule that is set up for a particular file to control who can edit, read or write on the file

user interface: the way in which a user interacts with a computer system

Key terms

graphical user interface:
(known as GUI), a user
interface which relies mainly
on windows, icons, menus,
pointers

command line interface: the
user has to type in all of the
commands for the operating
system instead of using a
mouse to point at and select
menu options or double-
clicking on icons

Many operating systems provide a graphical user interface (GUI), e.g. Windows and iOS. When using a GUI, the user communicates with the operating system using **W**indows, **I**cons, drop-down **M**enus and **P**ointers (WIMP).

Complete the Cambridge Computing Online activity
www.cambridge.org/links/kose4036

Before GUIs came into use, all operating systems provided a command line interface, where the user has to type in commands for the operating system, e.g. to print, copy, delete and move files.

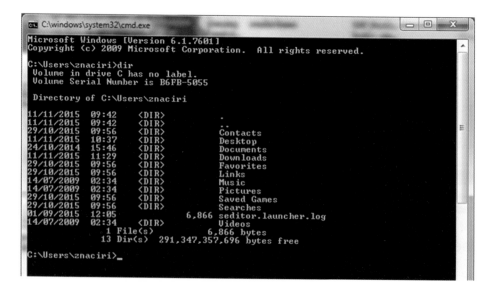

Command line interfaces are less convenient because the user has to learn all of the commands, e.g. to print, copy and move files. They then have to type them in correctly.

Download Worksheet 12.1 from Cambridge Elevate

Utility systems software

Utility programs perform specific tasks related to computer functions, resources, files and security. They help to configure the system, analyse how it is working and optimise it to improve its efficiency. Some examples are security programs and system optimisation programs.

Security programs can include:

- anti-virus software (scans for and removes malicious files)

- encryption software (uses an algorithm to scramble (encrypt) a file according to the key which is used; the key is needed to decrypt the file back to its original form)

- a firewall (prevents unwanted access to a computer over a network, e.g. a local network or the internet).

- spyware detectors (block and remove programs designed to collect personal information and transmit it to another user).

System optimisation programs can include:

- system clean-up tools (to search for and remove files no longer needed)

- disk defragmentation tools (used to rearrange the parts of files on the disk drive: when a file is saved to disk, parts of the file might be saved in different areas of the disk these tools try to move all the parts to the same area for quicker access)

- file compression software to make files smaller so that they take up less storage space and can be transmitted to other users more easily.

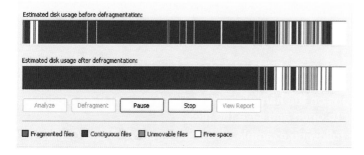

This image shows the fragmented files on the hard disk drive and how they will be arranged after defragmentation.

Backup programs

One of the most important tasks for any computer user is to back up their data in case of file loss or corruption. Backing up involves copying the files to a second medium such as disk, tape or to a storage company on the internet so that they can be restored if there are problems with the originals. Backup programs, which are usually included in operating systems, can be configured to back up sensitive data at specific times. Often they also compress the data so that it takes up less storage space.

They can be configured to perform full backups, where all of the specified data is backed up, or incremental backups, where only new files or ones that have changed since the last backup are saved in order to save time. The software will manage the various backups and find a file if it needs to be restored.

 Key terms

full backup: all of the files specified by the user will be backed up

incremental backup: only new files or files that have been changed since the last backup will be backed up and kept with the last full backup

Complete Interactive Activity 12b on Cambridge Elevate

Remember

1. The operating system:
   a. is a collection of software and forms part of the systems software
   b. manages all of the other software applications and memory allocation
   c. communicates with users through a user interface
   d. controls hardware devices (e.g. printers, hard disk drives, monitors) through the use of device drivers.
2. Utility programs:
   a. Perform specific functions to maintain and optimise the computer operations and ensure the security of the system.
   b. Include system clean-up and update tools, such as disk defragmentation tools, anti-virus programs and file compression tools.

Download Worksheet 12.2 from Cambridge Elevate

Practice questions

One of the functions of an operating system is multitasking.

a. Explain one reason why multitasking is needed in an operating system.

b. State two other functions of an operating system.

Download Self-assessment 12 worksheet from Cambridge Elevate

Your final challenge

- As files are saved, edited, enlarged and resaved they can become fragmented so that different parts of the file are located at different positions on the hard disk drive. This fragmentation means that it takes longer to open and save the files.

- In the following example, there are three (**A**, **B** and **C**) files spread across the drive. After defragmentation, they are all placed in order on the drive.

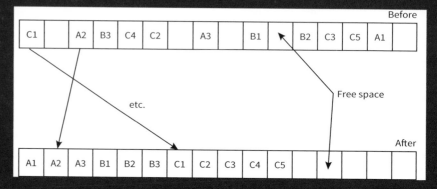

- Your challenge is to create an algorithm and to code and test a program that will rearrange the file segments as shown.

Tip

Using a two-dimensional array will help with the solution.

13 Networks

Learning outcomes

By the end of this chapter you should be able to:

- explain what is meant by a computer network and list the different types of networks
- describe the differences between client server and peer-to-peer networks
- explain the functions of the hardware needed to connect computers
- explain how computers communicate using cable and microwave
- describe network topologies
- explain how users connect to and use the Internet
- explain how data is transmitted across networks
- explain the use of protocols
- explain how virtual networks can be set up.

Challenge: act as a consultant

- You have to give professional advice to organisations on the setting up of networks.
- Your challenge is to give professional-sounding and accurate advice to your clients.

Why networks?

The networking of computing devices has had a profound impact on our lives and the ways in which we work, communicate with each other, buy products and services and find out information in our daily lives.

- Networks allow us to live in a connected world.

- Worldwide communication is possible for everyone.

- Our personal devices can be networked so that they can communicate with each other. Our laptops can be networked with our mobile phone, printers, mice, speakers and headphones.

- The Internet is a huge network of networks and the World Wide Web allows us to connect and communicate with people and services throughout the world.

- Thanks to networks, we can tell the world what we are thinking and what we are feeling (including what we are having for lunch). We can publish our photographs and videos to a world wide audience and keep in touch with our friends wherever we are.

Thanks to networks, we can publish our photo and videos to a world wide audience and keep in touch with friends wherever we are.

Computer networks

A computer network allows computers and devices to share data. This includes:

- computer-to-computer communication

- computers communicating with devices such as printers, mice and keyboards

- mobile phone networks

- smart televisions

- tablets and media players downloading videos and music and playing them through external devices such as speakers and digital projectors.

We live in a networked world where people and things are interconnected.

There are different levels of networking. Some of these are outlined below:

Personal area network (PAN)

A personal area network (PAN) is a network communicating up to 10 metres between computer devices such as laptops, mobile phones, tablets, media players, speakers and printers. They may be devices belonging to one person, or to several.

Key term

personal area network (PAN): network used for data transmission over short distances by devices such as laptops, mobile phones, tablets, media players, speakers and printers

Bluetooth-enabled devices can use a PAN to connect with each other.

The PAN may just connect the local devices or allow them to connect to higher-level networks such as the Internet.

Local area network (LAN)

Computers in a site such as an office building use a local area network (LAN) to connect with each other.

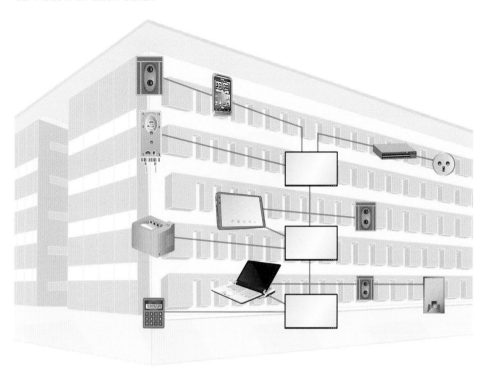

A local area network (LAN) is a computer network within a small geographical area such as a home, school, office building or a group of buildings on a local site.

Wide area network (WAN)

A wide area network (WAN) is a network that connects separate LANs over a large geographical area. This ensures that computers in one location can communicate with computers and users in other locations.

The Internet is a huge wide area network.

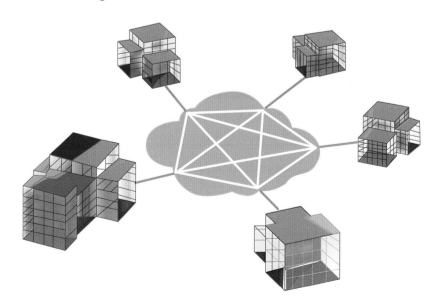

Network types

There are two network types: client-server networks and peer-to-peer networks. Peer-to-peer networks are used to connect a small number of devices, for example in a home or office where there are just a few users. They are cheaper to set up and maintain. Client-server networks are more expensive to set up and maintain as a more powerful computer is required to act as the server, network software is needed and specialist knowledge is needed to administer the network.

Client-server networks

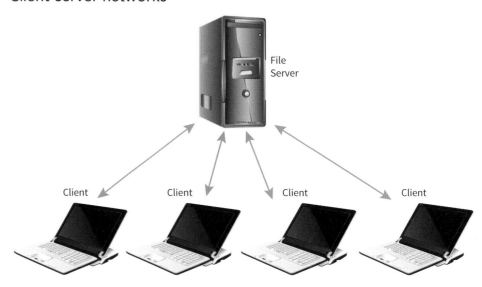

In a client-server network there are two types of computers: the computers that control access to the network (servers) and the computers on which the users work (clients).

- From the client machines, the users log into the network servers in order to be able to access programs and peripherals and save data on the servers.

- The server is therefore responsible for the security of the network, expecting users to log in with a username and password. As all files are stored on the server the data can be backed up centrally.

 Key terms

server: a computer that provides files on demand to client machines
client: a computer that acts as a desktop for users and which relies on a server for its operations

Peer-to-peer networks

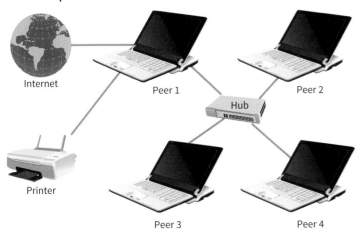

Internet

Peer 1

Peer 2

Hub

Printer

Peer 3

Peer 4

In a peer-to-peer network, the computers are simply connected together without any one computer having any superiority over the others. All of the computers on a peer-to-peer network are equal.

- Through sharing rights granted by the users any computer can share the programs of another, save data onto their hard disk and use printers connected to them.

- Each computer acts as both a client and a server and can communicate directly with all of the others.

- Security is distributed and the users of each computer have to be able to grant access rights to its resources and allot passwords.

- As data is stored on all of the computers and is not held centrally, all the users are responsible for backing up procedures.

Complete the Cambridge Computing Online activity
www.cambridge.org/links/kose4037

ACTIVITY 13.1

a. Describe the characteristics of

   i. a personal area network

   ii. a local area network

   iii. a wide area network.

b. Describe the difference in roles between a client computer on a client-server network and one on a peer-to-peer network.

Complete Interactive Activity 13a on Cambridge Elevate

 Remember

1. A computer network allows devices to share data and resources.

2. Include personal area networks (PANs), local area networks (LANs) and wide area networks (WANs).

3. In client-server networks there are two types of computers:

   (a) the computers that control access to the network (servers)

   (b) the computers on which the users work (clients).

4. In a peer-to-peer network all computers are equal - they operate as both clients and servers.

5. Security, data storage and the backing up of data is centralised in a client-server network but is distributed in a peer-to-peer network

Key terms

microwaves: electromagnetic waves that can be used to carry data between computers

protocols: agreed rules for requesting and sending data across networks

How do computers connect to a network?

In order to connect to a network, a computer needs some hardware (physical devices) and also some software that allows it to communicate with the other computers. Devices can be connected using cables. The most commonly used are 'twisted pair' cables in which pairs of copper wires are twisted together and carry electrical signals, and optical fibre cables, which are made of glass. As they transmit information encoded in beams of light the data transmission is much faster. The connection can also be microwaves, including radio waves.

Network interface card (NIC) or network adapter

A network interface card (NIC) or network adapter is a component that connects a computer to a network. It formats the data sent from the computer into a required format according to the protocols (rules) of the network.

Originally, the adapters for desktop PCs were on 'cards' that were installed in the computer but are now built into the motherboard. Network interface cards and adapters now support both wired and wireless network connections.

Every NIC is created with a hardware number permanently 'burned' into it. This permanent hardware number is known as the MAC (Media Access Control) address. MAC addresses are 48 bits in length and are usually displayed as a 12-digit hexadecimal number.

Every MAC address is unique so that all data on a network can be sent to the correct component, just like letters delivered to the correct house or text messages and voice calls to the correct phone number.

Network hubs, wireless access points, switches and routers

Hubs

A hub is used to link the computers as cables from each one feed into the hub.

- All of the computers on the network plug into a port on the hub using a cable.

- When a message is received through the cable from one of the computers, the hub transmits it to all of the other computers.

- Because the hub transmits every message to every part of the network and not just to the computer it is intended for, there are a lot of unnecessary transmissions or network traffic, resulting in a reduction in the speed that data is transmitted as the network becomes overloaded.

Key term

network traffic: the overall network usage caused by all of the data that is being transmitted at a given time

Wireless access points

Wireless access points allow wireless devices to connect to a wired network.

- They convert data they receive through cables into a wireless signal and vice versa.

- They are commonly used in public buildings to provide 'Internet hotspots'.

- They are similar to hubs: they cannot direct messages to particular devices.

Switches

Network switches are sometimes used instead of hubs.

- Network switches have a similar function to hubs in a single network, but they read the messages passing through.

- They can read the destination addresses and send them to only the intended computers.

- They can do this because they build up a table of all of the MAC addresses on the network.

- They therefore cut down on unnecessary network traffic.

- Switches can send and receive information at the same time, so they are faster than hubs.

Routers

Routers connect different networks together.

- They are similar to switches in that they read the address information and forward the messages to the correct network. A switch does this within a single network, but a router does this across several networks.

- Routers are commonly used in the home to allow many computers to share an Internet connection. The router links the home network to a much larger one: the Internet.

- The router will transmit the incoming web pages, streamed audio, etc. to the correct computer on the network.

- Routers can have both cable and wireless connections.

 Complete the Cambridge Computing Online activity
www.cambridge.org/links/kose4038

ACTIVITY 13.2

1. A small business has decided to network the five computers used in its office. To connect to the network each computer will require a network adapter.

    a. Explain why each computer will require a network adapter in order to connect to the network.

2. The business has decided to buy a router for the network.

    b. Explain the advantages to the business of buying a router.

Complete Interactive Activity 13b on Cambridge Elevate

Remember

1. Computers need a network adapter to connect to a network.
2. Hubs and switches are used to allow messages to be transmitted between computers in a single network.
3. Routers are used to transmit messages between computers on different networks.
4. Cables and radio waves can be used to carry the data.

Transmission media

The two main ways that devices use to communicate over a network are by cable or microwaves; in other words, 'wired' and 'wireless'.

Cable

The traditional method for networking computers is to connect the computers using cables. In large networks there is usually a combination of twisted-pair copper wire and also fibre optic cable.

Copper wire carries the data as electric currents, and in fibre optic cable they are transmitted as pulses of light generated by a light emitting diode (LED) or a laser.

Fibre optic cables have a far greater bandwidth and can carry signals far faster than copper cables. The signals can also travel over greater distances without needing to be boosted.

In order to transmit data over the cables, there are rules, called protocols, concerning how the data is packaged and how collisions are detected or prevented. The most widely standard is Ethernet.

Microwave

Microwaves consist of electromagnetic radiation travelling in waves with a frequency higher than 1 gigahertz (billions of cycles per second). Radio waves are a type of microwave and they are used to transmit data across networks in frequencies of between 2.4 and 5GHz.

Each frequency range is divided into separate channels. For example, in the 2.4GHz range used in most networks, there are 14 channels spaced 5MHz apart. Devices operating on channels close to each other may cause interference and so users can change the operating channel of their Wi-Fi device.

A wireless access point and a router can be used to connect wired and wireless networks.

The most commonly used standard of data transmission using radio waves is Wi-Fi. Others include GSM (Global System for Mobile communications), used for mobile phones, e.g. 3G and 4G; Bluetooth and Wi-Fi direct.

Tip

Bandwidth is the amount of data that can pass through the transmission medium per second. It is often called the 'bit rate'. It does not measure how fast the bits are travelling, only how many can get through a particular point in a second. Bandwidth is measured in bits per second (bps) or megabits per second (Mbps). (Note: bandwidth is measured mega**bits** and not mega**bytes**.)

Key terms

Ethernet: a set of technical standards for connecting computers

frequency: the number of waves per second

channel: the smaller sub-ranges into which a frequency range can be divided

Comparison of wired and wireless networks

	Wired	Wireless
Bandwidth	Very high bandwidth up to 100Gbps.	Far lower bandwidth. The latest version of Wi-Fi can offer speeds from 433Mbps to 2 or 3Gbps.
Installation	Setting up is more difficult. Cables have to be run all over the site.	Easy. All that is needed are wireless access points.
Cost	Cables and hardware can be expensive. Also cost of work being done.	Cheap. Just cost of wireless access point.
Cost	Security is good. A user has to physically plug their computer into the network using a cable.	Security is poor. Anyone within range can see the network and connect to it to use it. The access point must be secured with a security password. Some form of encryption must be set up.
Interference	There should be no interference with the signal on a network cable.	The signal can be affected by walls and electronic equipment such as microwave ovens. It is also affected by distance from the access point and the number of connected computers.
Mobility	Not very mobile. You have to plug the computer into a wall socket and cannot use it in a room without one. Contact is lost as soon as it is unplugged if you want to move to another room.	Very mobile. Users can access the network from anywhere on the site. Can move from room to room and remain connected.

Key term

bandwidth: the amount of data that can pass through the transmission medium per second, often called the bit-rate

---

ACTIVITY 13.3

Discuss the benefits and drawbacks of setting up in the home either a wired or wireless network.

Key terms

topology: the structure of the network

node: places on the network where there are items of equipment

Network topologies

A network topology describes how all of the parts of a network are arranged and connected together. The topology includes the nodes (e.g. computers, printers, modems) and the connecting lines (cables).

Star topology

Using star topology, each computer is connected individually to a central point, which can be a file server or switch.

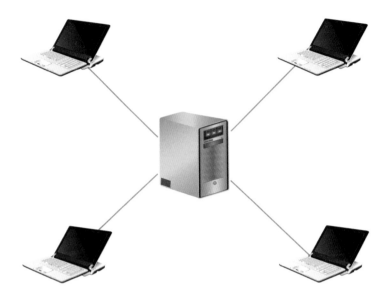

Advantages

- Adding or removing devices is easy, and can be done without affecting the entire network.

- Data packets can be directed to the intended node directly without having to pass along the complete network.

- There will be less network traffic and fewer collisions.

- If one link fails, all the other devices will continue to operate.

Disadvantages

- Network operation depends on the functioning of the central component (file server or switch) and if this fails, then so will the entire network.

- It requires a lot of cable as each computer is connected individually to the central component and so will be expensive.

Mesh topology

Each of the network nodes, servers, client computers and printers, are interconnected with one another. Every node not only sends its own signals but also relays data from other nodes. Every node is connected to every other node.

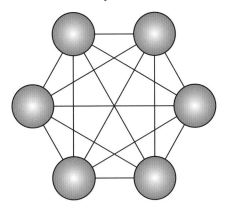

Advantages

* Data can be transmitted from different devices simultaneously.

* Even if one of the components fails there is always an alternative route for the data.

* It can handle high volumes of data traffic.

* Adding more devices will not hamper the transmission of data as all nodes help to transmit the data.

Disadvantages

* The overall cost is expensive compared with other topologies.

* Very difficult to manage as it requires continuous supervision.

ACTIVITY 13.4

A small business uses a star topology for its local area network. List three benefits of using a star topology.

The Internet

The Internet is a global system of interconnected computer networks that serves billions of users worldwide and is therefore a wide area network. The Internet provides many services including email and the World Wide Web (www).

The Internet is often called a 'network of networks' because it consists of millions of private, public, academic, business, and government networks that are linked by different networking technologies.

The World Wide Web was first proposed by the British scientist, Tim Berners-Lee in 1989. He created the first website in 1990.

 Remember

1. Data can be transmitted in networks by cables and radio waves.
2. The most widely used standards for transmission are Ethernet for wired and Wi-Fi for wireless.
3. Topology is the arrangement of the computers and other devices in the network and how they are connected together.
4. Topologies include star and mesh arrangements.

 Complete the Cambridge Computing Online activity www.cambridge.org/links/kose4039

 Download Worksheet 13.1 from Cambridge Elevate

 Complete Interactive Activity 13c on Cambridge Elevate

Hosts

A host is a computer which can be accessed by users working at remote locations using networks, including the Internet. Web hosting companies rent space on their servers where people can develop their own websites that can be accessed by users all over the world using the World Wide Web.

In 1969 there were four host computer systems and today there are tens of millions. The Internet Society was established in 1992 to oversee the policies and protocols that define how we use and interact with the Internet.

Hosting companies are specialists in web hosting. It is possible to host a website on your own computer at home but there are problems with doing this. Here are some of the problems that you may encounter:

- You need to have a static Internet address that stays the same. Most home computers are given a different address by their service provider every time they connect to the Internet.

- You need to keep your computer switched on at all times, otherwise clients might be unable to connect to your website.

- You need a very fast broadband connection capable of handling a very large number of users, all wanting to use your website at the same time.

- When a computer failure takes place, you need the technical knowledge to repair it quickly, or you need another computer that will instantly take over delivery of your website.

- You need a great deal of technical knowledge in addition to that needed to design your website.

- You need to be able to protect your website against the threats from hackers and various other unscrupulous users.

- You need to be insured against any losses that users might suffer from as a result of using your website.

Web hosting companies solve many or all of these problems by maintaining teams of engineers, software programmers, legal and administration staff. It is much less expensive to use one of these companies because you share most of these costs with hundreds or thousands of other clients.

There is a huge infrastructure of cables forming the backbone of the Internet. These cables are provided and maintained by large corporations such as IBM and AT&T and they charge for access.

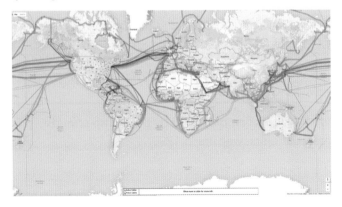

Connecting to the Internet

To connect to the Internet, computers require the following:

Hardware	<ul><li>A network adapter (as described in the networking section).</li><li>A modem.</li></ul>
Access to cable infrastructure	Large organisations can negotiate their own access with the corporations that control the infrastructure, but smaller ones and individual users will require the services of an Internet Service Provider (ISP) to organise that access. ISPs also provide storage space, called 'hosting', for the websites of their users.
An address	Every computer needs a unique software address in order to communicate over the Internet. This is provided by the IP address.<ul><li>IP stands for Internet Protocol, the set of procedures used by computers accessing the Internet.</li><li>Every computer accessing the Internet must have a unique identifier. This is their IP address.</li></ul>

Key terms

modem: short for 'modulator-demodulator'; modulates and demodulates signals (converts them from digital to analogue and vice versa) sent from and received by a computer over a communications network

IP address: a unique software address used to communicate over the Internet (see below for more details)

IP addresses

An IP address is a set of numbers used to identify one particular computer. The IP address is like a postal address and it will allow Internet data and messages to be sent directly to the correct computer. IP addresses originally consisted of 4, 8-bit numbers for version 4 addresses (IPv4), e.g. 216.27.61.137. This provided only 4 billion unique addresses, so IPv6 was introduced. IPv6 uses 128 binary bits to create a single unique address on the network. An IPv6 address is expressed by eight groups of hexadecimal numbers separated by colons, as in 2001:cdba:0000:0000:0000:0000:3257:9652. 128 bits provide 3.4×10^{38} unique addresses.

Complete the Cambridge Computing Online activity
www.cambridge.org/links/kose4040

Domain names

Domain names are used to identify one or more IP addresses. They are more convenient to use and easier to remember than the four octets of binary numbers, for example the IP address of the domain name of Cambridge University Press (www.cambridge.org) is 174.35.68.38. When the domain name is used, it will be converted to the correct IP address by the Domain Name Service (DNS) and the contact will take place.

Complete the Cambridge Computing Online activity
www.cambridge.org/links/kose4041

Key terms

domain name: a user-friendly name for a particular website

packet: a small block of data that is transmitted from one computer to another

Packets

When devices transmit data, the data is broken down into small pieces called packets. These are sent separately, and then joined up at the end so that the message is complete.

Rules are needed so that all of the computers on the network work together. For example, how will the receiving computer know when the message is complete or if there has been a transmission error?

A packet consists of:

- A header, containing the source and destination addresses and the position of this packet in the complete message or file.

- The body, containing part of the complete message data (also known as the payload).

- A footer (also known as the trailer), that informs the receiving device that it has reached the end of the packet and can also be used for error checking to ensure the complete packet has been delivered intact.

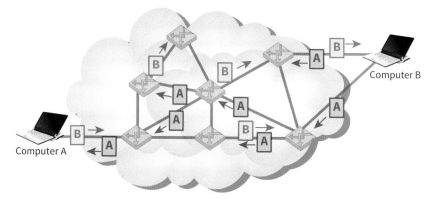

The packets sent between computers A and B take different routes across the network.

The packets are then sent out on their various journeys to the recipient computer. They do not all follow the same route. In fact, they do not all arrive in the correct order but, because they are labelled, the receiving computer can put them back together in the correct order.

The journey of the packets across a large network like the Internet is extraordinary. They could be travelling from the east coast of America to your bedroom! Here's how it works:

- The source computer splits the file into packets and addresses them with the recipient's IP address.

- The file is split because the transmission of a large file would consume all the bandwidth and slow the network.

- These packets are then sent onto the network using cables or microwaves as in a wireless network.

- Routers on the network inspect each packet and decide the most efficient path for the packet to take on the next stage of its journey.

- In order to do this, each router has a configuration table containing information about which connections lead to particular groups of addresses.

- The routers can balance the load across the network on a millisecond-by-millisecond basis.

- If there is a problem with one part of the network while a message is being transferred, packets can be routed around the problem, ensuring the delivery of the entire message.

- The final router can direct the packet to the correct recipient.

Thousands of miles in less than a second and all put back together again!

This method of data communication is called packet switching. It is more efficient because it means that there does not have to be a dedicated line between the two communicating devices. Compare this with making a telephone call on a landline, where there is a dedicated line between the two telephones. That method is called circuit switching.

In packet switching the same line can carry parts of billions of communications at the same time and if there is a problem or the line is full, then another route can be quickly found.

 Complete the Cambridge Computing Online activity
www.cambridge.org/links/kose4042

 Complete the Cambridge Computing Online activity
www.cambridge.org/links/kose4043

Protocols

There must be rules so that computers on all networks can communicate with each other when they are requesting and providing data and services. With such complicated processes as sending data packets, rules, called protocols, are essential.

TCP/IP stands for Transmission Control Protocol/Internet protocol. It is actually a suite or set of protocols arranged in four layers. Data to be transmitted (or when it is received) must pass through the layers where packaging data is added or read.

The four layers are:

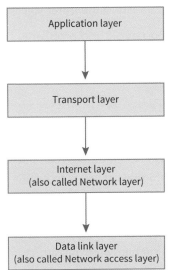

The application layer is where applications such as web browsers and email clients reside. This is where requests are made to web servers or emails are originated by the applications. Protocols used in this layer include HTTP, FTP and SMTP. The requests are passed to the next transport layer.

The transport layer is where the TCP protocol is active and is concerned with host-to-host communication. It divides the data received from the application layer into packets of the correct size. It also checks that the packets have arrived safely. If data is being received it sends an acknowledgement to the computer that sent the packet.

The Internet layer is where the IP protocol is active and adds the source and destination IP addresses to the packets and routs them to the recipient computer.

The data link layer is concerned with transmitting the data through the cables of the local network using the protocols of the specific network, e.g. Ethernet.

 Key term

packet switching: when certain areas of the network are too busy to carry the packets, they are automatically switched to emptier circuits

 Download Worksheet 13.2 from Cambridge Elevate

 Complete Interactive Activity 13d on Cambridge Elevate

Protocols of the application layer

The table below shows some of the protocols of the application layer.

FTP	File Transfer Protocol: provides the rules that must be followed when files are being transmitted between computers.
HTTP	Hypertext Transfer Protocol: the rules to be followed by a web server and a web browser when requesting and supplying information. HTTP is used for sending requests from a web client (a browser) to a web server and returning web content from the server back to the client.
HTTPS	Secure HTTP: ensures that communications between a host and client are secure by ensuring that all communication between them is encrypted.
SMTP	Simple Mail Transfer Protocol: the protocol for sending email messages from client to server and then from server to server until it reaches its destination.
POP	Post Office Protocol: used by a client to retrieve emails from a mail server. All of the emails are downloaded when there is a connection between client and server.
IMAP	Internet Message Access Protocol: unlike POP, the messages do not have to be downloaded. They can be read and stored on the message server. This is better for users with many different devices as they can be read from each rather than being downloaded to just one.

Benefits of using networking layers

Networking technologies are separated or compartmentalised into layers, each one containing specific hardware and software protocols. Each layer performs specific tasks and interacts with the adjacent layers in the 'network model'.

The benefits of this approach are:

- It simplifies the overall model by dividing it into functional parts.

- Each layer is specialised to perform a particular function.

- The different layers can be combined in different ways as required.

- One layer can be developed or changed without affecting the other layers.

- It makes it easier to identify and correct networking errors and problems.

- It provides a universal standard for hardware and software manufacturers to follow so that they will be able to communicate with each other.

Virtual networks

A virtual network is created through software rather than hardware. A large LAN can be subdivided into a series of virtual LANs (VLANs) so that teams can have their own virtual LAN and communicate and share information just with each other. This makes it easier to configure software used just by a particular team and reduces network traffic because data will be sent only to members of the VLAN. It also increases security as the sensitive data of each team can be kept separate from the others. These VLANs share the same hardware infrastructure but through software they are separate logical LANs.

Download Worksheet 13.3 from Cambridge Elevate

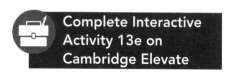
Complete Interactive Activity 13e on Cambridge Elevate

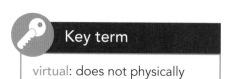
Key term

virtual: does not physically exist, although it appears to

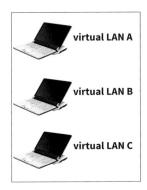

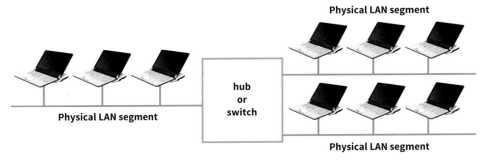

A virtual private network (VPN) is similar but it is set up within a large WAN such as the Internet. Users across the world can log in, work and collaborate on their own private network. As it only appears to be, and is not really, a private, unique network it is said to be virtual. The network is established through software and uses encryption and other software to ensure that all communication is secure.

In a VPN, the packets that are sent are placed within an outer packet that only that particular VPN can understand using special protocols. The process is usually called tunnelling.

The cloud

In Chapter 11 we looked at the advantages of 'cloud storage': the saving and backing-up of data on remote storage devices using the Internet. Cloud computing now allows users to access and use applications such as word processors and spreadsheets stored on remote servers.

There are advantages for individuals and businesses:

- Lower maintenance costs: software does not need to be installed, maintained or upgraded on the local computers or servers.

- Software does not have to be 'bought' and businesses only have to pay for those parts that they need to use (this is known as 'software as a service').

- All software is automatically upgraded.

- As long as they have Internet access, employees can work from anywhere in the world.

- All data is automatically backed up at the remote site.

- Employees can collaborate on the same documents because they are not stored on one particular computer.

> ### Key terms
>
> **virtual private network:** a network that appears to the users as a unique network but which is part of another network
>
> **tunnelling:** process by which packets are placed inside an outer packet that only members of the VPN can read

Download Worksheet 13.4 from Cambridge Elevate

Remember

1. The Internet is a huge network of networks.
2. To connect to the Internet, a user needs a network adapter and a modem.
3. Protocols are the rules computers use for communicating on networks.
4. An ISP provides access to the Internet infrastructure for the users.
5. A user needs an IP address.
6. Domain names stand for IP addresses as they are easier to remember.
7. DNS resolves the names back into IP addresses.
8. TCP/IP is a suite of these protocols.
9. The TCP/IP protocols have four layers:
   a. the application layer
   b. the transport layer
   c. the Internet layer (also called the network layer)
   d. the data link layer (also called the network access layer)
10. Virtual networks are private, secure networks within larger WANs such as the Internet.

Practice questions

1. Protocols are used by computers communicating over networks.
   a. Explain what is meant by a 'protocol'.
2. TCP/IP is a collection of network protocols acting in layers.
   a. With the aid of a diagram give example protocols operating in each layer and their roles in network communication.
   b. List three benefits of arranging the protocols in layers.

Download Self-assessment 13 worksheet from Cambridge Elevate

Your final challenge

You have two clients:

1. 'Smith and Brown' are a small firm of solicitors. There are two solicitors and they also have a general office with two clerical workers. They would like a network so that they can share facilities and work collaboratively.
2. 'The Academy' is a secondary school with two main buildings and 50 classrooms, two of which are computer rooms. They would like a network so that all the pupils can log in using their laptops wherever they are in the school.

Your task is to give the clients advice such as:

- The type of network that is best suited to them.
- The hardware they will require to network their computers.
- Any software needed to set up the network.
- The infrastructure they will need.

You can present your advice as a written report or a presentation.

14 System security

Challenge: design and code an information point

- System security or cyber security is the use of technology, working practices and precautions designed to protect networks, computers, programs and data from attack, damage or unauthorised access.
- Information points are useful places where users can seek information about security threats. They can be placed in strategic places such as libraries.
- Your challenge is to design and code an information point that will allow users to use a menu system to select information about security threats and how they can be prevented and combatted.

Why system security?

Everyone takes the security of their homes and possessions seriously but they often don't take any precautions to protect their personal data from online hackers.

- Sometimes banks or large companies are targeted. But individuals are at risk too.

- Any individual with an Internet connection and an email address is likely to be targeted, often having their personal details and credit card numbers stolen. This is known as identity theft.

- There were 34,151 confirmed instances of identity fraud in the UK recorded in the first three months of 2015!

Threats posed to networks

There are many threats to network security. Most target the computers and communications software, but many target far weaker links: the people who use them.

A study released in 2015 found that human error was the root cause of 52% of all security breaches to networks. The biggest problems were failure to follow general policies and procedures, general carelessness and a lack of knowledge of threats.

Hackers have remotely disrupted Internet-enabled cars, adjusting the temperature, windscreen wipers and wiper fluid, and even disabling the brakes and taking over the steering.

Key term

social engineering:
psychologically tricking people
into divulging their secret
information or doing things
that they wouldn't otherwise do

Some of the methods used need no knowledge of programming or computers. They are low-tech 'con tricks', referred to as social engineering, aimed at enticing vulnerable people to disclose their personal information.

Examples of social engineering are blagging, phishing and shouldering.

Blagging

Blagging, sometimes called pretexting, can be done face-to-face or by telephone as well as by computer. The criminal invents a scenario to try to get the victim to divulge information, e.g. pretending to be a charity or an official such as a police officer, bank employee or an insurance claims investigator.

Phishing

This is when fraudsters send emails claiming to be from a bank or building society e-commerce site in order to find out your personal and financial details.

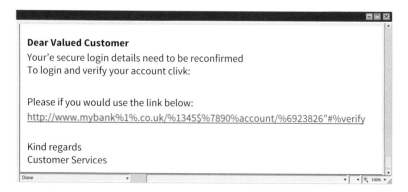

Phishing emails can often be recognised by:

- **Urgency**: they want you to respond quickly, without thinking.

- **Careless use of language**: they sometimes contain spelling errors and a careless writing style.

- **Impersonal**: you may not be addressed personally but only as 'Dear customer', although as the criminals become more sophisticated they are able to find your personal details from various sources such as social networking sites.

- **False links**: you are asked to click on a link that leads to a website controlled by the criminals.

- **Attachments**: sometimes you are asked to open programs or documents sent with the email; these attachments may contain spyware.

The term 'phishing' comes from 'fishing': bait is spread across the Internet in the hope that people will bite. Spear phishing is where individuals or particular groups who might have specialist information are targeted. It has been estimated that over one billion pounds a year is stolen through phishing scams.

Shouldering

This is sometimes referred to as 'shoulder surfing' and it involves finding login names, passwords, credit card and PIN (personal information numbers) by direct observation, such as:

- someone in an office watching others entering passwords

- watching someone enter their PIN at a cash machine (ATM)

- an employee at a shop or petrol station watching PINs being entered

- criminals using binoculars or closed circuit television to watch from a distance or record users entering sensitive information.

To prevent shoulder surfing, shield the keypad from view by using your body or cupping your hand over the keypad. When working on a laptop, keep your back to a wall with no open sides. Extra care should be taken when entering a password.

ACTIVITY 14.1

Catherine has just received the following email:

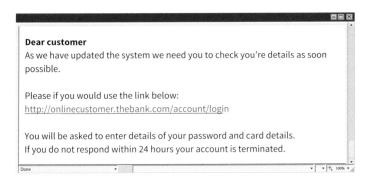

Dear customer
As we have updated the system we need you to check you're details as soon possible.

Please if you would use the link below:
http://onlinecustomer.thebank.com/account/login

You will be asked to enter details of your password and card details.
If you do not respond within 24 hours your account is terminated.

a. What is the name given to this type of email?

b. State three clues that might suggest that it is a bogus email.

Download Worksheet 14.1 from Cambridge Elevate

Complete Interactive Activity 14a on Cambridge Elevate

Malware

Malware is short for **Mal**icious soft**ware** and includes any software designed to

- disrupt the functioning of a computer system

- gain unauthorised access to a computer system

- gather information from the users without their knowledge.

Remember

1. Social engineering means getting people to disclose private and sensitive information by deception.
2. This information can then be used to steal money and valuable data.
3. Methods include blagging, phishing and shouldering.

Key term

malware: software that has been designed to gain unauthorised access to a computer system in order to disrupt its functioning or collect information without the users' knowledge

Types of malware include:

- pharming (via DNS)

- virus

- worm

- Trojan (or Trojan horse)

- spyware

- adware.

Key term

antivirus software: software designed to prevent, detect and remove malware

Malware	Explanation	Precautions
Pharming	In Chapter 13, we saw that domain names are used to represent IP addresses and how they are translated back into the IP address when you enter the name in your browser. If you have visited the site before, then this IP address will be stored on your computer (in the DNS cache) and your browser will connect without using the Domain Name Service. Malware that you may have received in an email can change the IP address of the domain name to a bogus one that you will then visit instead. Malware can also infect the DNS servers themselves so that everybody is directed to the bogus site!	• Check that the http address of the site is the one you intended to visit. • Check that there is a secure connection (https) if you have to enter sensitive information. • Check the site's security certificate. • Install the latest security updates. • Install antivirus software.
Virus	A virus is a computer program that is hidden within another program or file. It can replicate itself and insert itself into other programs or files, which are then often passed by a user to other computers. Viruses usually have a harmful effect, e.g. corrupting or deleting data on a disk.	• Install a firewall to ensure software is not downloaded without your knowledge (see later in this chapter).
Worm	A worm is different to a virus in that: • It has an independent existence: it does not have to exist inside another program or file. • It does not need human action to spread it: it can travel to other computers, e.g. through a network or by sending itself in emails to everyone in a user's address book unaided. As the worm is making thousands of copies of itself it will use the computer's resources and cause other programs to run slowly. On a network it will consume bandwidth and affect performance. Some worms cause damage by deleting data or by creating a 'back door' so that the hacker can take over the infected computer with potentially catastrophic consequences.	• Ensure that the operating system is up to date. • Install the latest security updates. • Install antivirus software and ensure that it is constantly updated. • Ensure that the antivirus software can scan emails. • Use adware removal software.

Trojan or Trojan horse	A Trojan does not replicate or attach itself to other files. It must be installed by a computer user who thinks they are installing legitimate software or by opening an email attachment (that is why they are called Trojan horses). • Trojans can just be annoying, e.g. by changing the desktop and adding new icons. • They can also be malicious, e.g. by deleting files and destroying system information. • They can also create 'back doors' to computer systems, allowing criminals to access your personal data, e.g. they can transmit your screenshots or key presses to the criminal's computer.
Spyware	This is similar to Trojans in that it 'spies' on the computer and sends information to a criminal. The difference is that it comes packaged with other software e.g. free software that you download, so that the user does not know they are installing it.
Adware	Adware is the name given to programs that are designed to: • display advertisements on the computer • redirect search requests to advertising websites • collect marketing-type data about users (e.g. the types of websites that you visit) so that customised adverts can be displayed. When this is done without a user's consent, it is considered to be malware. Adware is often bundled with freeware and shareware programs, or a computer can be infected by visiting a malicious website. Adware can also be used to refer to free programs that have adverts within them. The user can often register the program and pay a fee to have the adverts removed.

- Install anti-spyware protection software that removes or blocks spyware
- Avoid opening emails and attachments from unknown sources.
- Surf and download more safely:
  - Only download programs from trusted websites.
  - Read all security warnings, license agreements, and privacy statements.
  - Never click 'Agree' or 'OK' to close a window. Instead, click the red 'X' in the corner of the window.
  - Be wary of popular 'free' music and movie file-sharing programs.

Key term

Trojan horse: a phrase used to describe unintentionally accepting a hidden enemy attack; from an ancient Greek myth where a large wooden horse (in which enemy soldiers were hidden) was left as a gift for the city of Troy, and the people of Troy took it into the city, sealing their fate

ACTIVITY 14.2

a. Describe the differences between a virus, a worm and a Trojan horse.

b. Describe the precautions that users should take to prevent infections by the malware listed in part (a).

Complete Interactive Activity 14b on Cambridge Elevate

Remember

1. Malware describes software intended to prevent a computer functioning correctly, to corrupt or destroy data or to collect user information without their knowledge.

2. Malware includes viruses, worms, Trojan horses, spyware, pharming and adware.

3. Users can protect their computer systems and use software to destroy malware.

Methods of attack

When criminals are targeting large organisations there are various methods of attack.

Type of attack	Description of attack
Brute force attack	This is a general attack on a network and requires no specialist knowledge of the individuals or the organisation. It is a trial-and-error method of obtaining login names and passwords to allow the hacker to access the network. For example, automated software can be used to generate and try millions of login names and passwords. Success is based on computing power and the number of combinations tried rather than an ingenious algorithm. That is why it is called 'brute force'.
Denial of service (DoS) attack 	This type of attack is designed to make a network or website grind to a halt by flooding it with useless network communications, such as repeated login requests. The criminals may use malware to take control of lots of computers ('zombies'), which all send login and information requests at the same time. The criminals may use these attacks to extort money from the company to stop the attacks. They may offer their services to a rival company to 'take out' the competition. They may be used by activists (known as 'hacktivists') to punish a company that they deem to be unethical.
Data interception and theft	In Chapter 13, we saw that data travels across all networks, including the Internet, in packets. This data traffic can be intercepted. The criminals use packet analysers or 'packet sniffers' to intercept the packets, which are then analysed and their data is decoded. The criminals can therefore steal sensitive data such as logins, passwords, credit card numbers and PINs.
SQL injection	Websites, e.g. social networking sites and online banking sites, use databases to store users' details. In order to query these databases and search for information, structured query language or SQL may be used. When a user enters their username and password, SQL is used to check if these are correct and stored in the database. Criminals can input specially created commands instead of a username or password. These commands can bypass the login requirements and gain access to the database so that the criminals have access to the data, e.g. names, addresses, credit card details. Organisations must carefully check the SQL commands entered to filter out these dangerous commands. This is called input sanitisation. →

Type of attack	Description of attack
Zero-day attack	Before new software is released it is tested as much as possible but there may be a security fault, unknown to the developers, that allows illegal access. This security hole can then be accessed by hackers who may then be able to gain network access. The day that the flaw is discovered is known as 'day zero' and then there is a race between the hackers who want to exploit the flaw and the developers who want to fix it.

ACTIVITY 14.3

Here is a headline from a fictitious online newspaper.

> ### Internet activists blame a foreign government for cyber-attack that brought down GitHub
>
> Activists battling Internet censorship in an undisclosed foreign country said on Monday they had proof of a massive online assault on their websites that had been coordinated by members of the government's information service.
>
> In recent days, popular coding service GitHub faced a massive denial of service (DoS) attack.

a.   Explain what is meant by a 'denial of service' attack (DoS).

b.   Carry out research to find out what is meant by a 'distributed denial of service' attack.

c.   Suggest a reason for such an attack in this instance.

d.   Can you find some recent examples of DoS attacks that have been in the news?

Key term

input sanitisation: when any inputs from users that could be harmful to its systems are filtered out and removed

 Download Worksheet 14.2 from Cambridge Elevate

Securing a network

There are many methods that can be used to preserve network security.

 Complete the Cambridge Computing Online activity
www.cambridge.org/links/kose4044

Physical security

The first line of defence is to prevent unauthorised people from entering the buildings where the network equipment is located.

* Keep access doors locked and fit them with security recognition measures, e.g. keypads or biometric systems such as fingerprint pads or iris scanners.

* Use swipe cards containing users' details.

- Install closed circuit television to monitor the exterior and interior of the building.

- Install burglar alarms and monitors in all rooms.

- Fit radio frequency identification (RFID) chips to all equipment so that an alarm will sound if the equipment is taken out of the building.

- Use chains and locks to attach equipment to work benches.

User security

People are the weakest points in any system causing the greatest security risks. The following methods can be used to minimise the risks:

- Network access control: a user's access rights can be set, e.g.:

  - they may not even be able to see certain folders and files

  - they may be able to read them but unable to edit or delete them.

- Good security practices should be followed for login names and passwords, e.g.:

  - passwords should be at least 8 characters long

  - they should contain both numbers and letters

  - they should contain both upper- and lower-case letters.

  - they should contain at least one non-alphanumeric character (!, $, ?, etc.)

  - they should never use user identifiable items such as name, date of birth, phone number, postcode, car registration, etc.

  - all passwords should be changed regularly

  - previous passwords must never be reused

  - passwords must never be written down

  - passwords must never be shared with other users.

Complete the Cambridge Computing Online activity
www.cambridge.org/links/kose4045

Encryption

All data that is transmitted or stored on a network must be considered at risk of being read by unauthorised personnel. It should therefore be converted into a form that they cannot understand.

- Encryption is the scrambling of data into a form that cannot be understood by unauthorised recipients.

- The encrypted data must be decrypted back to its original form.

- The encryption is carried out using a 'cipher'.

- A common method is the use of a 'public' and a 'private' key.

- All users have both a public and a private key.

- The public key is freely available to anyone but the private key is only known to the owner.

- Messages encrypted by a particular public key can only be decrypted with the corresponding private key.

- If person A wanted to send an encrypted file to person B, person A would encrypt it with person B's public key. On receipt, person B would then decrypt the file with their private key.

Firewalls

Firewalls are either software or hardware devices that protect against unauthorised access to a network, and are primarily used to prevent unauthorised access from the Internet. They can be configured to prevent communications from entering the network and also to prevent programs and users from accessing the Internet from within the network.

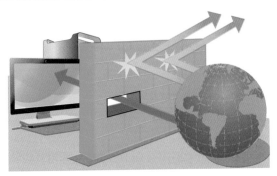

 Download Worksheet 14.3 from Cambridge Elevate

 Complete the Cambridge Computing Online activity
www.cambridge.org/links/kose4046

Network forensics

Network forensics is the monitoring, recording and analysis of network events to help guard against attacks on the security of the network. Software can be used to analyse any unusual activity made by network users as well as external threats.

As well as guarding against security threats, the analysis can be used as legal evidence if prosecutions are brought against the perpetrators.

Network policies

Network administrators should have procedures in place to prevent problems occurring and plans to follow if there is a problem. It is essential that good procedures are rigorously applied.

 Complete the Cambridge Computing Online activity
www.cambridge.org/links/kose4047

Acceptable use policy

An acceptable use policy is a set of conditions or rules that a network user must agree to comply with before they are allowed to use the network.

An acceptable use policy is required in order to:

- ensure that all laws are complied with (see Chapter 15)

- ensure that the network is not harmed in any way or that its security is not jeopardised

- ensure that all users have fair access to the network and that they are not bullied or abused in any way.

The policy could include the following items for network users:

- must not install software

- must not use their own devices, e.g. USB flash drives on the network

- must not download files from the Internet

- must not access any program or data for which the user has not been authorised

- must at all times comply with the law.

Backup policy

The backup policy is about the copying of programs and data stored on the network to safeguard them in case of natural or man-made disasters. The policy could include the following items:

- who is responsible for the backup

- which data will be backed up, e.g. all the data or only data that has changed since the last backup (incremental backup)

- when the backup is to be made, e.g. during the night

- how often backups will be made, e.g. weekly, daily or even hourly if the data changes constantly

- how the backups will be done, e.g. tape, DVD, cloud storage

- where the backups will be kept, e.g. on site, off site

- how long the backups will be kept.

Disaster recovery policy

The disaster recovery policy is a set of procedures that the organisation will follow to restore normal network operations if there is a natural disaster (e.g. fire or earthquake) or a man-made one (e.g. deliberate sabotage of data and equipment). It could include the following items:

- how often it should be tested: many organisations never test the plan until there actually is a disaster, only to find that it doesn't work or is inadequate

- a list of all of the possible threats and what should be done to counteract them

- a statement of where all data backups are kept

- the name or position of the person who is responsible for planning and carrying out the actual restoration of data and facilities

- a description of which data should be restored and the order in which it should be restored

- a list of all outside agencies (hardware and software suppliers) who are involved, and who will need to be contacted.

 Complete the Cambridge Computing Online activity
www.cambridge.org/links/kose4048

Identifying vulnerabilities

The security of a network should be constantly tested to see if it is vulnerable to attacks by hackers. This is called 'penetration testing'. Penetration testing is the testing of a computer system, network or web application to find vulnerabilities that an attacker could exploit. The test then indicates how those vulnerabilities could be exploited to demonstrate the havoc that could be caused.

The main objective is to determine security weaknesses. It can also be used to test an organisation's security policy, the security awareness of the users and the organisation's ability to identify and respond to security incidents.

A penetration test asks: 'How effective are our current security controls?'

 Key term

penetration test: tests a computer system or network to find vulnerabilities that an attacker could exploit

 Remember

1. There are many ways in which criminals can attack network systems and steal data.
2. Methods include brute force, denial of service (DoS), SQL injection and zero-day attacks.
3. Networks must be kept as secure as possible using methods such as
   a. access control
   b. user security
   c. firewalls
   d. encryption.
4. Organisations should have network policies in place to detect and withstand attacks and recover if their security is breached.
5. Penetration testing is carrying out controlled attacks to test the safeguards in place.

 Complete Interactive Activity 14c on Cambridge Elevate

216

Practice questions

1. A mail order company stores thousands of customers' details, including debit and credit card details, on its computer network. The company is concerned about the security of this information.

   a. Explain **three** measures that the company could take to prevent unauthorised access to their computer system.

   b. Describe a measure that the company could take to prevent employees from accessing information that they are not permitted to view.

   c. List **three** items that should be included in an acceptable use policy to prevent users from endangering the security of the network.

Download Self-assessment 14 worksheet from Cambridge Elevate

Your final challenge

Your final challenge is to design, code in the programming language you are studying, and test an information point for people searching for information about computer security.

It should:

- have a menu and sub-menu system so that users can select the options they need
- have details about all of the risks faced by computer users
- provide information about how these threats can be avoided and combatted.

216

15 Ethical, legal, cultural and environmental concerns

Learning outcomes

By the end of this chapter you should be able to:

- investigate and discuss the following issues in relation to the development and impact of computer science technologies:
  - environmental
  - ethical
  - legal
  - cultural
- discuss issues of data collection and privacy
- describe the legislation relevant to computer science.

Challenge: design and code an online test

- An increasing number of examinations are now taken online, using a computer rather than pen and paper.
- From the driving theory test to school tests and examinations, greater use is being made of computerised testing and marking systems.
- Your challenge is to design and code an online test that can be taken online and marked by computer, based on the issues raised in this chapter.

Why computer science technology?

- Computer science technology provides huge benefits in all areas of people's lives.

Impact of computer science technologies

Here are two examples of how things were in the past:

- To send a written message, you had to post a letter. The fastest it would get there would be the next day.

Typewriters were mechanical machines for writing text. They were heavy, the text was difficult to correct and there was no spell checker! It was also difficult to make multiple copies of the documents.

If you wanted to make copies of your typing, you put two pieces of paper in the typewriter at the same time with a piece of special paper, called carbon paper, between them to make a 'carbon copy' (this is why we write 'cc' on an email when we want to copy someone in).

Computer science can allow paralysed people to walk again using their own muscles by transmitting nervous impulses from their brains.

- Portable music players looked like this 50 years ago. They had very short battery life, scratched records and terrible sound quality.

Have a look on Cambridge Computing Online at some examples of how many ways computer science technologies have changed our lives.

 Complete the Cambridge Computing Online activity
www.cambridge.org/links/kose4049

 Complete the Cambridge Computing Online activity
www.cambridge.org/links/kose4050

These technologies have had a huge impact on everyone in the world. Even if people do not personally have access to them, or choose not to use them, they cannot escape their consequences.

Now, we should consider the impact of technologies on our world.

Environmental impact

The impact of computer science on the environment has been both positive and negative. Follow the link below and think about the issues that it raises.

 Complete the Cambridge Computing Online activity
www.cambridge.org/links/kose4051

By 2030, about 40% of the world's energy consumption will be due to the use of digital devices.

Negative impact: energy consumption

All electronic devices use electricity in order to work. Even if they use solar cells to provide the electricity, they are still using energy, and the production and disposal of solar cells has some environmental impact.

- All electronic equipment consumes electricity when it is working and also when it is recycled.

- In the production of computer equipment, huge quantities of electricity are used in addition to non-renewable and in some cases, dangerous materials.

- As more people are using computers, tablets and smartphones, more electricity is required and electricity production has harmful effects on the environment.

- Social networking makes the problem worse because all those tweets, status updates and selfies have to be stored somewhere. They are stored on servers in huge data centres; in 2011 it was calculated that there were half a million worldwide. Data centres consume vast amounts of electricity for the running of the stacks of servers and more importantly for cooling them down.

Negative impact: e-waste

Many people do not dispose of digital devices properly. 'E-waste' is any waste created by electronic devices that have been thrown away as well as waste substances created in their manufacture and use.

- Landfill sites take up areas of land that could be used for other purposes.

- Toxic substances, such as lead, mercury and cobalt, can get into the soil and the water supply from the landfills and cause health problems.

- Some companies illegally send e-waste to third world countries. Ghana in Africa has become a huge dumping ground for e-waste from developed countries.

- Computers from British firms, universities and colleges and even from government departments have been found on tips in these countries.

- Here people are exposed to toxic substances either when trying to extract them or when the huge piles are buried or burned.

E-waste can be disposed of safely:

- Many firms and organisations pay private companies to recycle their old computers safely.

- Councils also pay these companies to recycle electronic items collected at their household waste recycling centres.

- Another solution is to donate the equipment to charities who distribute it to people who need it but cannot afford to buy it.

Positive impact: monitoring climate change

Digital devices are used to monitor climate change by collecting information, transmitting the data around the world and analysing it.

Computers use the data to build complex models that are used to understand the factors affecting climate change and make predictions for the future.

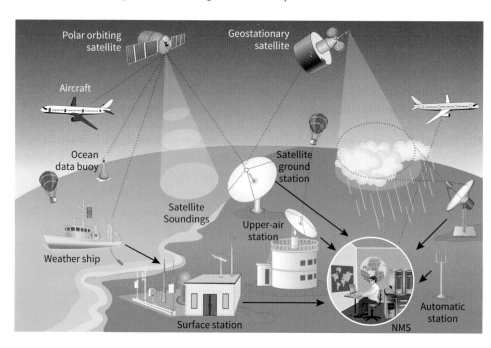

Positive impact: conservation

Digital tracking devices can be attached to animals to study their behaviour.

Conservationists use digital tracking devices using GPS and digital maps to track and study the lives of endangered species. The results are analysed by computer to help improve conservation strategies.

Mobile phone apps are also used by environmental groups to share information and educate people about the consequences of their actions.

Positive impact: energy production

Computer software is used to design efficient devices to produce electricity from wind and wave power. The designs can then be tested using computer models without having to build and then modify them in the light of the results. Computer software is also involved in their production and installation.

Wind turbines and tidal energy technologies are designed and tested using computer science.

ACTIVITY 15.1

'Computer scientists have a role to play in combatting global climate change.'

Discuss this statement.

Remember

1. Computer science technology has detrimental effects such as:
   a. use of electricity in production and functioning
   b. disposal in landfill sites
   c. release of toxic chemicals when burned.
2. Computer science technology has environmental benefits such as:
   a. monitoring and modelling of climate change
   b. use in animal conservation
   c. design and development of 'green energy' sources.

 Complete Interactive Activity 15a on Cambridge Elevate

 **Download Worksheet 15.1 from Cambridge Elevate**

Ethical issues

There are several laws that govern the use of computer systems and data but ethics is about good practice and behaving in a morally correct way. Ethical actions are different from lawful actions. Sometimes actions can be legal; but are they also ethical?

What are the ethical responsibilities of a computer scientist?

Obviously obeying the law is of primary importance but what about a computer scientist's ethical responsibilities to other people and society?

The Computer Ethics Institute has written 10 commandments for computer scientists. Here are four of them:

1. Thou shalt not use a computer to harm other people.

2. Thou shalt not use a computer to steal.

3. Thou shalt think about the social consequences of the program you are designing.

4. Thou shalt always use a computer in ways that ensure consideration and respect for your fellow humans.

These commandments stress that a computer scientist must always consider how their work can affect other people.

Ensuring that their programs are correct and are fully tested, especially when failure can lead to fatal consequences, is important for 1 and 4 above.

Have a look at this example.

The Therac-25 was a radio-therapy machine used to treat patients with cancer by directing beams of electrons or X-rays at tumours. Between 1985 and 1987 there were six accidents where patients were given massive overdoses of radiation resulting in severe injury or death.

 Key terms

ethics: a system of moral principles, often shown by doing things that society recognises as being good or by acting in ways that individuals and societies think of as reflecting good values

lawful: abiding by the laws and rules of a particular country or jurisdiction

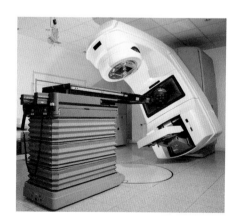

The previous model, the Therac-20, used electronic control systems to prevent overdoses but it was decided to use software control in the Therac-25. The software was developed by one person, and was not properly documented or tested.

The programmer obviously failed in his responsibilities to the users of the device and his software. But was the programmer aware of this? Had he received proper training from the company? Should the software have been developed by a team? Should it have been independently reviewed?

ACTIVITY 15.2

Carry out research into the Therac-25 case and report your findings discussing the causes and the ethical responsibilities of both the computer scientist and the company.

Surveillance cameras

Computer scientists have been involved in the development of software for cameras and surveillance systems. They have developed and perfected number plate and face recognition systems so that every individual person in a city like London can be tracked.

Obviously there are benefits in doing this, such as crime prevention, but should computer scientists consider the possible misuse of these systems? Have they given the authorities too much power in being able to track its citizens 24 hours a day, secretly?

Social consequences

One of the commandments states 'Thou shalt think about the social consequences of the program you are designing.'

The pictures show two developments based on software developed by computer scientists, the use of robots in manufacturing processes and ATMs (automated teller machines) that allow people to withdraw cash from their accounts.

Both developments have led to people losing their jobs in the manufacturing and banking industries. Should computer scientists have considered this when creating the software?

ACTIVITY 15.3

Technological developments that cause social change, such as those of the industrial revolution, are often resisted if they are not managed correctly. The term 'Luddite' is often used as meaning anyone who resists all new technology, but the original Luddites were not fighting against the new technology (most of them were actually using it). They were fighting against the effects it had on their livelihoods and living conditions because the new technology allowed employers to pay them less and as a result many were starving.

What is your opinion? Is it justified to oppose new technology if it has a negative impact on your living conditions? Is it justified to use new technology to enrich yourself even if it leads to other people starving?

You can find information about the Luddites on these websites:

*   www.cambridge.org/links/kose4061

*   www.cambridge.org/links/kose4062

Drones

It is now possible to fire missiles at people and drop bombs on them thousands of miles away using drones, making it easier to kill thousands of people.

Computer scientists developed the control and guidance software to allow this to happen but the same software has had other, beneficial uses for ship and commercial airline safety? What is your opinion on the ethics of developing the software?

ACTIVITY 15.4

Robots have rapidly evolved from being human controlled to being automated and now they are becoming fully autonomous.

Autonomous robots are designed to make their own decisions without human involvement or guidance. Who is responsible for their actions?

Discuss the ethical issues raised for computer scientists developing these systems.

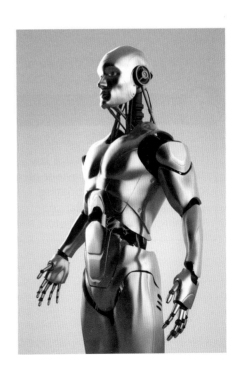

 Key term

autonomous: the ability to act on their own without human input

ACTIVITY 15.5

A computer scientist develops and programs systems for various companies, both large and small.

Inevitably, as her programs are used, bugs are discovered and enhancements are requested.

There are more bugs to fix and enhancements to be made than she can cope with and has to prioritise her work.

She has an ethical dilemma. Should she:

- drop everything and fix each bug as it appears?

- fix the bugs of the larger companies first as they pay more money?

- decide which bugs are the most serious and fix them first?

How can she decide which bug is more serious than another or how much harm it will do?

Discuss what she should do in order to act in an ethical way.

Security and Privacy

Everyone who owns a mobile phone is being tracked by mobile phone masts around the world.

The service providers keep records of locations, calls they have made, texts that they have sent and sites they have visited.

This data is useful for marketing and targeting adverts at particular users.

Internet service providers keep similar records of all online activity.

What we do online using computers and phones, every minute of every day is recorded!

Under the Regulation of Investigatory Powers Act (RIPA) the data can handed over without a warrant or any other safeguards to the police and security services to prevent terrorism and organised crime as part of their surveillance methods which can also include footage from surveillance cameras and having police officers actually following people around.

Most people would accept this intrusion on their privacy to prevent terrorism, but what if it was used for other purposes such as checking if a family put their bins out on the wrong day? Using the data for a purpose other than for which it was intended is called 'mission creep'.

Key term

Regulation of Investigatory Powers Act (RIPA): this is a law that regulates the behaviour of officers who are investigating crime; it covers surveillance, listening to phone calls, etc.

ACTIVITY 15.6

Local councils have used data collected under the Regulation of Investigatory Powers Act to check on people in the following circumstances:

- to check on families to make sure they were not cheating on school catchment area regulations

- to check if they are putting out their bins on the correct day.

Thinking about the original reason that the law was passed, what are your views on extending its scope in these ways?'

Impact on culture and society

Computer science technologies have had a profound effect on the ways in which people live, work and relate to each other.

Mobile phones have had a huge impact on societies and culture around the world. As well as improving communications in areas where there are no cables and infrastructure, they have allowed everyone to record and report on what is happening. This has been especially important in countries where there are repressive governments who prevent free speech. The use of mobile phones and social media has assisted with many popular revolutions.

Computer science technology has led to improvement in medicine.

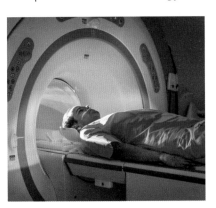 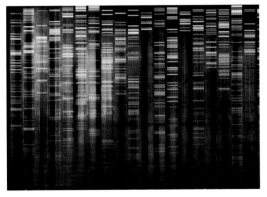

Full body scanners assist in the early diagnosis of cancer, cardiac disease, and other abnormalities.

Computers are used in medical research such as the analysis of DNA.

They are also used to store patient records and allow easy access to them in emergencies.

Modern cars use computer control through an Electronic Control Unit (ECU) for their engine management systems. Problems are diagnosed and fine-tuning is done by computer. Gone are the days when a mechanic 'tinkered' with the engine to set the timing or ensured there was a correct mixture of petrol and air.

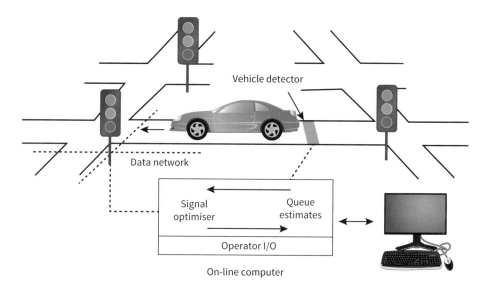

Vehicle detector

Data network

Signal optimiser	← Queue estimates →
Operator I/O	

On-line computer

All of the traffic lights in a town or city are computer controlled and centrally coordinated using wireless networks. But that can be a problem if the networks aren't secure. Read this article about commuters who hacked into the system to ensure they had green lights all the way to work: www.cambridge.org/links/kose4063

Computers have had an impact on education and the way information is presented and used. Now most classrooms have an interactive whiteboard that can be used like a large, touch-screen laptop.

The computer games market is huge and is expected to reach 103 billion dollars by 2017. Over 70% of people in the United Kingdom played a computer game in 2014 with women making up 52%. The largest group are aged over 44, with young people and teenagers making up 22%. The most successful entertainment product of all time, beating blockbuster films, is a British game. Can you discover which game it is? It took over 1 billion dollars worldwide in just three days.

ACTIVITY 15.7

Here are some areas of society and culture on which the use of digital technology has had an impact.

For each one give **three** examples of that impact.

a. the ways in which people interact with each other

b. work and employment

c. education

d. leisure.

The digital divide

People without access to technology, or who don't know how to use it, are at a disadvantage to those who do. This is known as the digital divide. There is a digital divide between countries and also between individuals within the same country. For example, in England, there are areas without high-speed Internet access.

The digital divide can have a huge impact on people who have little or limited access to computer science technologies.

- Having poor IT literacy can lead to low-paid employment or even being unemployed.

- The Office for National Statistics has calculated that in 2015 over 3.5 million of households in the United Kingdom have no Internet access and in 2013 it was estimated by the charity, Age UK, that it costs those households £276 per year because they cannot shop or pay bills online.

- 38% of those who are not online are also unemployed, but

    - from 2013 they have had to prove that they are actively searching for jobs **online** using the government's Universal Jobmatch website.

    - if they do not do this, their benefits can be stopped. They therefore have to travel to libraries for access.

ACTIVITY 15.8

What is your opinion? Should people be penalised if they cannot afford to pay for Internet access?

Is it ethical to force unemployed people to travel miles to access a government website?

Are they being punished for being unemployed?

Is that the type of society you want to live in?

Remember

1. Being ethical means behaving in a morally acceptable way by doing things that society recognises as being good.
2. Actions can be legal but not ethical, and vice versa.
3. Using digital devices such as mobile phones and the Internet enables organisations to track movements and daily activity.
4. There is a digital divide between those who have access to IT and digital devices and those who do not.

Legislation

The increased use of computerised systems and digital communications has led to the enactment of new laws to control that usage.

Personal data about everyone, including financial information, is held online. The Data Protection Act was introduced to protect this personal data. It tells organisations which collect and store this information exactly how they can and can't use it. It also gives people whose data is stored the right to access and change it.

The act imposes conditions on organisations that collect and store data and gives rights to those whose data is stored: the data subjects.

Download Worksheet 15.2 from Cambridge Elevate

Legal responsibilities of data holders	Rights of data subjects
Data must be processed fairly.	A right of access to a copy of the information comprised in their personal data.
It can only be used for the purpose for which it was collected.	A right to object to processing that is likely to cause or is causing damage or distress.
Only data that is actually needed should be held.	A right to prevent processing for direct marketing.
Data must be accurate and up to date.	A right in certain circumstances to have inaccurate personal data rectified, blocked, erased or destroyed.
Data must not be held longer than it is needed for.	A right to claim compensation for damages caused by a breach of the Act.
Data will be used in accordance with the rights of the data subjects.	
Data will be kept safe.	
Data will not be transferred to any country where they don't have similar laws.	

ACTIVITY 15.9

The Data Protection Act was a response to people's concerns about the storage of personal details online.

a. List **five** reasons why online storage is less secure than paper-based storage.

b. List **five** advantages of online storage over paper-based storage.

The Computer Misuse Act 1990 was enacted to counteract hacking.

This act lists three types of offence:

1. Unauthorised access to computer material: using a computer to attempt to access a program or data to which you know you are not authorised. Just trying to access the information is an offence, even if you aren't actually successful in doing so.

Key term

hacking: the unauthorised access to a computer system and the data it contains

2. Unauthorised access with intent to commit further offences: to attempt to access a computer system with the intention of committing a further offence. This could, for example, be trying to access personal details with the intention of committing identity theft.

3. Intentional and unauthorised destruction of software or data: to gain unauthorised access to a computer with the intention to change the data or impair the running of the computer, e.g. by planting a virus.

ACTIVITY 15.10

Identify which of the three crimes in the Computer Misuse Act is being committed in the following examples:

a. A user sees that another user has left their computer unattended and alters and deletes files from their personal area.

b. A user accesses a computer to find out a person's credit card number and security code so they can use it to buy goods online.

c. A student tries to guess the password of a class member and tries to log into the network as that person.

The Freedom of Information Act was set up to end a culture of secrecy in government. Before its introduction, the UK had no legislation obliging the public sector to make information available to the general public.

The act creates a right of access to information held by public authorities, which include central and local government, the health service, schools, colleges and universities, the police and courts.

The person requesting the information does not have to give a reason but the holder does if they refuse a request. The requester can then appeal to the Information Commissioner.

There have been many disclosures of information in the press enabled by the Freedom of Information Act, including, in May 2015, details of expense claims made by leading politicians.

Key term

copyright: this is a law protecting the rights of the person who created their work to only use it themselves

Complete the Cambridge Computing Online activity www.cambridge.org/ links/kose4052

Key term

patent: a permission granted by a government to a person for a set period of time to stop other people from making use of their inventions without their permission.

Copyright Designs and Patents Act

Computer scientists, like artists, authors, photographers and musicians, earn their money by charging people to use their work, e.g. to use their software, listen to their songs or read their books. They own the copyright to their work – no-one can use it without paying for it, or asking them first. For example, only the creator has the right to make copies or perform it in public or give other people permission to do so. This is covered by the Copyright Designs and Patents Act 1988.

Sometimes people try to copy their work. Copying software such as games and applications, scanning books, downloading pirate tracks, etc., means the creators are not paid. This is illegal and unethical. The increased use of digital technology and the Internet has made piracy easier.

This has serious impact on the computer scientists, artists, musicians, photographers and writers, who cannot continue their work if they are not paid. It has been estimated 50% of jobs in the music and film industries will be lost in the next few years owing to illegal copying and downloading.

Even in pre-digital, analogue, times there were infringements when people copied vinyl records onto tape cassettes.

Oracle, the company that owns the patents and rights to the Java programming language, has sued Google for using Java APIs (application programming interfaces) in its Android operating system. Initially the courts found in favour of Google but then for Oracle when they appealed. A group of eminent computer scientists have now asked the courts to declare that APIs should not be covered by copyright laws.

Some companies have been fighting for years in the American courts over software and technology used in mobile phones and who owns the rights to special features. Eventually, one such company was ordered to pay another company a huge amount of money in compensation.

Several major companies formed a coalition to assist in claiming that the design patents covered only minor features and if the court upheld the judgment and forced damages to be paid, it would harm consumer choice and damage companies spending billions of dollars a year on research and development.

ACTIVITY 15.11

Can you find any examples of these kinds of cases on the Internet?

Creative Commons Licensing

Creative Commons is an organisation that provides licences that allow the creators to give the public permission to share and use their work under certain conditions. They give people the right to share, use, and even build upon a work that an artist, musician or writer has created.

There are several levels including:

- Public domain: there are no restrictions. It can be used without permission or attribution for any purpose.

- Attribution license: the work can be used, distributed and copied as long as the creator is given credit for having created it.

- Attribution-non-commercial license: as above but only if it is used for non-commercial purposes.

Proprietary and open source software

All users of digital devices use software that has been designed and created by computer scientists working for themselves or for large organisations.

Proprietary software

Like songs and books, software applications are subject to copyright and users must sign or agree to licenses that give them limited rights but have lots of restrictions that limit how they can use the software.

This type of software is called *proprietary software* and the source code cannot be modified by anyone but the person, team, or organisation that created it.

Advantages of proprietary software	Disadvantages of proprietary software
The software will be developed carefully and tested thoroughly because people will be paying money to use it and they will be cross if it doesn't work.	The producers will develop the software for the majority of users and will not necessarily meet the needs of individual users, who are not able to modify the software for themselves.
It is important that users are happy if they are to pay money for the software and come back for more. Therefore support is often provided.	The support and updates may be expensive.
The producers will provide regular updates.	The software must be paid for.

Open source software

Open source software is freely available on the Internet and is constantly upgraded by users who under the licence are obliged to charge no fee if they pass it on to other users.

The four key freedoms of the open source movement are:

1. The freedom to run the program, for any purpose.

2. The freedom to study how the program works and change it.

3. The freedom to redistribute copies.

4. The freedom to distribute copies of your modified versions to others.

Key term

open source: software whose source code is available for modification or enhancement by anyone, e.g. Open Office, Linux, Android

Advantages of open source software	Disadvantages of open source software
It is free to use.	It may need specialist knowledge to install and develop the software.
Users can modify the source code to adapt it to their needs.	It may not appear as professional as proprietary software or have such a user-friendly interface.
Constant upgrades are available.	It may not have been tested as thoroughly as proprietary software.
There is a community of dedicated enthusiasts who will provide help and support.	

Download Worksheet 15.3 from Cambridge Elevate

Complete Interactive Activity 15b on Cambridge Elevate

Remember

1. Legislation includes:
   a. Data Protection Act 1988.
   b. Computer Misuse Act 1990
   c. Copyright Designs and Patents Act 1988
   d. Freedom of Information Act 2000.
2. Creative Commons licenses allow creators of works to give rights to the users.
3. The source code of proprietary software cannot be modified by anyone but the person, team, or organisation that created it and maintains exclusive control over it.
4. Open source software is software whose source code is available for use, modification or enhancement by anyone.

Practice question

Discuss the ethical and economical arguments surrounding software piracy.

Download Self-assessment 15 worksheet from Cambridge Elevate

Your final challenge

Your final challenge is to design and code a program to test students' knowledge of the topics covered in this chapter.

The program should:
- include questions covering all of the items in the chapter
- be text based or have a graphical user interface.

The questions can be of any type, e.g. multiple choice, text entry, yes/no response, drag and drop. The users should be given their final score and told which questions are incorrect.

Non-exam assessment

The programming project contributes 20 per cent of the marks for the GCSE award.

It allows you to demonstrate your computational thinking skills to create an algorithm to solve a problem and then to code and develop the solution through testing and resolving any problems that you find.

Before you start

It is very important that you fully understand what the task is asking and what you will have to do.

- Read it and re-read it.
- Highlight important points.
- Make notes.
- Use a spider diagram or mind map to help you visualise all of the sub-problems and the components you will need for the solution. This will help you to identify the inputs, outputs and processing that will be required.

The assessment scheme is set out to reflect the formal method for creating a solution – programming techniques, analysis, design, development or implementation and testing, evaluation and conclusions. Although separate points on the specification, we have joined programming techniques and development together below, as they are closely intertwined. As you are getting to know the task, you should be thinking ahead about the programming techniques and constructs that you will need to use, for example: conditional statements and iteration.

Programming techniques that you studied and can be used in the project are listed in the specification and are listed below. You might use techniques other than the ones listed.

The first part of the assessment scheme assesses the use of programming techniques and it stresses that they must be used appropriately.

You do not have to stick rigidly to this scheme and you can revisit earlier stages in light of later problems or developments. **Your report should reflect this**.

The report

You must produce a report detailing all of the stages you have gone through to solve the problem and create and refine your solution. This report is very important as it provides evidence of the methods you have used to solve the problem you have been set.

Remember

You can use material from this book in the Non-exam assessment, but remember to reference anything that you use!

You will be awarded marks for the following areas:

Programming techniques	maximum of 12 marks
Analysis	maximum of 6 marks
Design	maximum of 8 marks
Development	maximum of 8 marks
Testing and evaluation and conclusions	maximum of 6 marks

An example problem illustrating the following methodology is given in Chapter 7.

Programming techniques and development

Your report should include a full description and explanation of the coding of the solution.

It is a good idea to write this as you are actually coding your solution, stating what you have done in each lesson – a development diary.

It should include:

- screen prints of your code as it develops
- explanations of testing you have carried out on the subroutines as you have developed them
- changes you have made in the light of your testing
- lists of the resources you have used, for example: function libraries or program add-ins for developing a graphical user interface.

Your code should:

- be modular, using functions and procedures, so that it is well organised
- use meaningful variable names all written in the same way (e.g. as camel case)
- be fully commented so that each section is fully explained.

To obtain full marks, your solution must be complete and successfully solve all parts of the task.

Your solution will also be assessed on your use of appropriate programming techniques.

Here is a list of the elements and techniques that you should consider using in your program:

- variables
- different data types including Boolean, string, integer and real
- arrays
- operators
- the three basic programming constructs used to control the flow of a program: sequence, conditionals, iteration
- suitable loops including count and condition controlled loops
- string and array manipulation
- file handling operations: open, read, write and close.

These are just the basics and you can use any suitable techniques that ensure an efficient and elegant solution – the code should be clear, simple and concise.

Solving the problem with 20 lines of clear, concise code is more elegant than solving it with 100 lines of code containing unnecessary variables and constructs.

Elegant code is the result of careful analysis and thoughtful algorithms.

An elegant solution will make someone say 'Wow. Why didn't I think of that?'

As you are developing your code, you should ensure:

- it is modular and broken down into its component parts
- it is fully commented to explain each part
- all of the techniques mentioned above are used appropriately
- the solution is coded efficiently, using as few commands and lines of code as possible to achieve the outcomes.

Analysis

This section allows you to use your skills in decomposing, abstraction and pattern recognition to fully inspect the problem, break it down into its component parts and resolve what has to be done to solve it.

In your report, you should include:

- an outline of the problem stating the main points
- a list of the main requirements of the solution – what it has to do
- a decomposition of the problem listing all of the sub-tasks. These should be fully explained
- a **requirements specification** listing what each of the solutions for the sub-tasks should achieve
- the **performance** or **success criteria** that will be used to judge whether the solution successfully solves the problem. These should reflect the requirements specification and be fully explained
- a list of all of the inputs and outputs required for the solution and the validation techniques that will be required
- the data structures that will be required (e.g. variables and arrays)
- a test plan listing all of the tests that will be carried out and the expected results; the tests should show that you are aware of all the problems that could arise when the program is used by another user. For example, a test could check that data has actually been entered and that data is within the expected range.

The following shows an example test plan:

Test number	Test data	Expected result	Actual result	Type of test
1	3	9	9	**Valid** or **in range** test
2	1	1	1	Boundary test
3	10	100	100	Boundary test
4	12	Message stating that the number should be between 1 and 10	The message was displayed as expected.	**Erroneous** or **out of range** test.

Design

This section of the report should explain the designs for the sub-tasks and requirements identified in the analysis.

In the design section there should be:

- full algorithms for solving all of the sub-tasks displayed as flow diagrams and pseudocode
- the algorithms should contain all of the variables, data structures and validation techniques identified in the analysis.

The pseudocode should be fully commented to describe how the subroutines (functions and procedures) are called by the main program and why they are included. The design should clearly show that the solution is modular and makes use of functions and/or procedures.

The design should contain features to ensure that you have taken account of:

- possible areas for misuse (e.g. entering erroneous data or selecting inappropriate options)
- validation and authentication.

There should be a consideration of a suitable user interface explaining how the user will interact with the system.

There should also be a discussion of the test plan, linking the algorithms to the tests to be carried out. The discussion should demonstrate that the tests are not merely proving that the program works as expected but are erroneously attempting to find faults.

The design should be complete enough for another competent person to use it to code a successful solution.

Development

Your report should include a full description and explanation of the coding of the solution.

It is a good idea to write this as you are actually coding your solution, stating what you have done in each lesson – a development diary.

It should include:

- screen prints of your code as it develops
- explanations of testing you have carried out on the subroutines as you have developed them
- changes you have made in the light of your testing
- lists of the resources you have used, for example: function libraries or program add-ins for developing a graphical user interface.

Your code should:

- be modular, using functions and procedures so that it is well-organised
- use meaningful variable names all written in the same way (e.g. as camel case)
- be fully commented so that each section is fully explained.

As you are developing your code you should ensure:

- it is modular and broken down into its component parts
- it is fully commented to explain each part
- all of the techniques mentioned above are used appropriately
- the solution is coded efficiently, using as few commands and lines of code as possible to achieve the outcomes.

Testing and evaluation and conclusions

Your report should show how you have thoroughly tested all aspects of your solution.

Your testing should not just involve expected data that demonstrates that your solution is a success but should show that you have actually tried to make your system fail by using extreme and unexpected data.

- Your test plan should cover all of the performance or success criteria that you identified in the analysis.
- It should list the test data to be used, the expected and the actual outcomes.
- You should also explain how you took remedial action to solve any errors you found that were highlighted by your tests.
- If there are any unresolved issues, you should explain how they could be solved given more time.

Evaluation

Your report must contain an evaluation comparing your finished solution against all of the performance or success criteria that you identified. As you write this, you can use your test results as evidence.

Finally, you should thoroughly check your report to ensure that it is presented in a structured way with all of the sections clearly labelled.

Ensure that grammar and spellings are correct and that you have used all technical terms accurately.

Checklist

A good way to ensure that your report covers all of the required items is to create a checklist and tick off each item when you are sure that it is adequately covered.

A sample one is shown below.

Item	Completed
Analysis	
Outline of the problem stating what the solution is expected to achieve.	
List of all of the sub-tasks.	
Requirements specification listing what the solutions for the sub-tasks should achieve.	
Performance or success criteria that will be used to judge the success of the solution.	
Inputs, outputs and validation are identified.	
A full test plan that contains test data for all of the success criteria.	

Item	Completed
Design	
Designs for all of the components are included.	
All variables have been identified and given meaningful names.	
All data structures have been identified.	
A user interface has been designed.	
The design is modular – using functions and/or procedures.	
Algorithms for all of the components are included.	
Algorithms displayed as flow diagrams.	
Algorithms displayed as pseudocode.	
All pseudocode is commented to explain what it is intended to do.	
Explanation of how the test plan will test the algorithms.	
Development	
Explanation of how the program developed at each stage.	
Screen prints showing development.	
Lists all of the problems encountered and changes made as a result of them.	
Tests carried out on each component with results and any changes made.	
List of all the resources used.	
The code	
Modular – use of functions and/or procedures.	
Comments explaining each module.	
All variables have meaningful names consistently displayed.	
The following techniques have been used (if required):	
• variables	
• different data types including Boolean, string, integer and real	
• arrays	
• operators	
• the three basic programming constructs used to control the flow of a program: sequence, conditionals, iteration	
• suitable loops including count and condition controlled loops	
• string and array manipulation	
• file handling operations: open, read, write and close	
• all of the techniques have been used appropriately.	
Testing, evaluation and conclusions	
The test plan covers all of the performance criteria.	
All tests include test data, expected results and actual results.	
Normal and extreme data is used.	
Explanation of how errors were rectified.	
Explanation of how unresolved errors could be rectified.	
The evaluation compares all of the success criteria against the finished solution and the test results.	
The report	
All sections are in ordered sequence.	
All spellings checked.	
All technical terms are used correctly.	

Glossary

A

address: a number assigned to a storage location in memory so that it can be accessed

alpha testing: testing done by the programmer

analogue: data that is continuously changing

antivirus software: software designed to prevent, detect and remove malware

applet: a small application or program created in the Java programming language that can be sent to a user along with the web page they have requested (e.g. animations, word processors and games)

application software: programs which perform specific tasks

applications: programs that are called up by the systems software, and which perform specific tasks

argument: the name for the data that is passed to a subroutine by the main program

array: a structure that contains many items of data, usually of the same type. The data is indexed so that a particular item of data can be easily found

assembler: a program which translates assembly language into machine code

assigning: giving a variable a value

authenticate: confirm that a user's password has been entered correctly

autonomous: the ability to act on their own without human input

B

bandwidth: the amount of data that can pass through the transmission medium per second, often called the bit-rate

base 10: each place value is ten times bigger than the place to its right

base 2: each place value is two times bigger than the place to its right

beta testing: testing done by a selected group of individuals to receive their feedback about how well the program works

binary digits: either a 1 or a 0. Computers can only communicate in 0s and 1s; series of 0s and 1s represent the codes for various instructions and data

BIOS: the **B**asic **I**nput/**O**utput **S**ystem controls the computer when it is first switched on. It tests the system hardware and loads the operating system. It is specially written for each motherboard and performs any other operations that are needed by that particular motherboard

boundary test: where the highest or lowest acceptable numbers are entered; these check any logical errors that may have been introduced using the <= and >= operators

bus: a bundle of wires carrying data from one component to another or a number of tracks on a printed circuit board (PCB) fulfilling the same function

byte: a group of eight bits

C

called: procedures are 'called' by the main program: this means that they are started up, given data, run and return data to the main program

casting: converting one data type to another

central processing unit (CPU): this is the component of the computer that controls the other devices, executes the instructions and processes the data

channel: the smaller sub-ranges into which a frequency range can be divided

character (often abbreviated to 'char'): a variable that holds one letter, number or symbol

character set: the list of binary codes that can be recognised by computers as being usable characters

client: a computer that acts as a desktop for users and which relies on a server for its operations

closed: when the computer has finished using the file, closing it saves it safely on to the disk for permanent retention

colour depth: the number of bits used to encode the colour of each pixel

command line interface: where the user has to type in all of the commands for the operating system themselves instead of using a GUI. The user has to type in all of the commands for the operating system instead of using a mouse to point at and select menu options or double-clicking on icons

comment: information typed in the program to provide information for the programmers. It is not executed by the computer. All programming languages allow comments but use different symbols to denote them. Often forward slashes are used (//) or the hash symbol (#)

compiler: a program that converts high level programming languages into machine code

compound statement: a statement where Boolean operators are combined and work together to examine if several conditions are true or false

compression: reducing the size of a file so that it takes up less storage space or bandwidth when it is transmitted

concatenation: the placing together of two separate objects so that they can be treated as one, e.g. two string variables can be joined end-to-end to produce a larger string

constant: a value that does not change while the program is running

control signals: electrical signals that are sent out to all of the devices to check their status and give them instructions

copyright: this is a law protecting the rights of the person who created their work

D

decision: when a question is asked (as in *selection*) the answer will lead to one or more different alternative actions

digital: representing data in discrete numerical form

driver: a program which is called by a peripheral manager to operate any devices for example a printer, the monitor, or a mouse, when they are called by an application

dry run: the program is run on paper and each stage is carefully analysed to see what values the various inputs, variables and outputs have. At this stage, a computer is not being used

dynamic array: an array that has not had its size defined and can change as data is appended

E

efficiency: how successfully and quickly an action is carried out. For a computer program it can be assessed by:

- how long it takes a program to generate a result

- how much code has been written to generate the result

- how much processor time and memory it uses

electrical storage: storing data using devices such as flash memory. This is sometimes called 'solid state'

erroneous test: data that should be rejected is deliberately input to check that authentication routines are functioning as expected (sometimes called an 'out-of-range test')

Ethernet: a set of technical standards for connecting computers

ethics: a system of moral principles. Ethical behaviour is often shown by doing things that society recognises as being good or by acting in ways that individuals and societies think of as reflecting good values

execute: to run a computer program or process

execution: when a program or part of a program is run by the computer

F

field: is one item of information, e.g. in a record of a car; make, model and maximum speed are all fields

file handle: a label that is assigned to a resource needed by the program. It can only access the file through the computer's operating system

flash memory: this is memory which can be programmed electrically but then keeps its data when the power is turned off

float: a numeric variable with a fractional value; it will have digits on either side of a decimal point. Commonly used to store currency values, e.g. 1.50 for £1.50

frequency: the number of waves per second

full backup: all of the files specified by the user will be backed up

G

global variable: a variable that is used in the main program. It can be used by any of the commands or subroutines in the program

graphical user interface: (known as GUI), a user interface which relies mainly on windows, icons, menus, pointers

H

hacking: the unauthorised access to a computer system and the data it contains

hardware: the physical components making up the computer, and its peripheral devices

heat sink: a metal device, glued to the CPU chip with thermally conducting paste, to transfer the heat away from the chip

HTML: HyperText Markup Language (HTML) is used to write web pages for the Internet as well as in ebooks, PDF documents, etc. The algorithm would be interpreted differently in JavaScript to create the game that could be played in a web browser

I

identifier: the 'name' given to a variable

incremental backup: only new files or files that have been changed since the last backup will be backed up and kept with the last full backup

index: a number that identifies each element of an array or string

input sanitisation: when a computer organisation uses programs to remove any inputs from users that could be harmful to its systems

instruction set: the set of instructions for a particular processor that it will understand and be able to process

instruction: an instruction to a microprocessor to perform a specific task

integer: a whole number without decimals (can be positive or negative)

interpreter: a program that will run a high level program directly, interpreting the instructions and converting them to machine code as the program is executed

IP address: a unique software address used to communicate over the Internet

iteration: when a task is repeated for a set number of times or until there is a required outcome

L

lawful: abiding by the laws and rules of a particular country or jurisdiction

local area network (LAN): network used for data transmission by computing devices with one building or site, such as an office building or a school or university campus

local variable: a variable that is used only within a function or procedure. When the function has completed its work, the local variable is discarded

logic circuit: a combination of standard logic gates used to perform complex logic operations, where the outputs of some gates act as the inputs to others

logic gate: an electronic device which either produces or does not produce an output depending on the inputs it receives and the logic rule it is designed to apply

logical error: a problem in the design of the algorithm

logical operator: operator such as AND, OR, NOT, etc., which performs a Boolean operation on some inputs

loop: part of a program where the same activity is specified once and then repeated for a fixed number of times or until a condition is met

lossless compression: no data is lost when a file is compressed and the file can be decompressed with all of its information intact

lossy compression: data is lost in the compression process and when the file is decompressed; it will not contain the full amount of information that it started with

M

machine code: the instructions in a form that the processor can execute; strings of 1s and 0s

magnetic storage: storing data using magnetic media such as a hard disk drive

malware: software that has been designed to gain unauthorised access to a computer system in order to disrupt its functioning or collect information without the users' knowledge

menu: a set of options to help a user find information or use a program function

microwaves: electromagnetic waves that can be used to carry data between computers

mnemonic: a tool or technique designed to help a person's memory (e.g. 'Richard of York gave battle in vain' used to help remember the order of the colours of the spectrum: red, orange, yellow, green, blue, indigo and violet)

modem: short for 'modulator-demodulator'; modulates and demodulates signals (converts them from digital to analogue and vice versa) sent from and received by a computer over a communications network

motherboard: the main printed circuit board of the computer; it has connectors that other circuit boards can be slotted into

multitasking: when the processor or the separate cores of a processor work on different programs at the same time

N

network traffic: the overall network usage caused by all of the data that is being transmitted at a given time

nibble: half a byte

node: places on the network where there are items of equipment

numeric variable: a variable that stores only numbers; numeric variables can be used in mathematical operations

O

opcode: the code for the instruction being given

open source: software whose source code is available for modification or enhancement by anyone, e.g. Open Office, Linux, Android

operand: the data the operator works on

optical storage: storing data using optical devices such as CDs and DVDs

overflow error: caused when a calculation produces a result that is greater than the computer can deal with or store

overwritten: if a file exists on the computer and a new file is created with the same name, the new file is kept and the old file is written over and lost

P

packet switching: when certain areas of the network are too busy to carry the packets, they are automatically switched to emptier circuits

packet: a small block of data that is transmitted from one computer to another

parallel processing: when the processor cores work on different parts of the same program

parameter: the names of the variables that are used in the subroutine to store the data passed from the main program as arguments

parentheses: brackets

patent: a permission granted by a government to a person for a set period of time to stop other people from making use of their inventions without their permission

penetration test: tests a computer system or network to find vulnerabilities that an attacker could exploit

permission: a rule that is set up for a particular file to control who can edit, read or write on the file

personal area network (PAN): network used for data transmission over short distances by devices such as laptops, mobile phones, tablets, media players, speakers and printers

pipelining: the process of allowing the microprocessor to execute many instructions at the same time. As one instruction is being decoded the next one can be fetched

pixel: short for picture element. The smallest unit of a digital image or the smallest possible dot on a computer screen

place value: the value that a digit's position in a number gives it, e.g. (for denary) in the number 356, the digit 5 has a value of 50 whereas in the number 3560, the digit 5 has a value of 500

printed circuit board (PCB): the base that supports the wiring and electronic components that are soldered to it or fit into sockets on the board

process: an activity that a computer program is performing

property: one of the characteristics or attributes of a data type; for e.g. one of the properties of a string variable is its length, or the number of characters it contains

protocols: agreed rules for requesting and sending data across networks

pseudocode: a language that is similar to a real programming language, but is easier for humans to understand although it doesn't actually run on a computer. It can easily be converted to a regular programming language

R

RAM: (also known as random access memory) memory that can be used by computer programs to store data and instructions, but all of its data is lost when the computer is switched off

read mode: the file is opened in such a way as to allow the data to be used by the program but not to allow the program to write any data to the file. Using read mode protects the data file from being accidentally changed by the program

redundancy: the number of items of data in a file which are repeated

register: a storage location that is inside the CPU itself

Regulation of Investigatory Powers Act (RIPA): this is a law that regulates the behaviour of officers who are investigating crime; it covers surveillance, listening to phone calls, etc.

relational operator: an operator that compares two items of data, e.g. <, >, =

resolution: the number of pixels per square inch in an image when it is displayed on paper or on the computer screen: the higher the resolution, the better the picture

run: a sequence of repeated characters e.g. aaaa

S

sampling: making a physical measurement at set time intervals and then converting the measurements to digital values

searching: looking through a file to see if a particular piece of data is there

secondary storage devices: devices that store information but which do not lose the data when they are switched off e.g. hard disk drives, DVD Roms.

selection: a question is asked, and depending on the answer, the program takes one of two courses of action

sequence: the order in which tasks are to be carried out

sequential: starts at the beginning and moves through the list one by one

server: a computer that provides files on demand to client machines

social engineering: psychologically tricking people into divulging their secret information or doing things that they wouldn't otherwise do

sorting: putting items of data into a precise order, for example alphabetical or numerical

static array: an array that is of a set size

storage location: a place in RAM where a single piece of data can be kept until it is needed

string traversal: moving through a string, one item of data at a time; sometimes this might just mean counting

string variable: a variable that holds characters (which can be letters, numbers, spaces and symbols including exclamation and question marks) that are always enclosed in quotation marks; mathematical operations are not carried out on string variables

subroutines: self-contained modules of code that can be 'called' by the main program when they are needed

substring: a smaller string which is part of another string

sub-tasks: the smaller steps that a larger task might be divided into

swap file: this is a file, kept on the hard drive or other storage device, used to store data and instructions while a program is running but when the RAM is full; it is not as quick as RAM

syntax error: a grammatical mistake in the code, which could be caused by a misspelling, e.g. 'prnit' instead of 'print' or by missing colons, semi-colons or brackets

syntax: the rules of spelling, punctuation and grammar of a language so that the meaning of what is being communicated is clear (humans can make allowances if the rules are broken, but computers can't!)

systems development cycle: a defined process of planning, designing, creating, testing and deploying an information system

systems software: software that operates and controls the computer hardware, allows software to run and provides an interface for computer users.

T

table: a collection of rows and columns forming cells which are used to store data and user information in a structured and organised manner

test data: carefully planned, sample data, used to try out programs to check that they give the correct outputs

testing plan: a plan for the way in which a program is to be tested

topology: the physical structure and layout of a network

trace table: while the dry run is being worked through, a table is drawn up showing each line of the program and showing the values of each variable, input and output for each line

traverse: go through an array or string sequentially one item at a time

Trojan horse: a phrase used to describe unintentionally accepting a hidden enemy attack; from an ancient Greek myth where a large wooden horse (in which enemy soldiers were hidden) was left as a gift for the city of Troy, and the people of Troy took it into the city, sealing their fate

true or false: indicate whether a logical statement is correct or incorrect; this could be represented in a computer as 1s (true statements) and 0s (false statements) respectively

truth table: a table that shows all the possible combinations of outputs which can occur with all of the different possible inputs; usually used with logic problems

tunnelling: process by which packets are placed inside an outer packet that only members of the VPN can read

U

user interface: what the user sees on their screen

V

valid test: ensures that the correct result will be produced with the expected data (sometimes called an 'in-range test')

validation: the process through which the program checks that data is sensible and that it is suitable for use by the program

variable: a container which is used to store values such as an attempts counter

virtual private network: a network that appears to the users as a unique network but which is part of another network

virtual: does not physically exist, although it appears to

volatile: data is permanently lost when power is switched off

W

wide area network (WAN): a network of networks connecting local area networks over a large geographical area

write mode: the program can 'write' to the file, in other words, change the data in the file

Index

Acknowledgements

The authors and publishers acknowledge the following sources of copyright material and are grateful for the permissions granted. While every effort has been made, it has not always been possible to identify the sources of all the material used, or to trace all copyright holders. If any omissions are brought to our notice, we will be happy to include the appropriate acknowledgements on reprinting.

p1t Andrey Esin/Shutterstock; p1b iurii/Shutterstock; p2 Eric Gevaert/Shutterstock; p3 5 second Studio/ Shutterstock; Andy Heyward/Shutterstock; p4tl and tr claudiodivizia/iStock/Thinkstock; p26t Sooa/Shutterstock; p26b Webitect/Shutterstock; p27 iStock/Thinkstock; p44t wanpatsorn/Shutterstock; p44b © OJO Images Ltd/Alamy; p47 Volodymyr Krasyuk/Shutterstock; p48c Powerbee-Photo/Shutterstock; p48b Reload_ Studio/Thinkstock; p53t Mopic/Shutterstock; p53b piotr_pabijan/Shutterstock; p57 Michael Schoppe | 8mb.de/Shutterstock; p61 Pavlo Burdyak/Shutterstock; p76t iStock/Thinkstock; p76b alice-photo/Shutterstock; p78 Only background/Shutterstock; p89t © Jay Brousseau/Getty Images; p89b © Georgia Barnett/ Alamy; p93 © OJO Images Ltd/Alamy; p95 Andrey_ Popov/Shutterstock; p103t © 2/Medioimages/Ocean/ Corbis; p103b © rinderart/Alamy; p106t © Library of Congress Prints and Photographs Division Washington, D.C. 20540 USA. [LC-DIG-ds-00175]; p106b © Leudej Rodjanapaitoon/Alamy; p112 © Tetra Imges/Corbis; p144tl, tr, bl, br © Courtesy of David Waller; p126t © Giuseppe Cesch/Getty Images; p126b © Shotshop GmbH/Alamy; p128 © tarczas / Alamy; p134 © Decollage Toucan/ESA/epa/Corbis; p140t © Jan Bruggeman/Photographer's Choice/Getty Images; p140b © Michelle O'Kane/Moment/Getty Images; p147 Maya Moody/Fotolia; p148 © Aerial Archives/Alamy; p155t, c, b © Courtesy of David Waller; p157t © Michelle O'Kane/Moment/Getty Images; p157b © Pictorial Press Ltd /Alamy; p162t © Kelly Redinger/Design Pics/Corbis; p162b © INTERFOTO/ Alamy; p164cl Route55/Thinkstock; p164cr PHOTOCREO Michal Bednarek/Shutterstock; p164b © Roman Milert/ Alamy; p165 © PhotoQuest/Archive Photos/Getty Images; p166 © Simon Belcher/Alamy; p179r © cogal/ E+/Getty Images; p179l scanrail/Thinkstock; p181t © Rafe Swan/Cultura/Getty Images; p181b Timashov Sergiy/Shutterstock; p184t and b, p185 © Courtesy of Microsoft; p187t alexskopje/ Thinkstock; p187b LanKS/Shutterstock; p197 Toria/ Shutterstock; p198t amasterphotographer/Shutterstock; p198b © www.cablemap.info; p205t © Nicolas Ayer/ EyeEm/Getty Images; p205b © Hannu Liivaar/Alamy; p206 © Fotosearch/Getty Images; p207tr © Image Source/Getty Images; p208 © Wavebreak Media ltd/ Alamy; p211 © Image Source/Getty Images; p212 © YAY Media AS/Alamy; p217t © Pete Farrington/ EyeEm/Getty Images; p217b © sturti/Getty images; p218t © trekandshoot/Alamy; p218b cybrain/ Shutterstock; p219 Huguette Roe/Shutterstock; p220t © PhotoStock-Israel/Alamy; p220c ER_09/ Shutterstock; p220b © OPD/LOOK AT SCIENCES/ SCIENCE PHOTO LIBRARY; p221 Alexander Tihonov/Shutterstock; p222t © Sean Pavone/Alamy; p222bl © Dario Sabljak/Alamy; p222br RainerPlendl/ Thinkstock; p223 ©SCIENCE PICTURE CO/SCIENCE PHOTO LIBRARY; p225br © Kheng Ho Toh/Alamy; p225bl © Cultura Creative (RF)/Alamy; p226t © Adam Hester/Getty Images; p226b ©BSIP SA/Alamy; p229 eldeiv/Shutterstock.